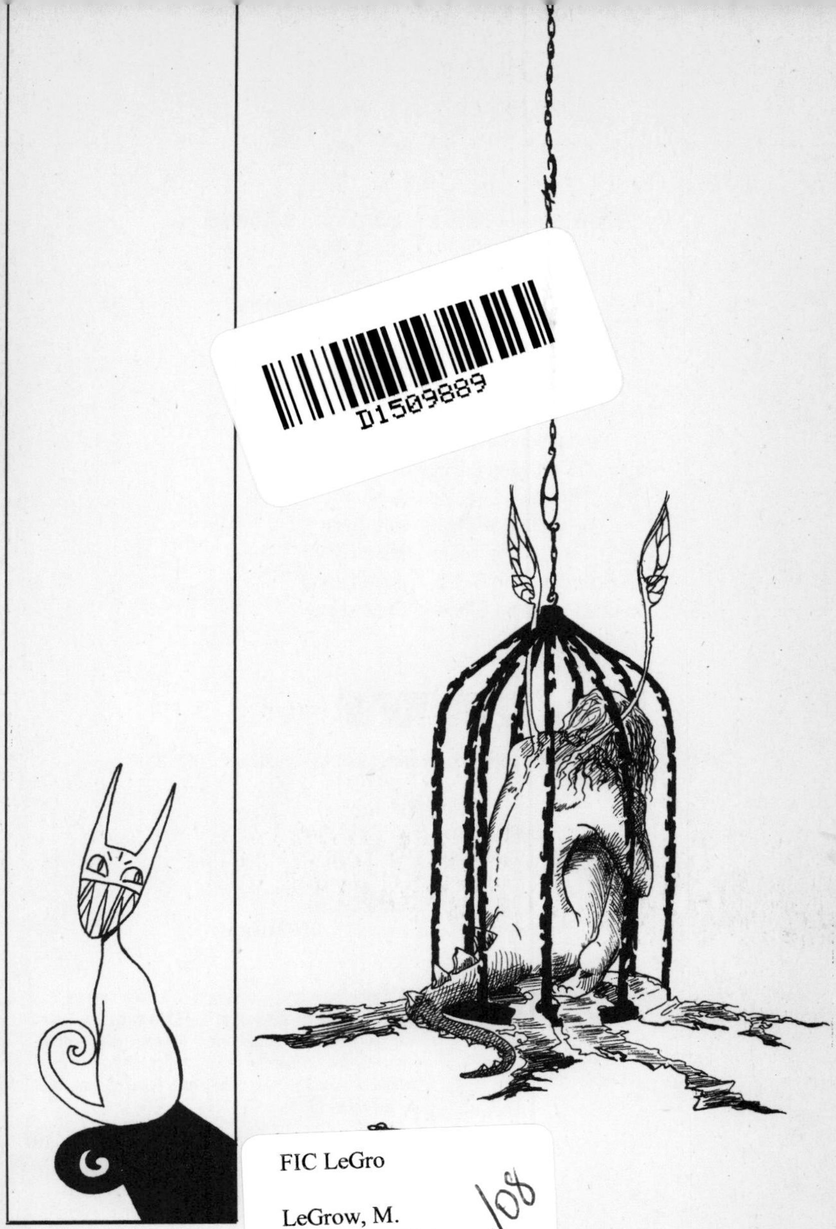

Bizenghast Vol. 4
Created by M. Alice LeGrow

Development Editors - Jodi Bryson & Aaron Suhr
Lettering - Lucas Rivera
Cover Concept Artist - Cor-Chan
Cover Designer - Chelsea Windlinger

Editor - Lillian Diaz-Przybyl
Digital Imaging Manager - Chris Buford
Pre-Production Supervisor - Erika Terriquez
Production Manager - Elisabeth Brizzi
Managing Editor - Vy Nguyen
Creative Director - Anne Marie Horne
Editor-in-Chief - Rob Tokar
Publisher - Mike Kiley
President and C.O.O. - John Parker
C.E.O. and Chief Creative Officer - Stuart Levy

A  Manga

TOKYOPOP and  are trademarks or registered trademarks of TOKYOPOP Inc.

TOKYOPOP Inc.
5900 Wilshire Blvd. Suite 2000
Los Angeles, CA 90036

E-mail: info@TOKYOPOP.com
Come visit us online at www.TOKYOPOP.com

ISBN: 978-1-4278-0484-6

First TOKYOPOP printing: December 2007
10 9 8 7 6 5 4 3 2 1
Printed in the USA

Bizenghast

Volume 4

By M. Alice LeGrow

HAMBURG // LONDON // LOS ANGELES // TOKYO

Bizenghast

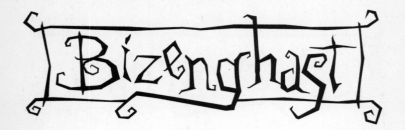

Contents

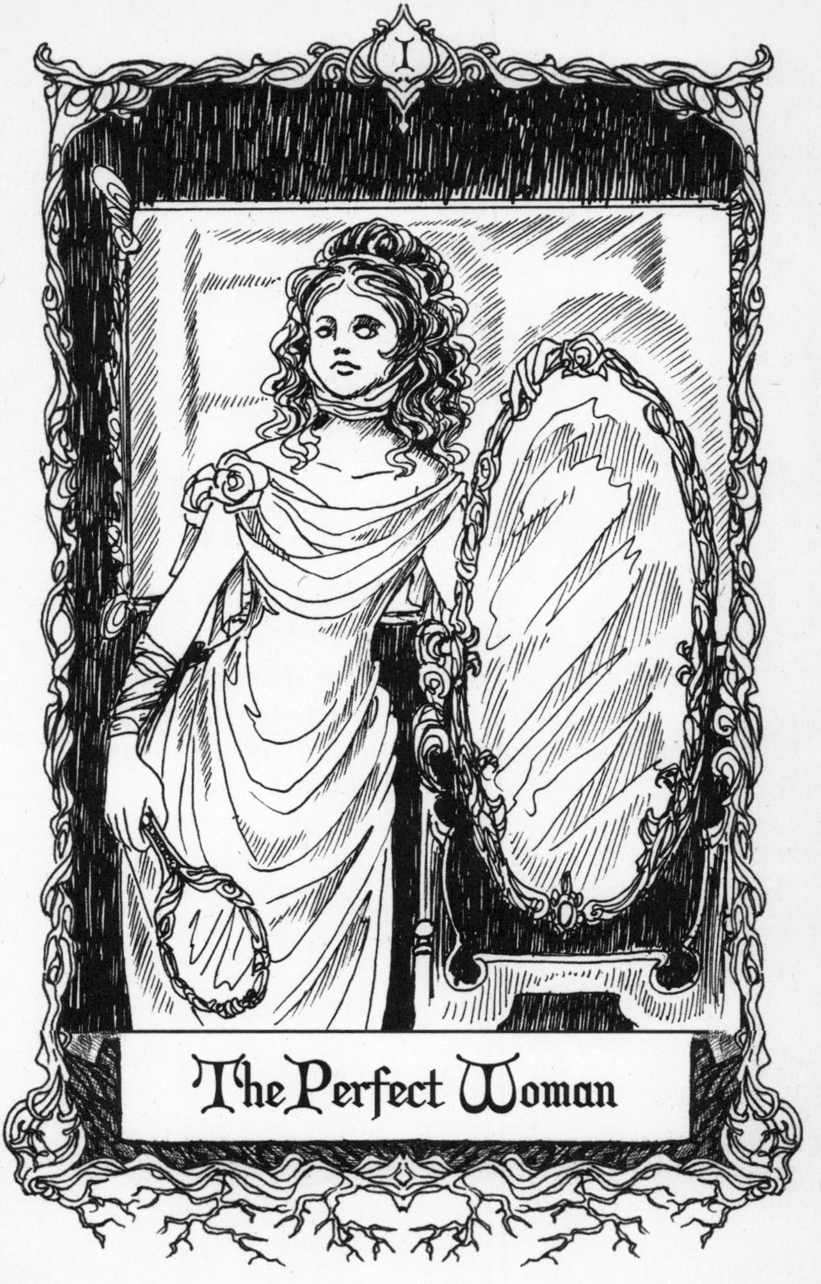
I
The Perfect Woman

This book is dedicated to
the following people:

The Four O'Clock Thieves
Captain Z
Snake-friends everywhere
And to my biggest fans, who tirelessly
campaigned for me, who never doubted
my determination and who supported me
through all the hard times...thanks,
Mom and Dad.

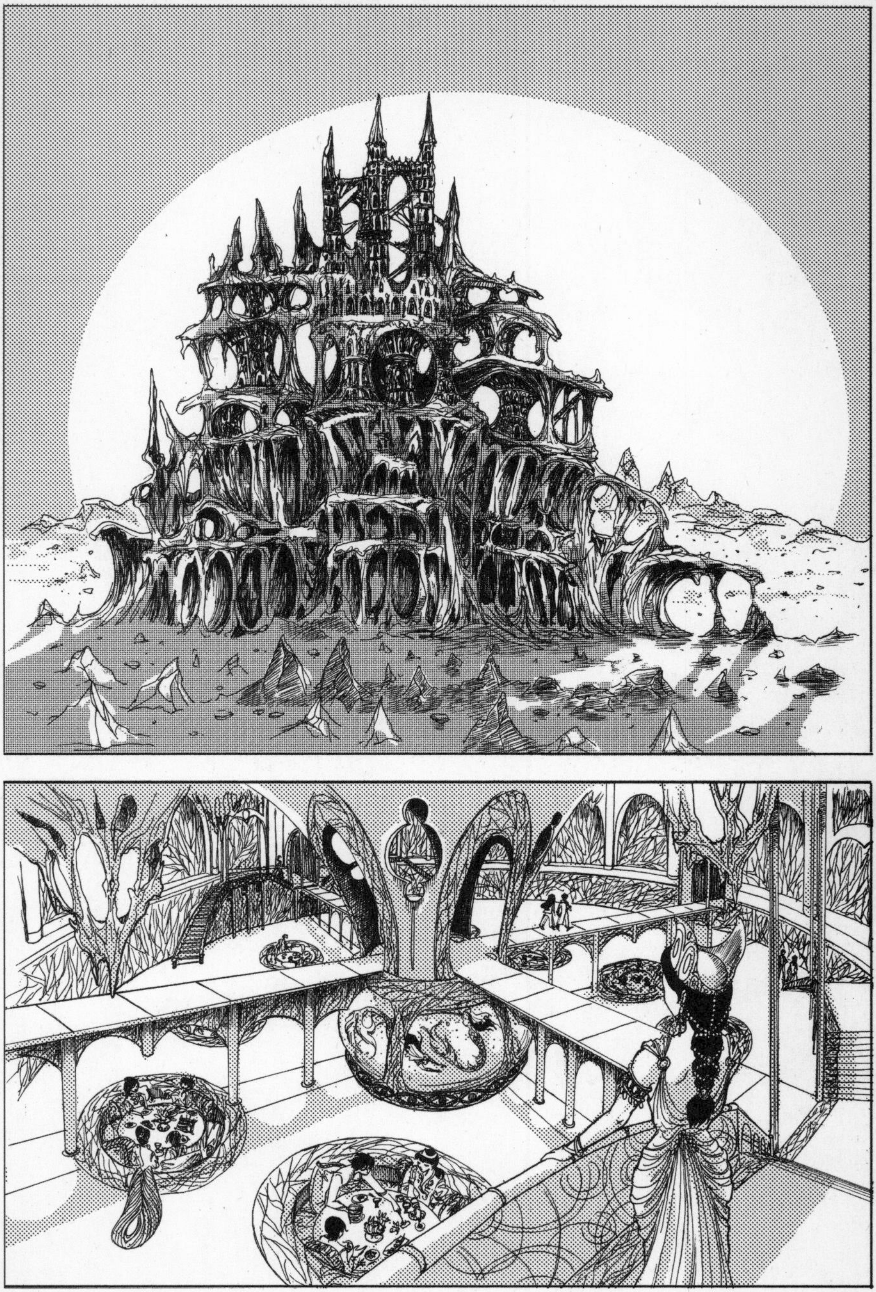

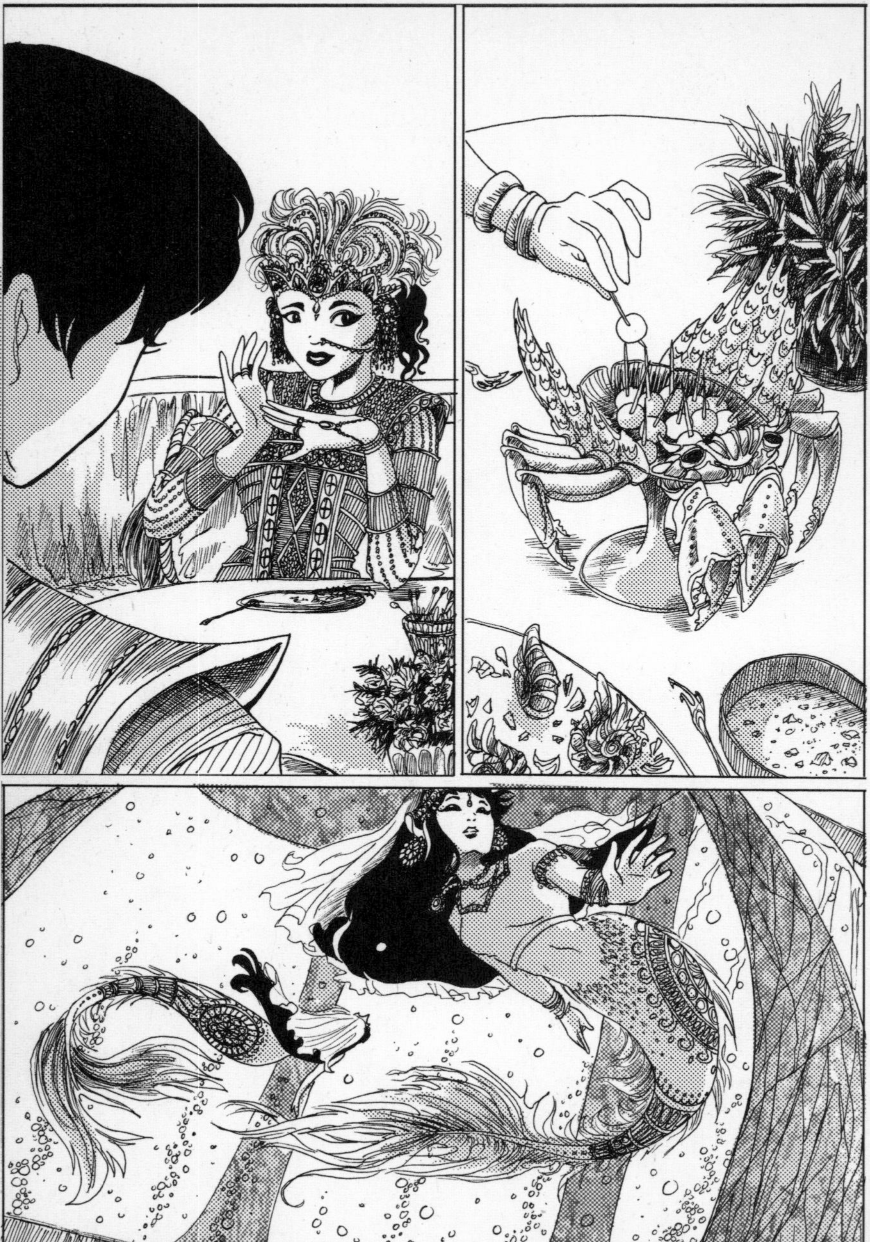

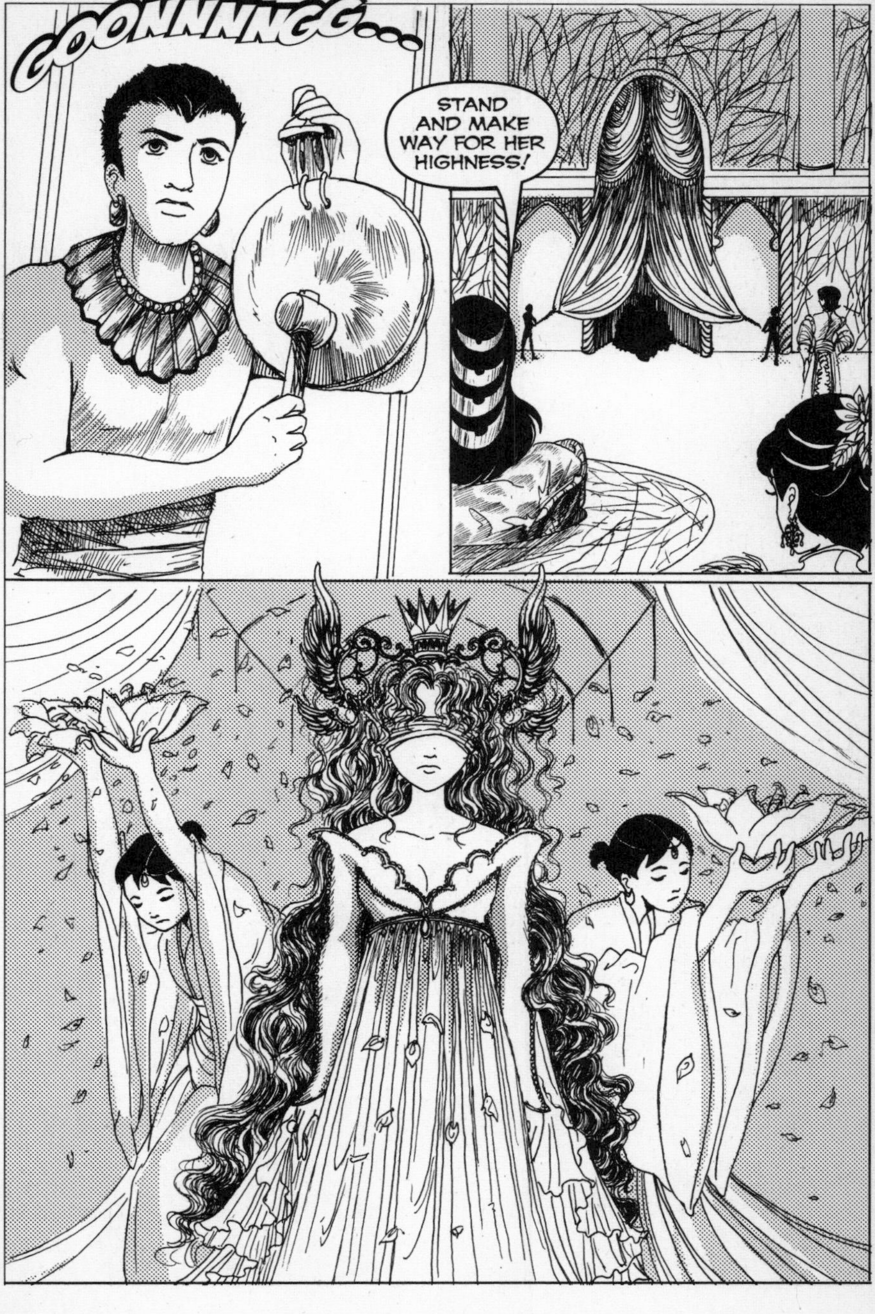
GOONNNNGG...
STAND AND MAKE WAY FOR HER HIGHNESS!

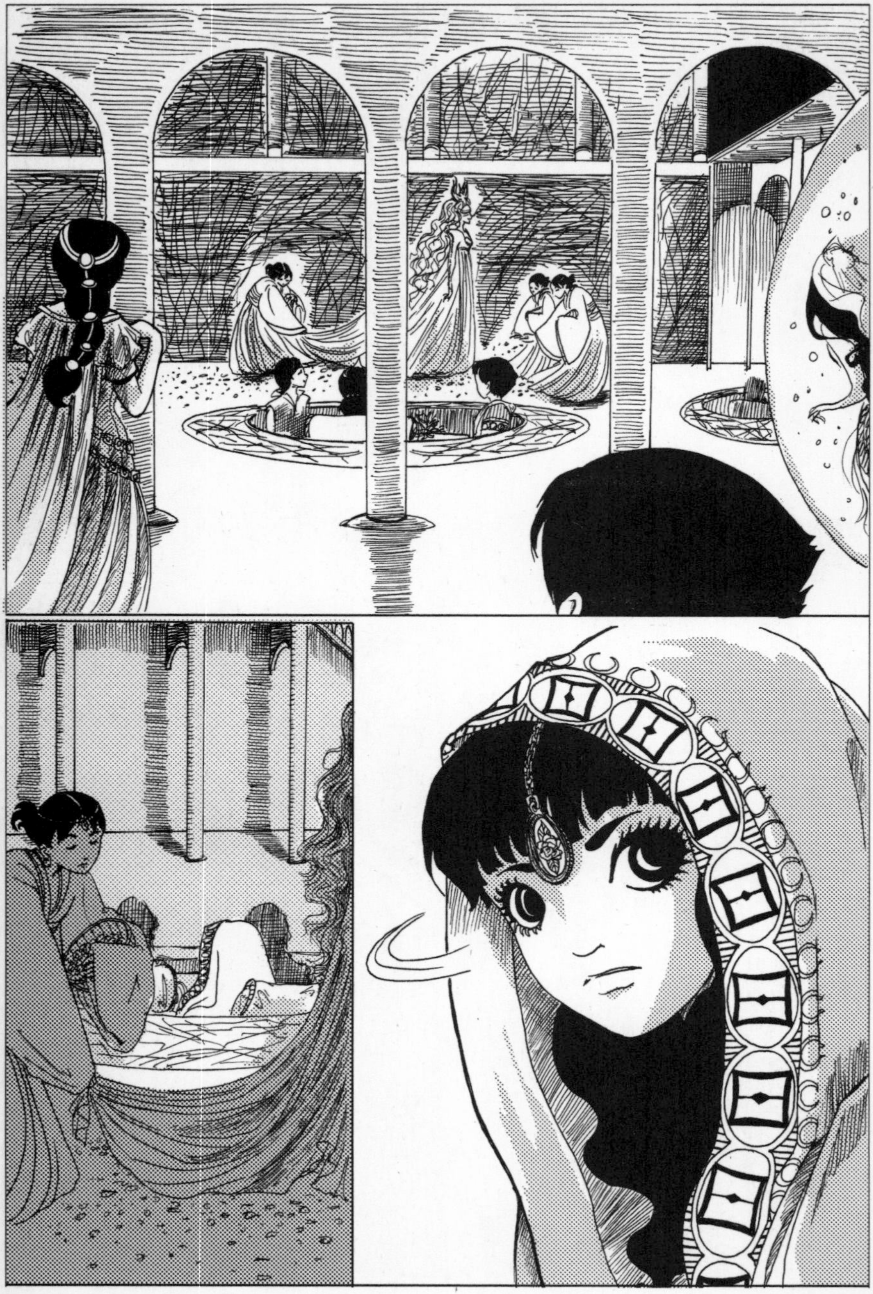

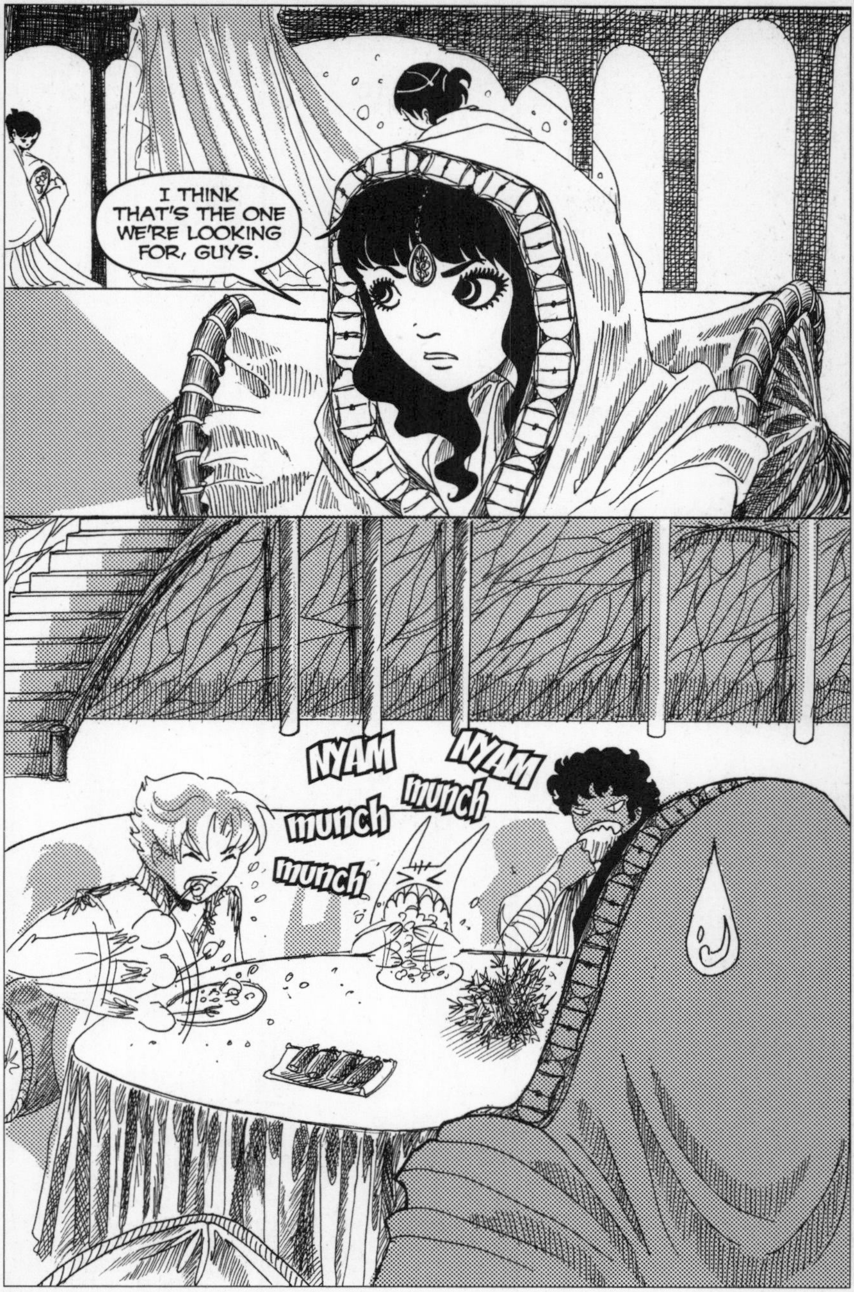
I THINK THAT'S THE ONE WE'RE LOOKING FOR, GUYS.
NYAM
NYAM
munch
munch
munch

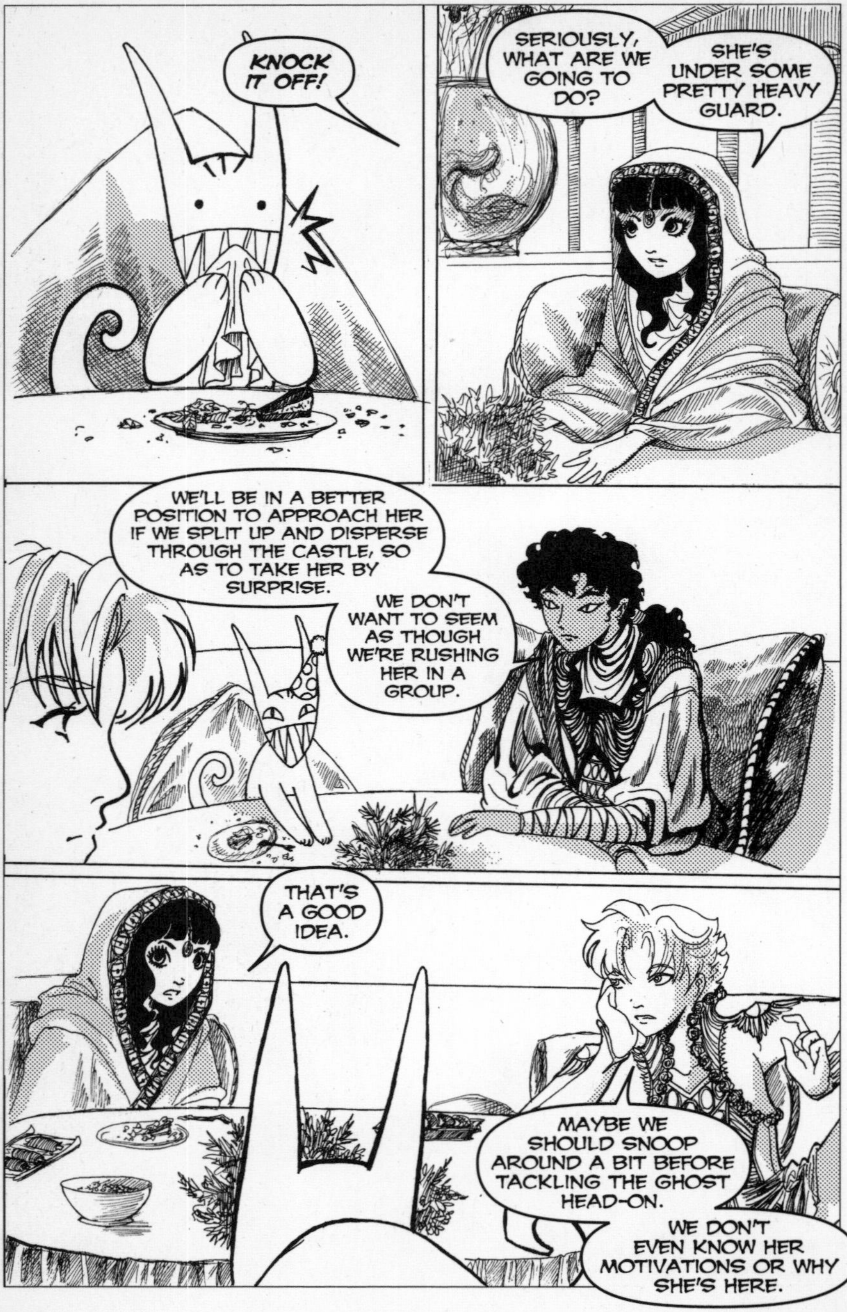
KNOCK IT OFF!
SERIOUSLY, WHAT ARE WE GOING TO DO?
SHE'S UNDER SOME PRETTY HEAVY GUARD.
WE'LL BE IN A BETTER POSITION TO APPROACH HER IF WE SPLIT UP AND DISPERSE THROUGH THE CASTLE, SO AS TO TAKE HER BY SURPRISE.
WE DON'T WANT TO SEEM AS THOUGH WE'RE RUSHING HER IN A GROUP.
THAT'S A GOOD IDEA.
MAYBE WE SHOULD SNOOP AROUND A BIT BEFORE TACKLING THE GHOST HEAD-ON.
WE DON'T EVEN KNOW HER MOTIVATIONS OR WHY SHE'S HERE.

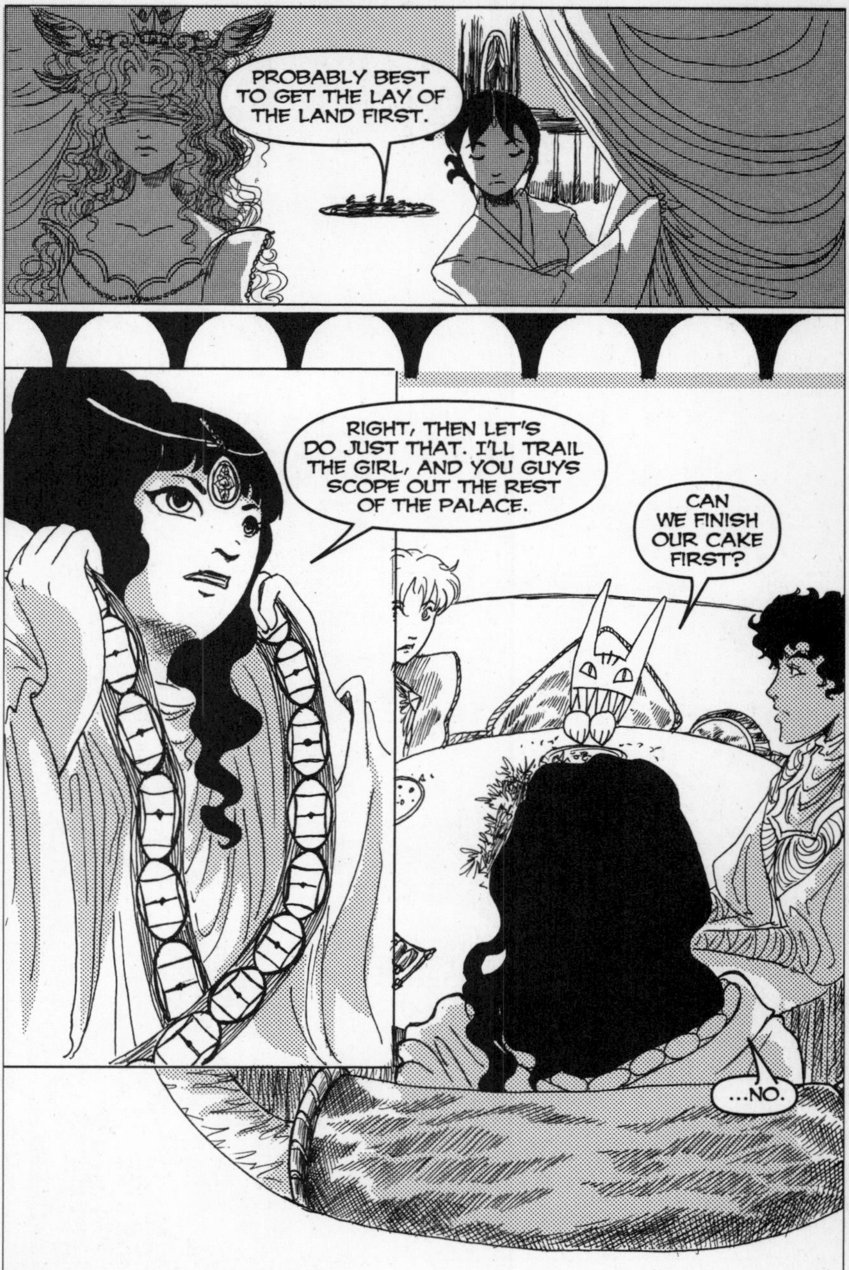
PROBABLY BEST TO GET THE LAY OF THE LAND FIRST.
RIGHT, THEN LET'S DO JUST THAT. I'LL TRAIL THE GIRL, AND YOU GUYS SCOPE OUT THE REST OF THE PALACE.
CAN WE FINISH OUR CAKE FIRST?
...NO.

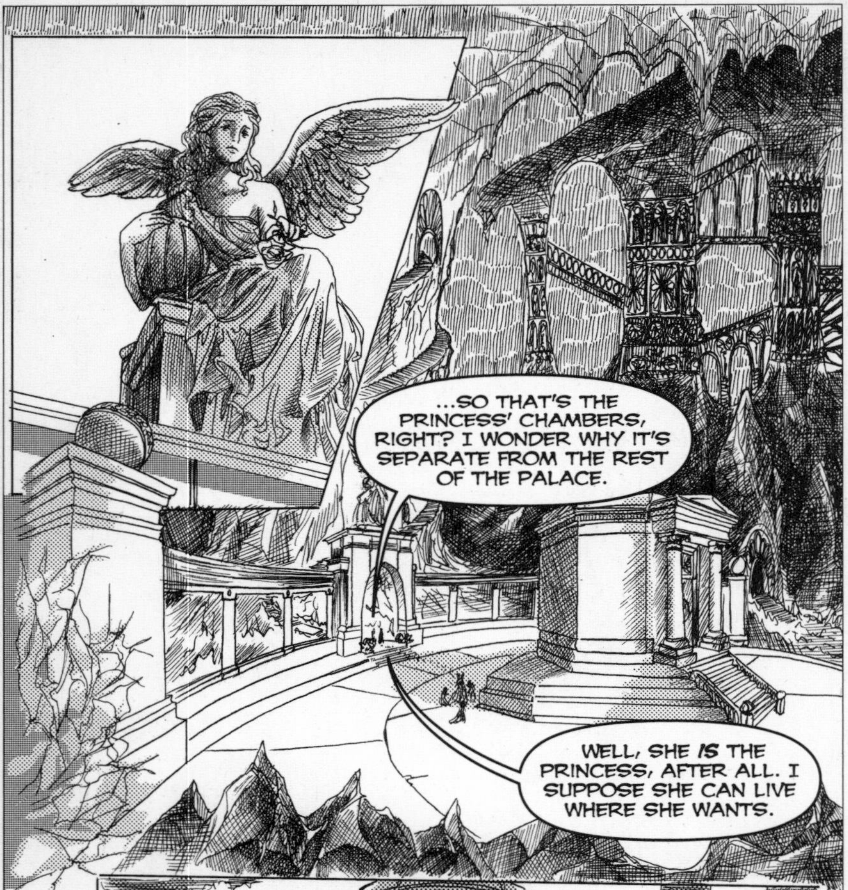
...SO THAT'S THE PRINCESS' CHAMBERS, RIGHT? I WONDER WHY IT'S SEPARATE FROM THE REST OF THE PALACE.
WELL, SHE *IS* THE PRINCESS, AFTER ALL. I SUPPOSE SHE CAN LIVE WHERE SHE WANTS.
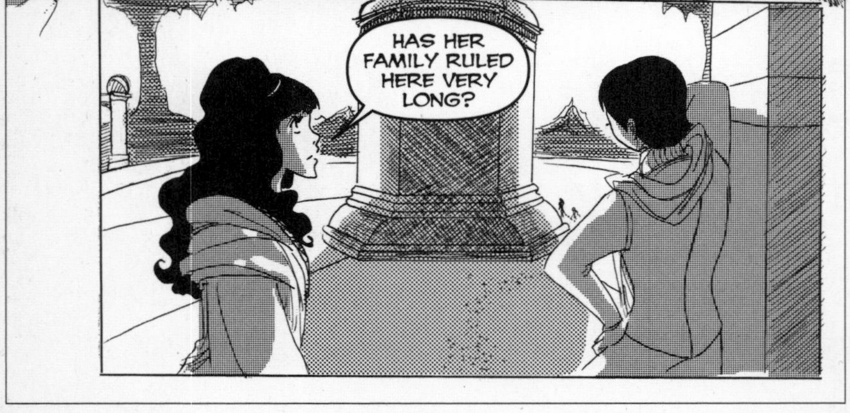
HAS HER FAMILY RULED HERE VERY LONG?

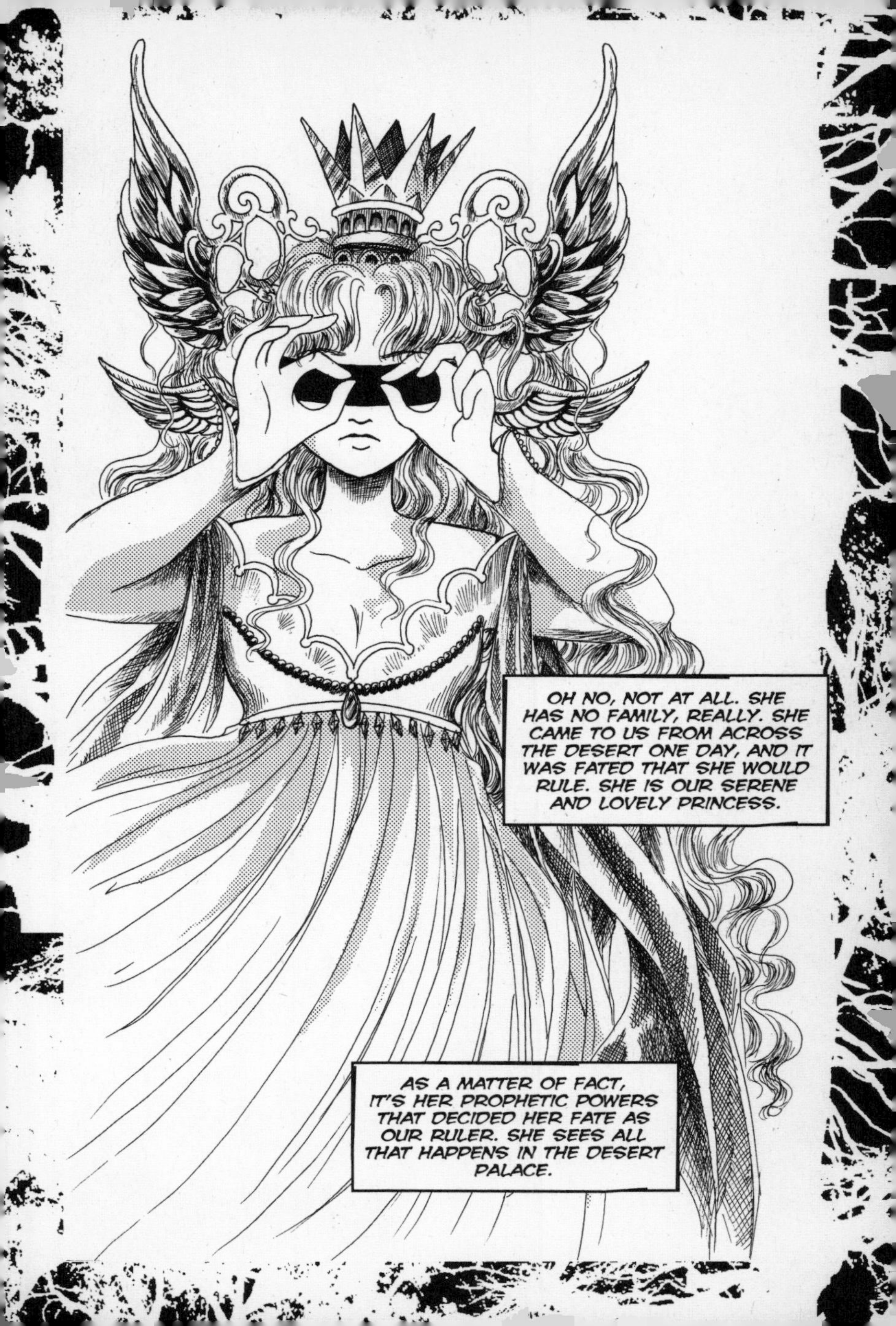
OH NO, NOT AT ALL. SHE HAS NO FAMILY, REALLY. SHE CAME TO US FROM ACROSS THE DESERT ONE DAY, AND IT WAS FATED THAT SHE WOULD RULE. SHE IS OUR SERENE AND LOVELY PRINCESS.
AS A MATTER OF FACT, IT'S HER PROPHETIC POWERS THAT DECIDED HER FATE AS OUR RULER. SHE SEES ALL THAT HAPPENS IN THE DESERT PALACE.

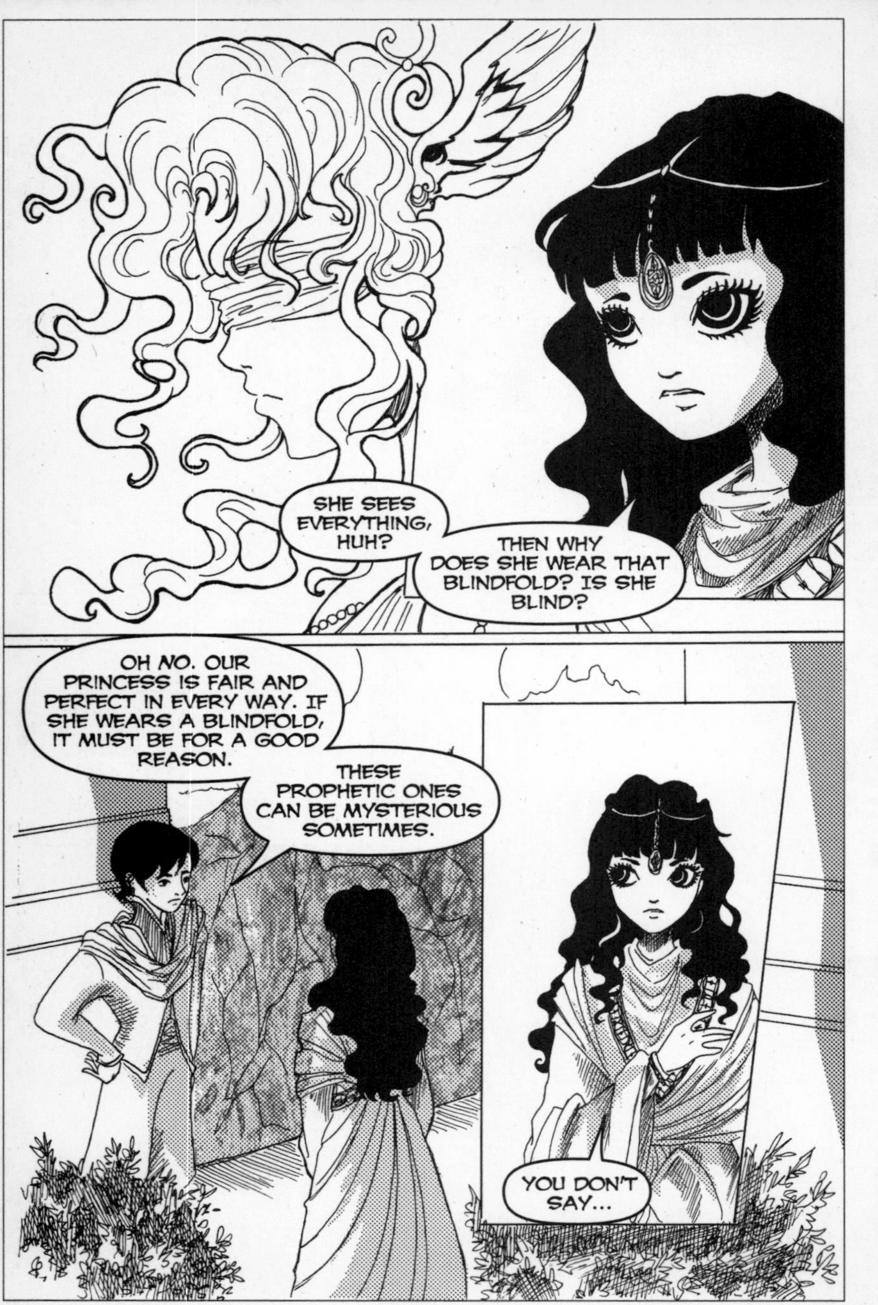
SHE SEES EVERYTHING, HUH?
THEN WHY DOES SHE WEAR THAT BLINDFOLD? IS SHE BLIND?
OH NO. OUR PRINCESS IS FAIR AND PERFECT IN EVERY WAY. IF SHE WEARS A BLINDFOLD, IT MUST BE FOR A GOOD REASON.
THESE PROPHETIC ONES CAN BE MYSTERIOUS SOMETIMES.
YOU DON'T SAY...

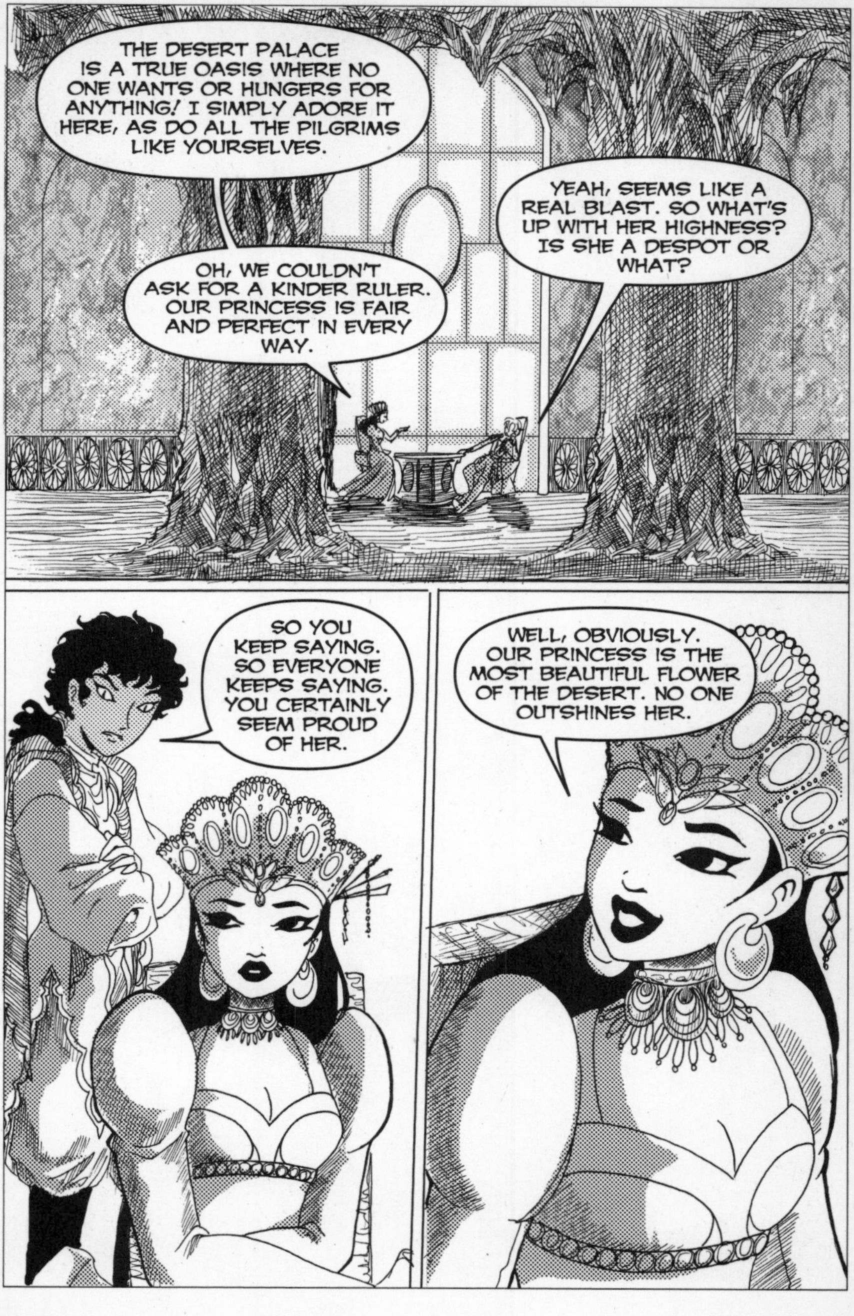
THE DESERT PALACE IS A TRUE OASIS WHERE NO ONE WANTS OR HUNGERS FOR ANYTHING! I SIMPLY ADORE IT HERE, AS DO ALL THE PILGRIMS LIKE YOURSELVES.
OH, WE COULDN'T ASK FOR A KINDER RULER. OUR PRINCESS IS FAIR AND PERFECT IN EVERY WAY.
YEAH, SEEMS LIKE A REAL BLAST. SO WHAT'S UP WITH HER HIGHNESS? IS SHE A DESPOT OR WHAT?
SO YOU KEEP SAYING. SO EVERYONE KEEPS SAYING. YOU CERTAINLY SEEM PROUD OF HER.
WELL, OBVIOUSLY. OUR PRINCESS IS THE MOST BEAUTIFUL FLOWER OF THE DESERT. NO ONE OUTSHINES HER.

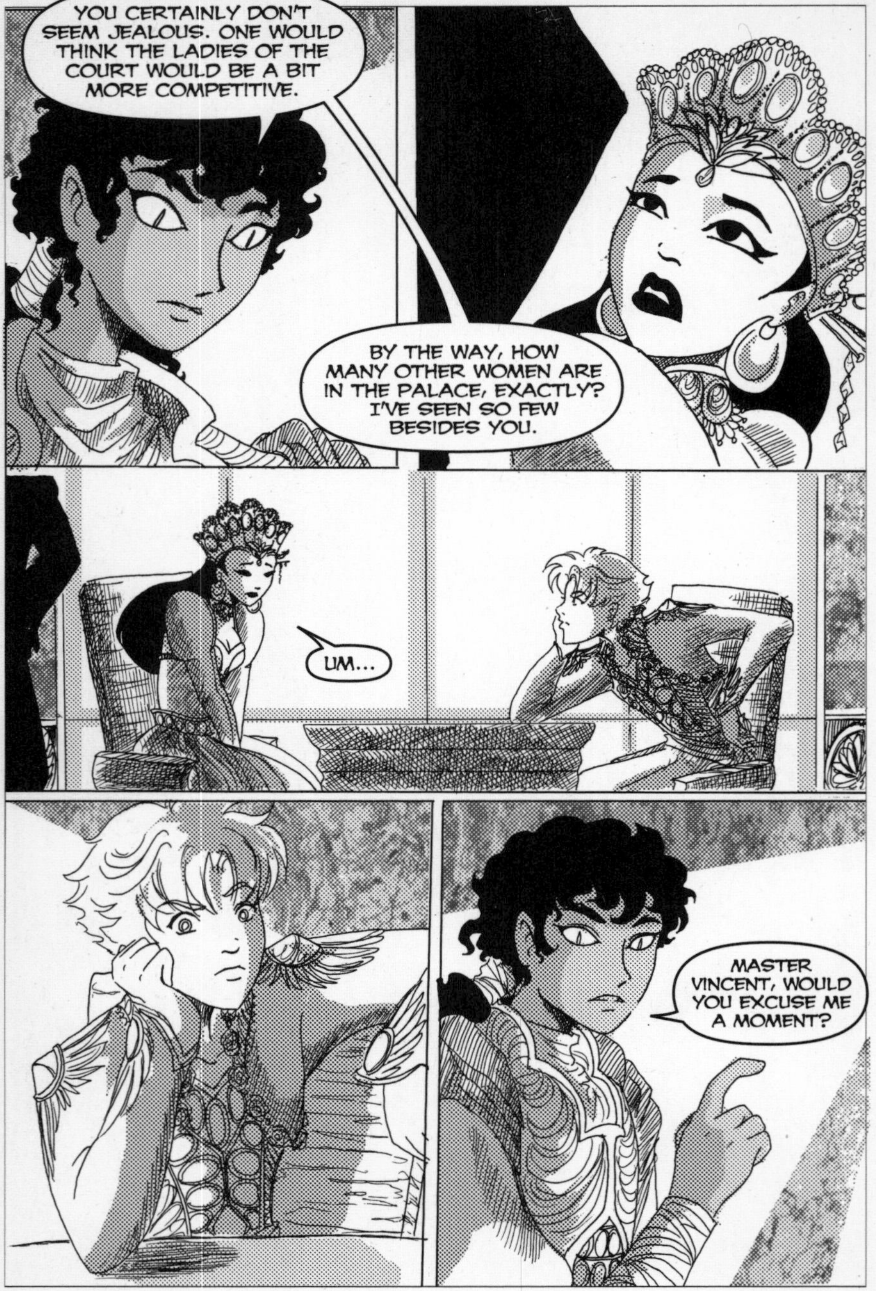
YOU CERTAINLY DON'T SEEM JEALOUS. ONE WOULD THINK THE LADIES OF THE COURT WOULD BE A BIT MORE COMPETITIVE.
BY THE WAY, HOW MANY OTHER WOMEN ARE IN THE PALACE, EXACTLY? I'VE SEEN SO FEW BESIDES YOU.
UM...
MASTER VINCENT, WOULD YOU EXCUSE ME A MOMENT?

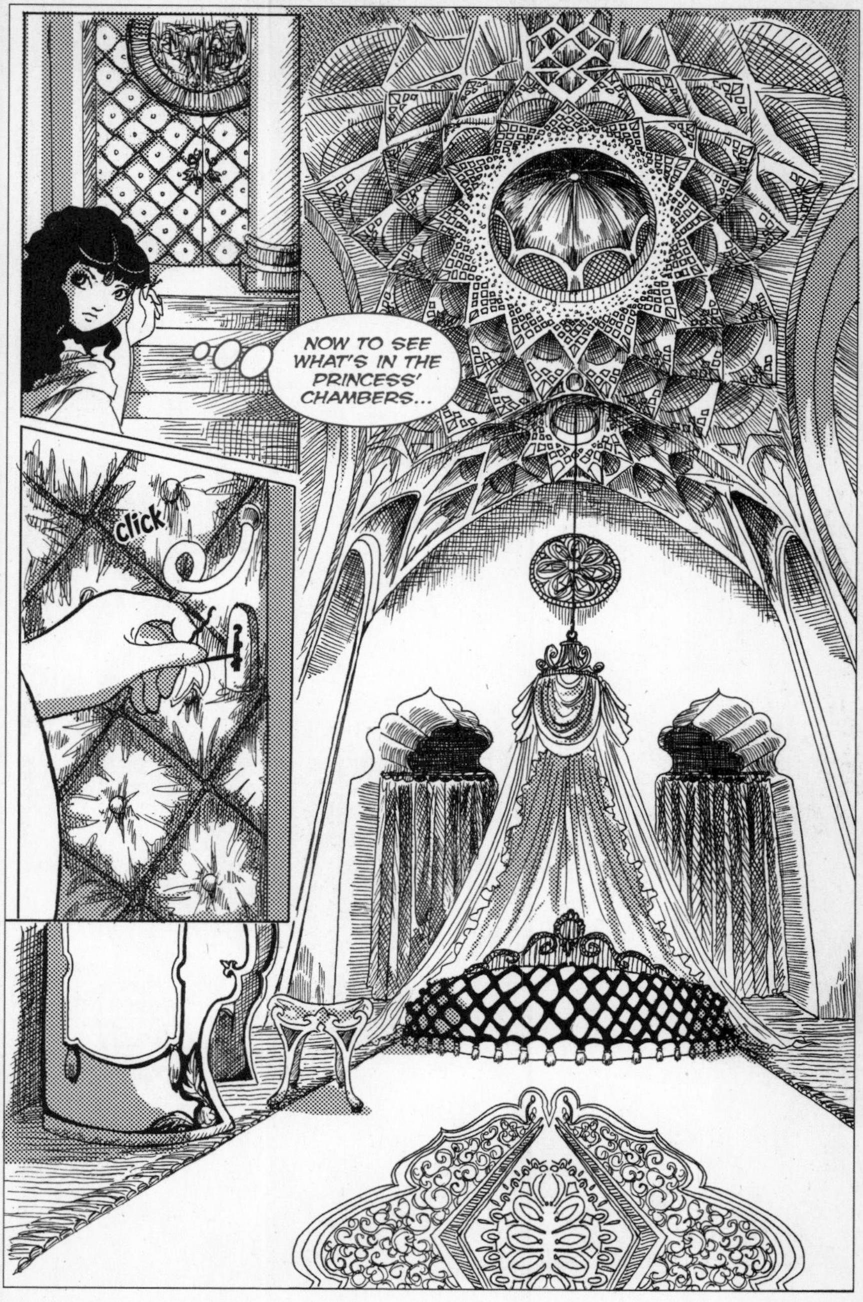

NOW TO SEE WHAT'S IN THE PRINCESS' CHAMBERS...
click

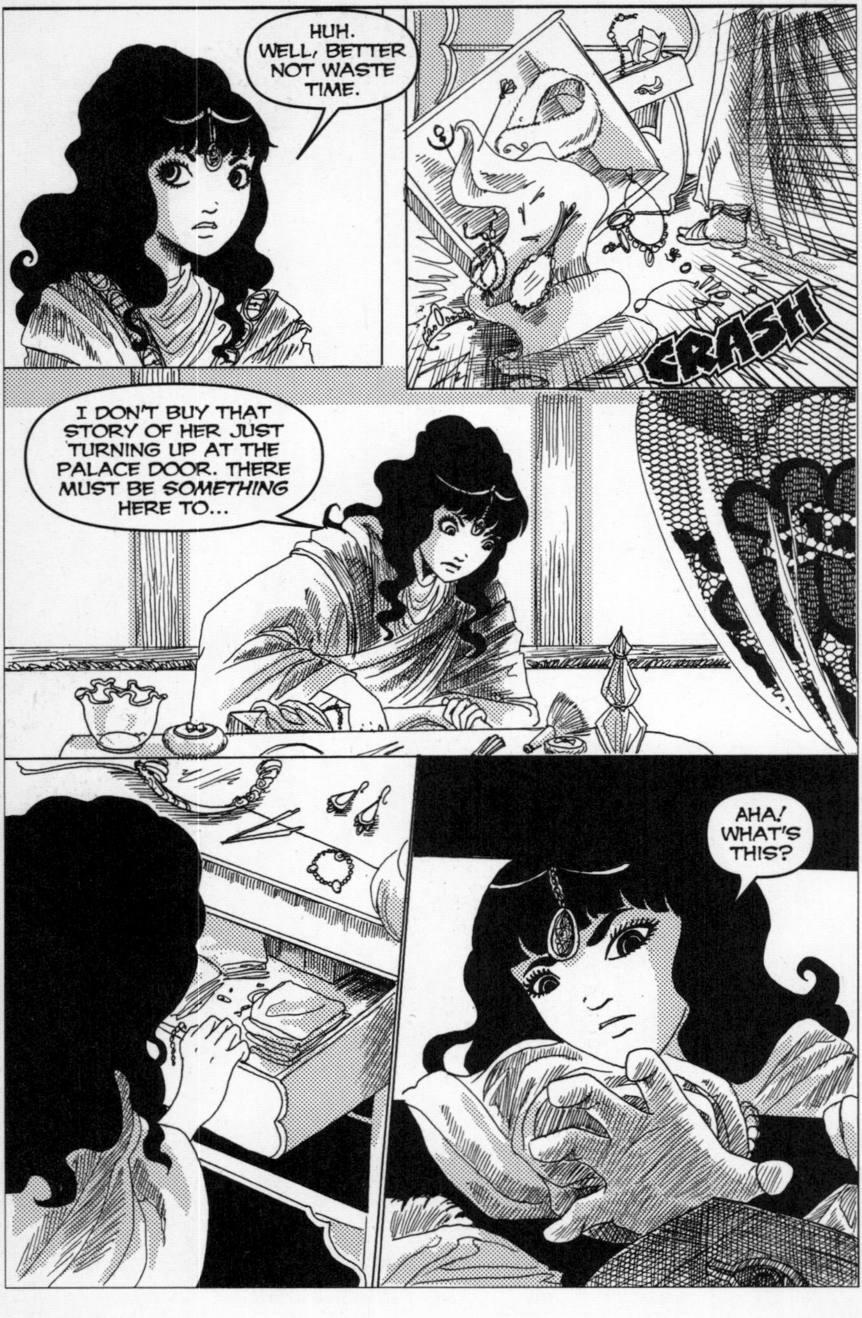
HUH. WELL, BETTER NOT WASTE TIME.
CRASH
I DON'T BUY THAT STORY OF HER JUST TURNING UP AT THE PALACE DOOR. THERE MUST BE *SOMETHING* HERE TO...
AHA! WHAT'S THIS?

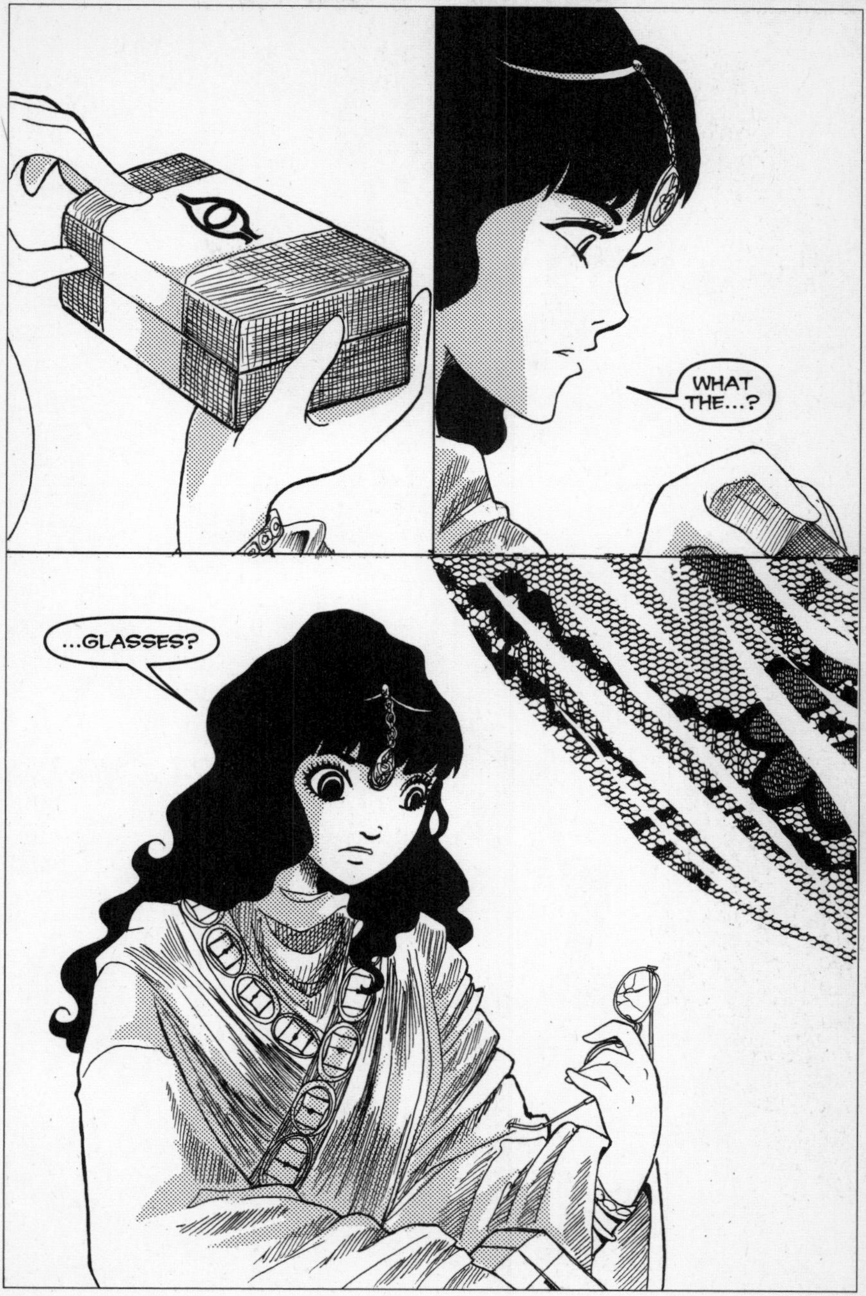
WHAT THE...?
...GLASSES?

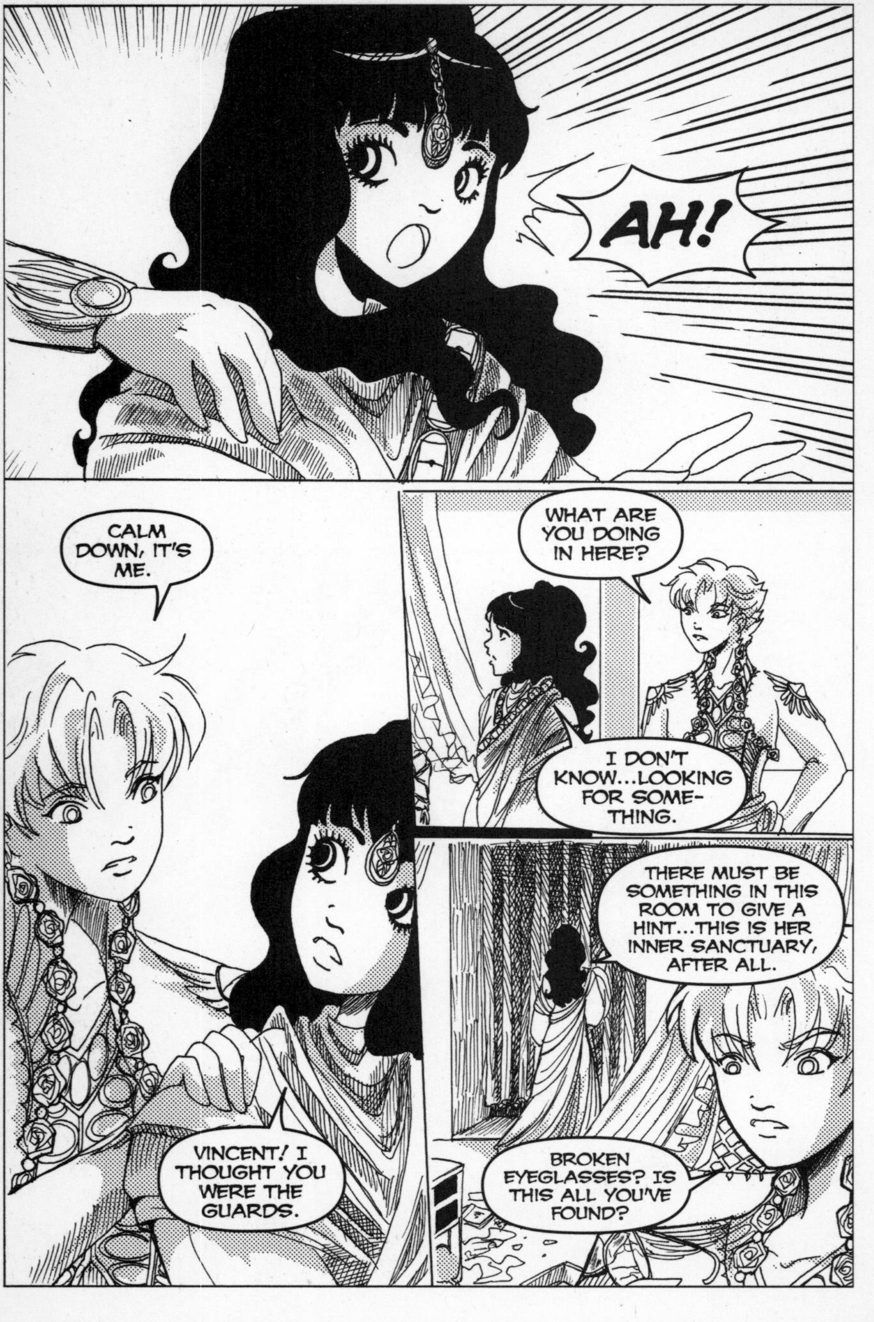
AH!
CALM DOWN, IT'S ME.
VINCENT! I THOUGHT YOU WERE THE GUARDS.
WHAT ARE YOU DOING IN HERE?
I DON'T KNOW...LOOKING FOR SOME-THING.
THERE MUST BE SOMETHING IN THIS ROOM TO GIVE A HINT...THIS IS HER INNER SANCTUARY, AFTER ALL.
BROKEN EYEGLASSES? IS THIS ALL YOU'VE FOUND?

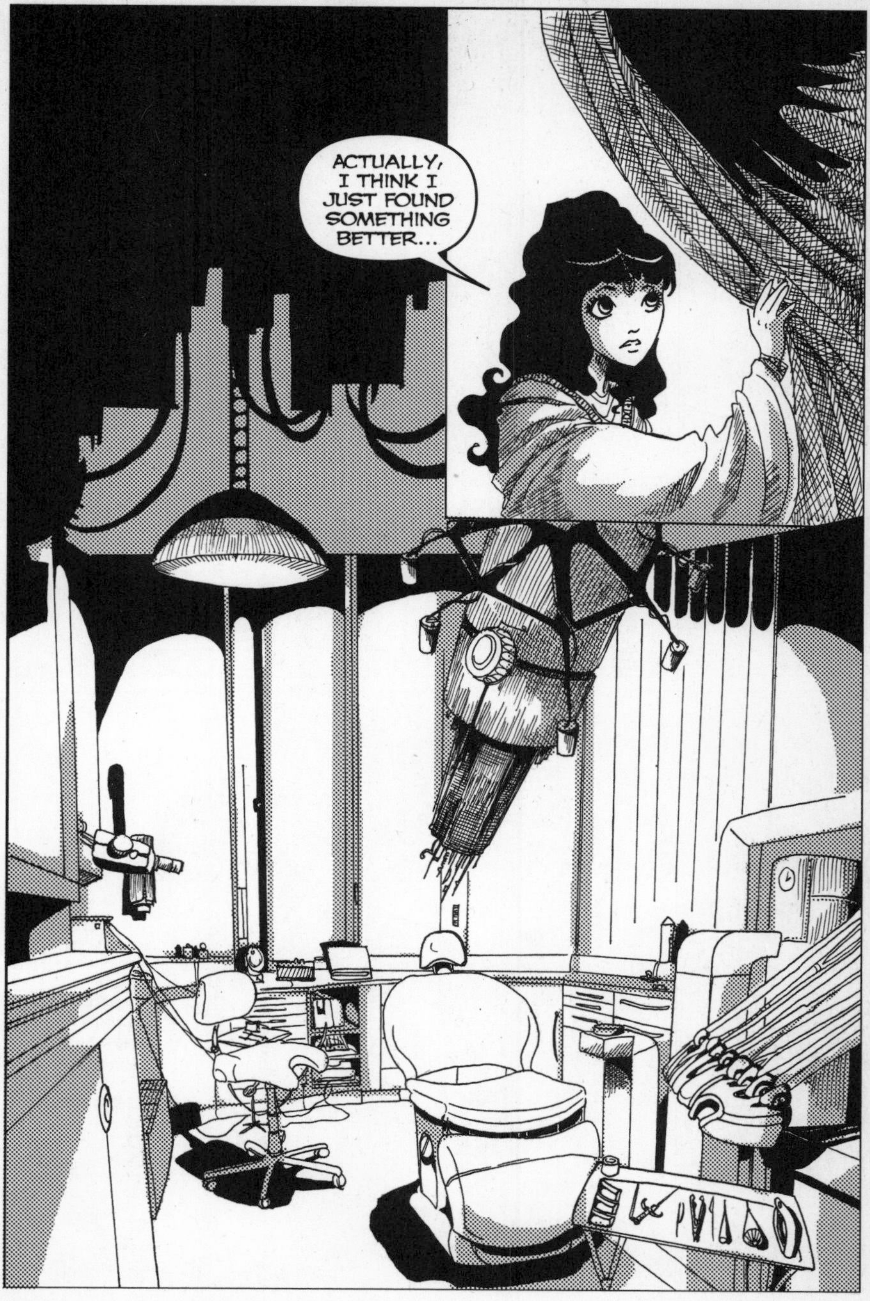
ACTUALLY, I THINK I JUST FOUND SOMETHING BETTER...

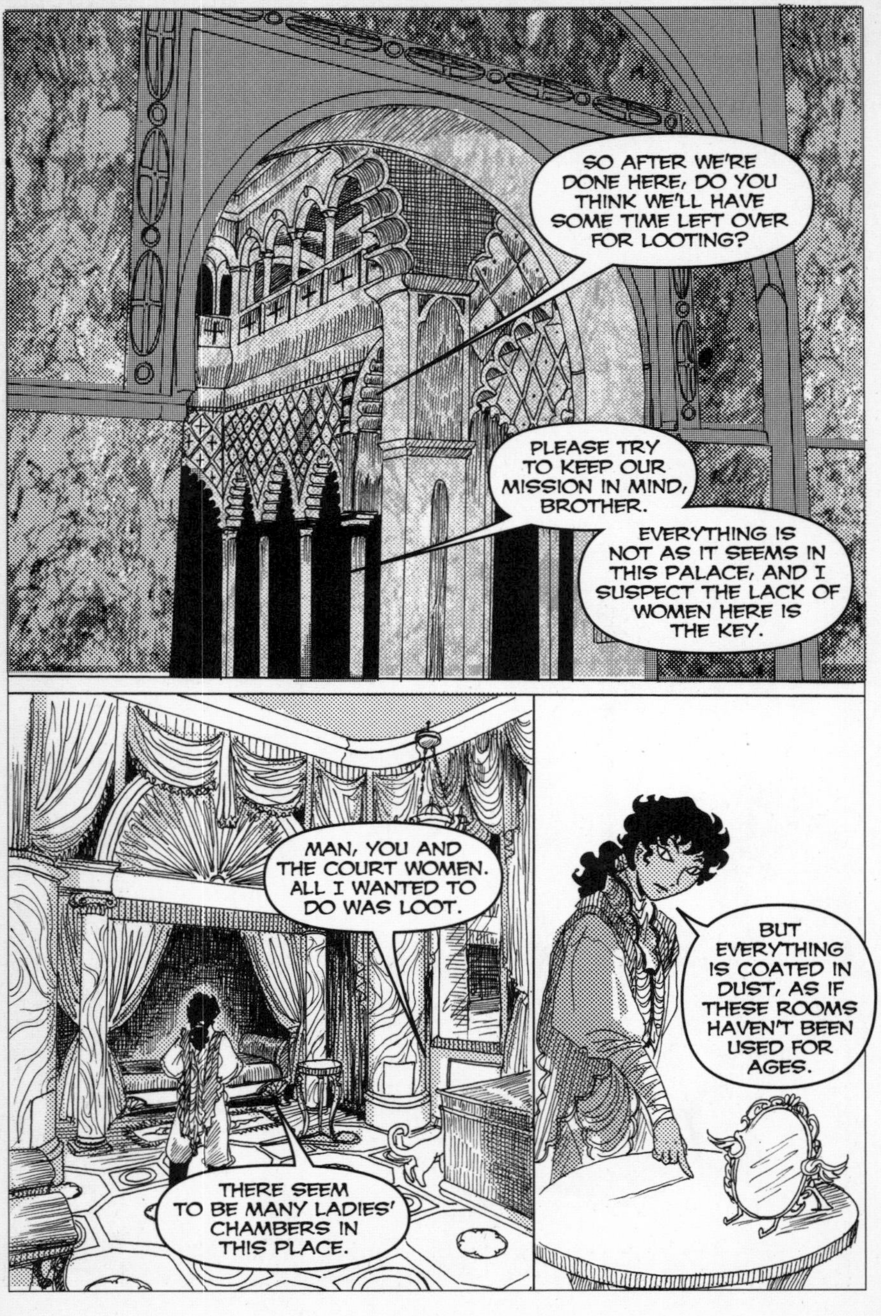
SO AFTER WE'RE DONE HERE, DO YOU THINK WE'LL HAVE SOME TIME LEFT OVER FOR LOOTING?
PLEASE TRY TO KEEP OUR MISSION IN MIND, BROTHER.
EVERYTHING IS NOT AS IT SEEMS IN THIS PALACE, AND I SUSPECT THE LACK OF WOMEN HERE IS THE KEY.
MAN, YOU AND THE COURT WOMEN. ALL I WANTED TO DO WAS LOOT.
THERE SEEM TO BE MANY LADIES' CHAMBERS IN THIS PLACE.
BUT EVERYTHING IS COATED IN DUST, AS IF THESE ROOMS HAVEN'T BEEN USED FOR AGES.

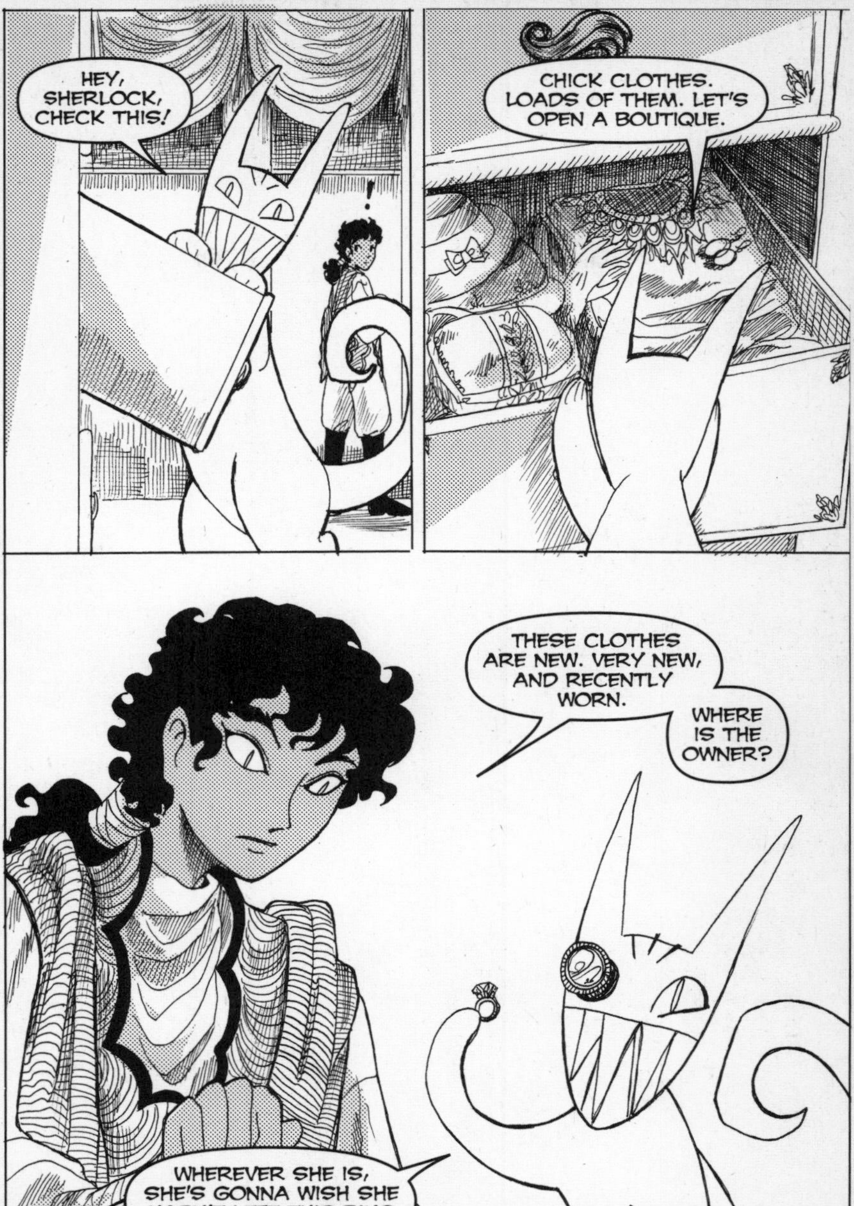
HEY, SHERLOCK, CHECK THIS!
!
CHICK CLOTHES. LOADS OF THEM. LET'S OPEN A BOUTIQUE.
THESE CLOTHES ARE NEW. VERY NEW, AND RECENTLY WORN.
WHERE IS THE OWNER?
WHEREVER SHE IS, SHE'S GONNA WISH SHE HADN'T LEFT THIS RING LYING AROUND.

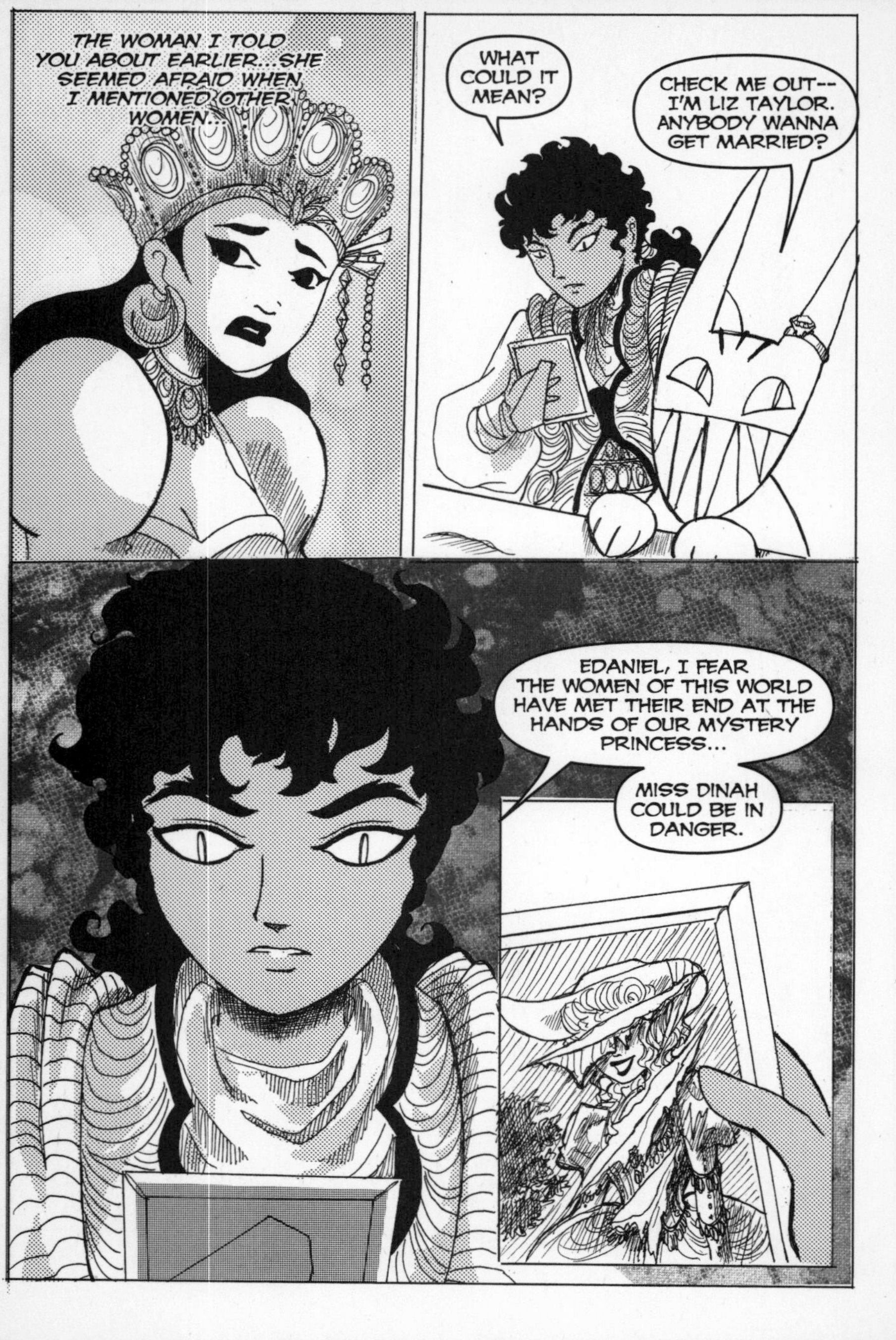
THE WOMAN I TOLD YOU ABOUT EARLIER...SHE SEEMED AFRAID WHEN I MENTIONED OTHER WOMEN...
WHAT COULD IT MEAN?
CHECK ME OUT-- I'M LIZ TAYLOR. ANYBODY WANNA GET MARRIED?
EDANIEL, I FEAR THE WOMEN OF THIS WORLD HAVE MET THEIR END AT THE HANDS OF OUR MYSTERY PRINCESS...
MISS DINAH COULD BE IN DANGER.

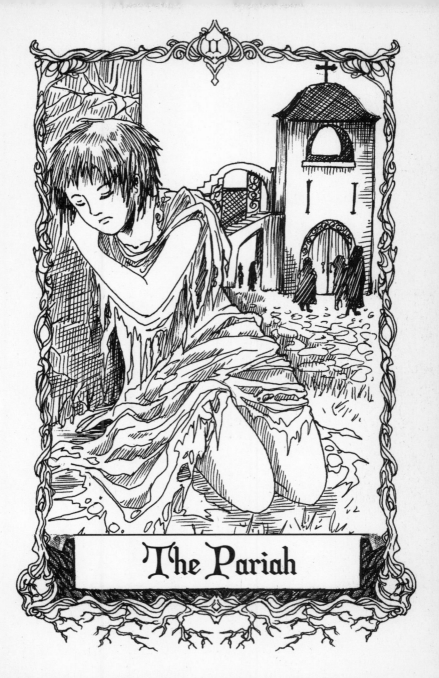

The Pariah

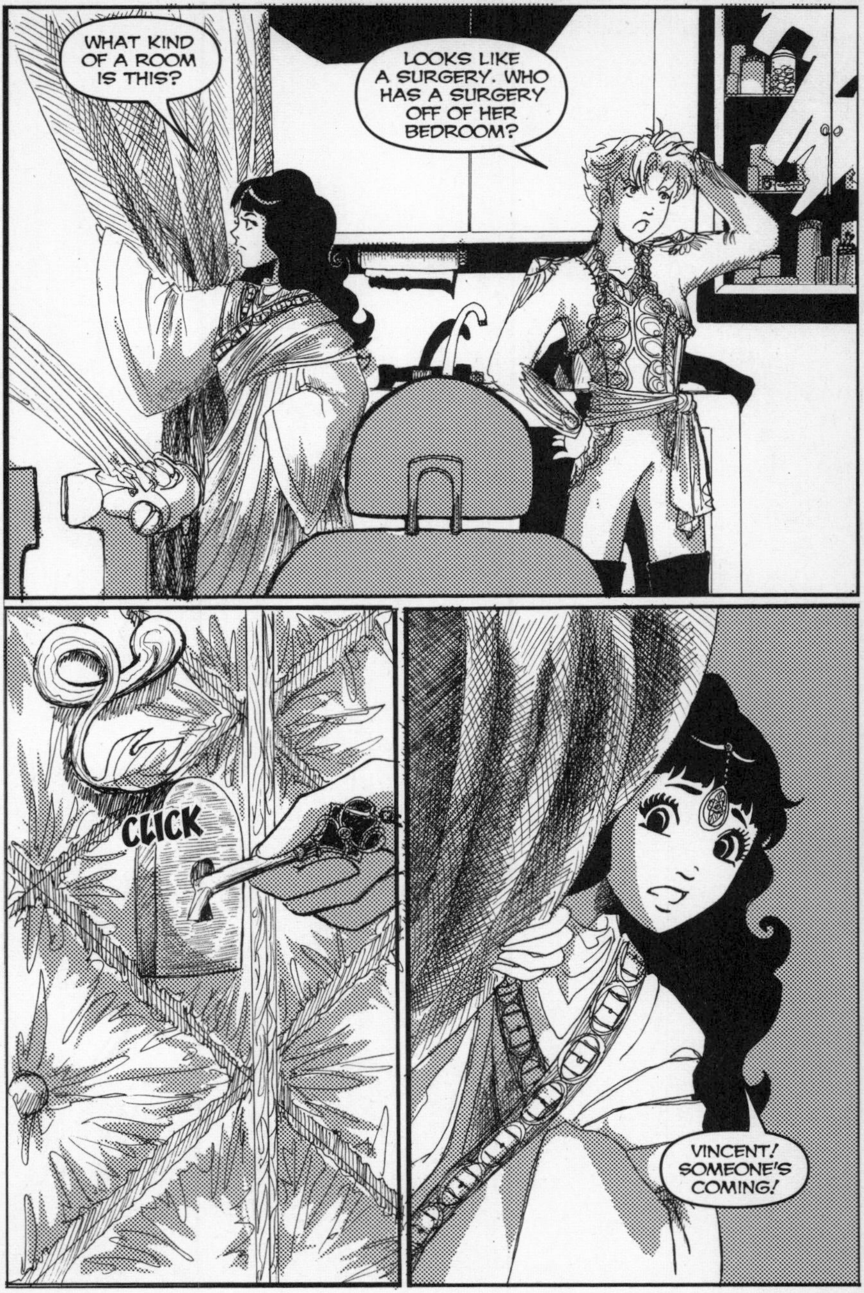
WHAT KIND OF A ROOM IS THIS?
LOOKS LIKE A SURGERY. WHO HAS A SURGERY OFF OF HER BEDROOM?
CLICK
VINCENT! SOMEONE'S COMING!

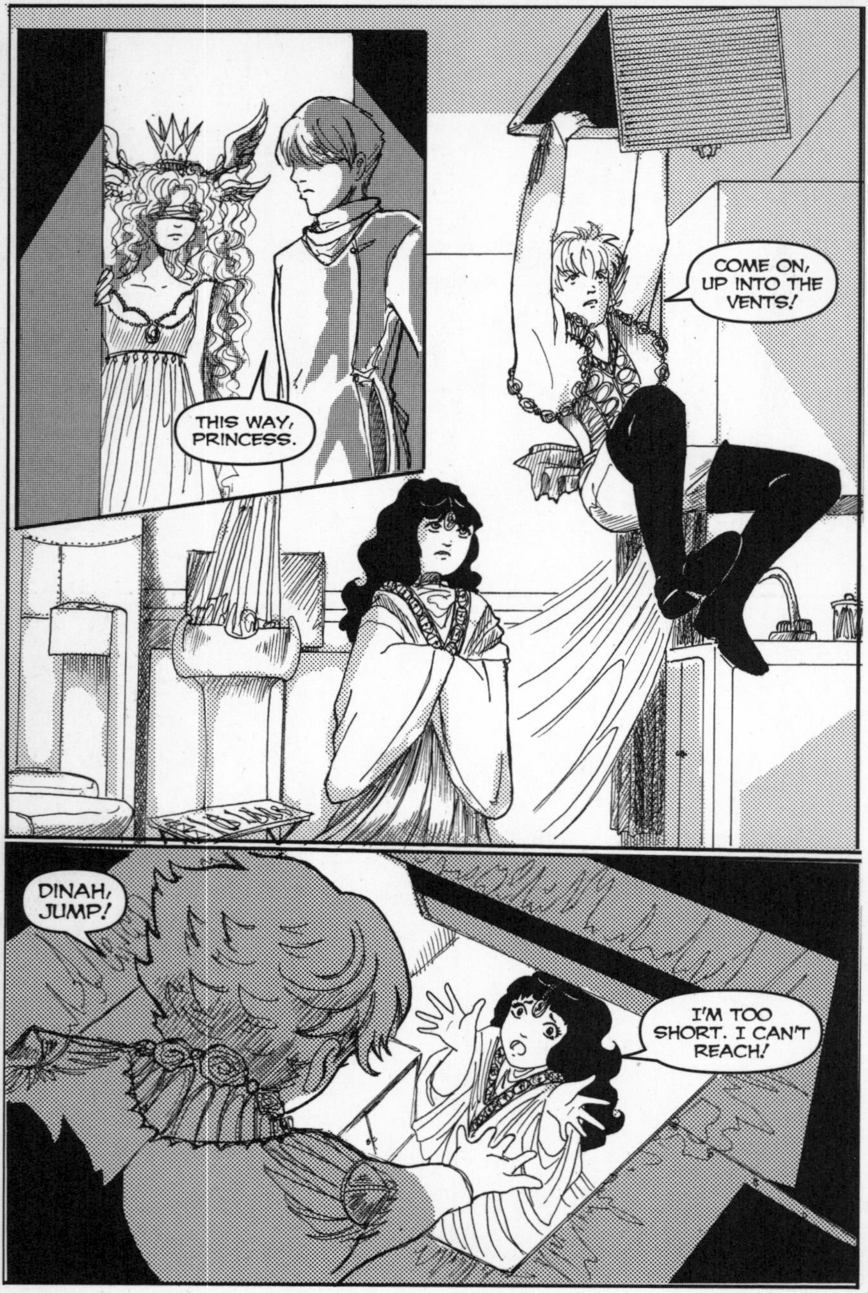
THIS WAY, PRINCESS.
COME ON, UP INTO THE VENTS!
DINAH, JUMP!
I'M TOO SHORT. I CAN'T REACH!

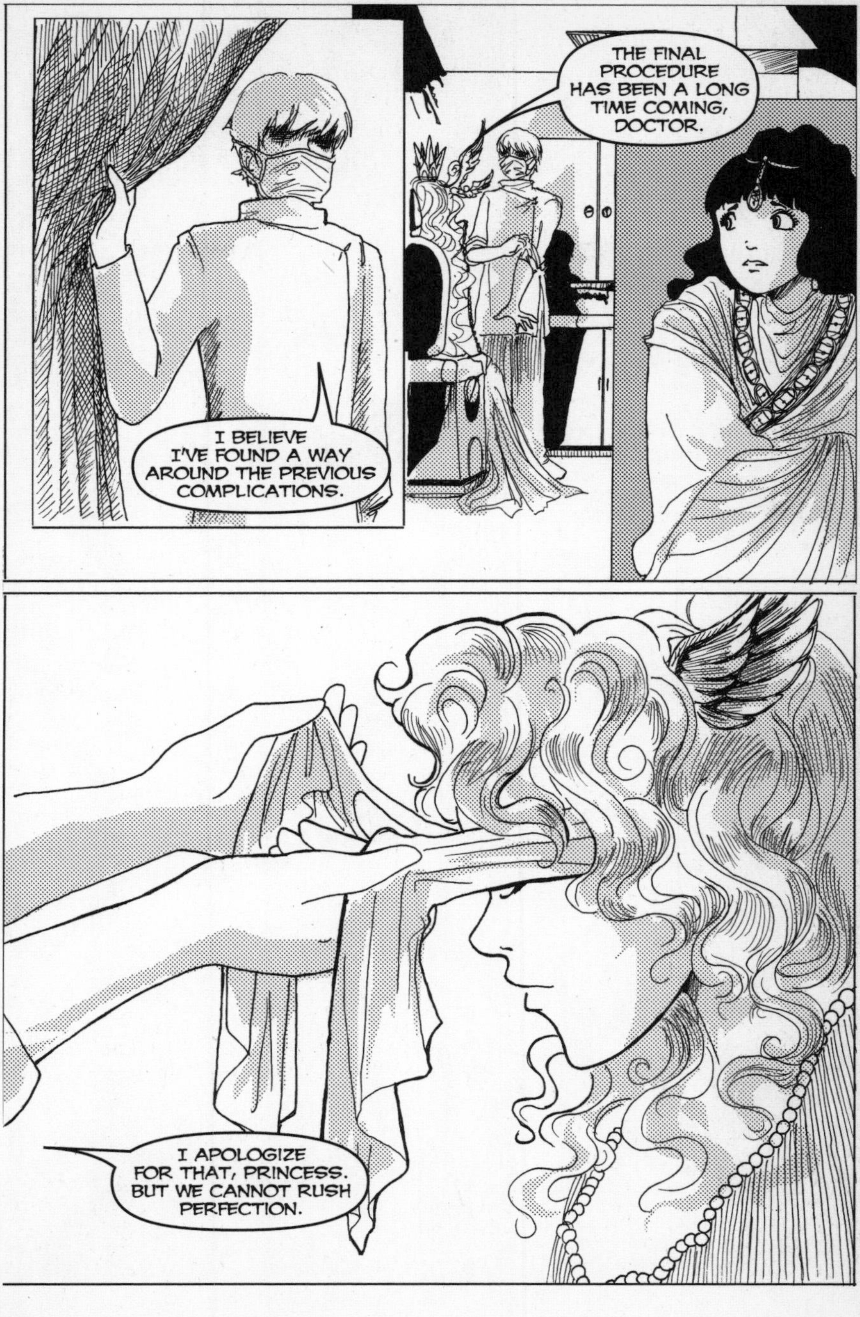
I BELIEVE I'VE FOUND A WAY AROUND THE PREVIOUS COMPLICATIONS.
THE FINAL PROCEDURE HAS BEEN A LONG TIME COMING, DOCTOR.
I APOLOGIZE FOR THAT, PRINCESS. BUT WE CANNOT RUSH PERFECTION.

YOU KNOW I DISLIKE DELAYS EXTREMELY.

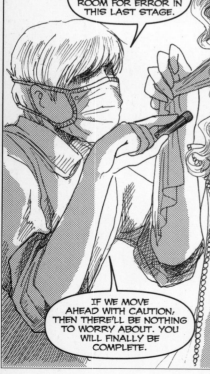

YOU MUST HAVE PATIENCE, MY PRINCESS. THERE'S NO ROOM FOR ERROR IN THIS LAST STAGE.

IF WE MOVE AHEAD WITH CAUTION, THEN THERE'LL BE NOTHING TO WORRY ABOUT. YOU WILL FINALLY BE COMPLETE.

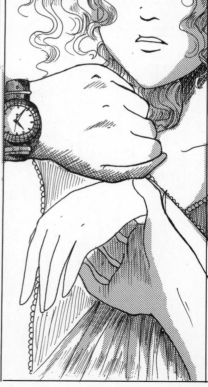

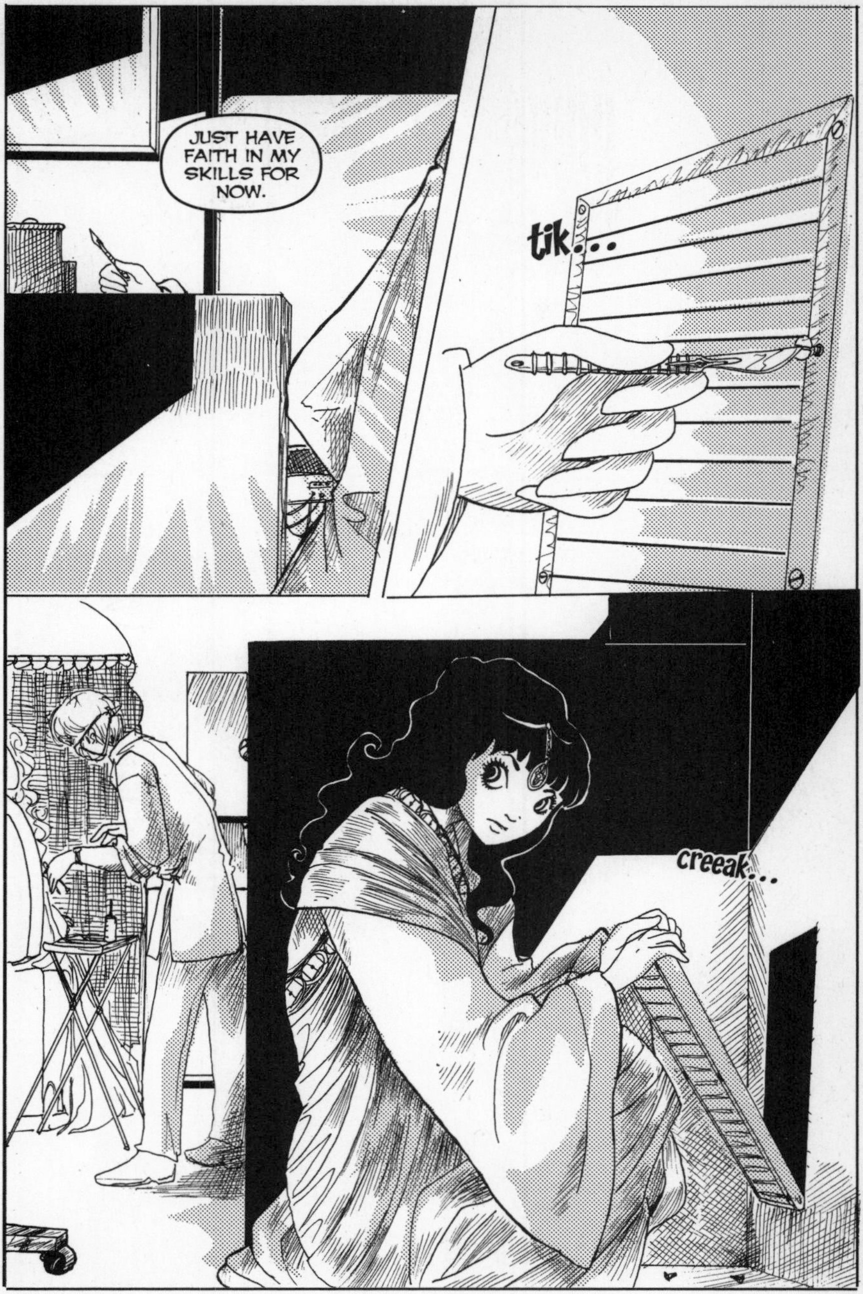

JUST HAVE FAITH IN MY SKILLS FOR NOW.
tik...
creeak...

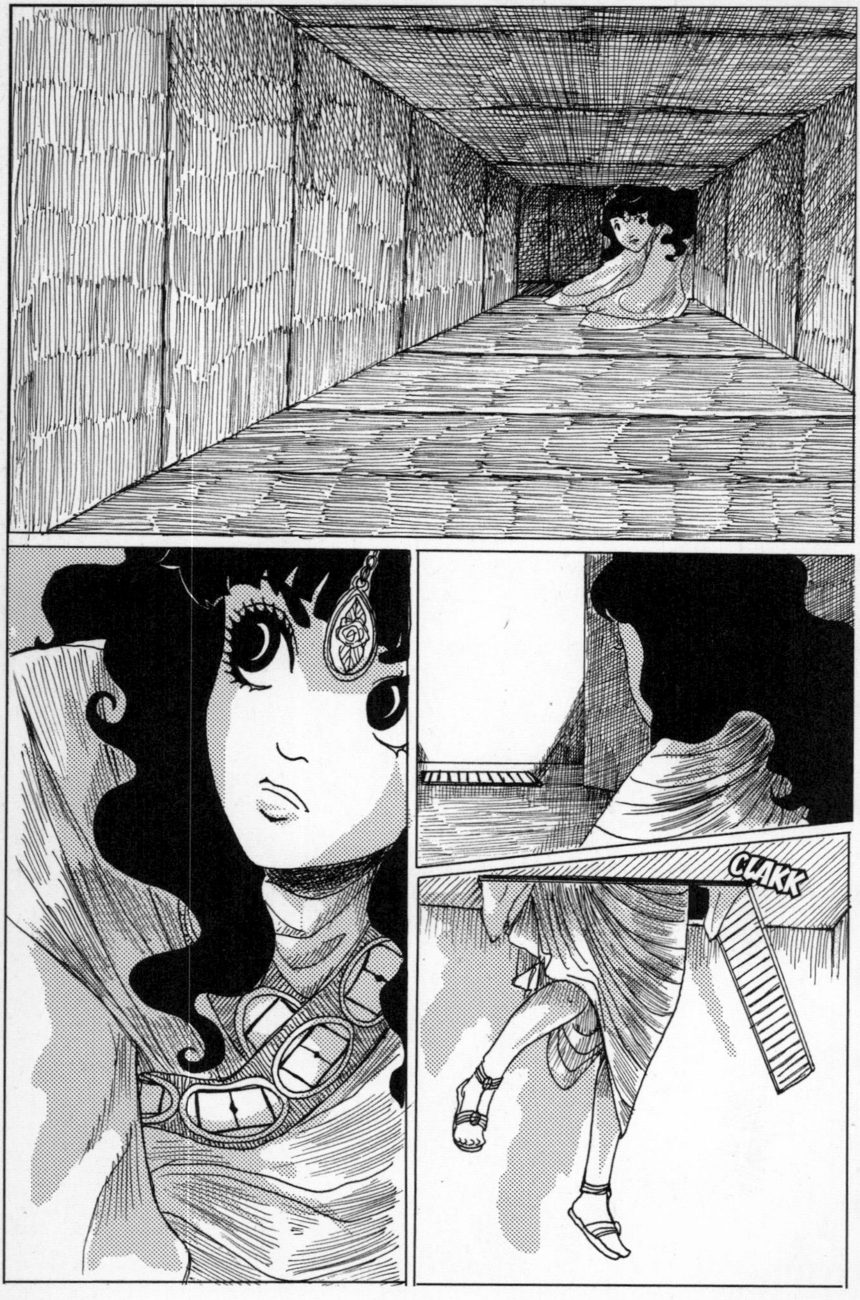
CLAKK

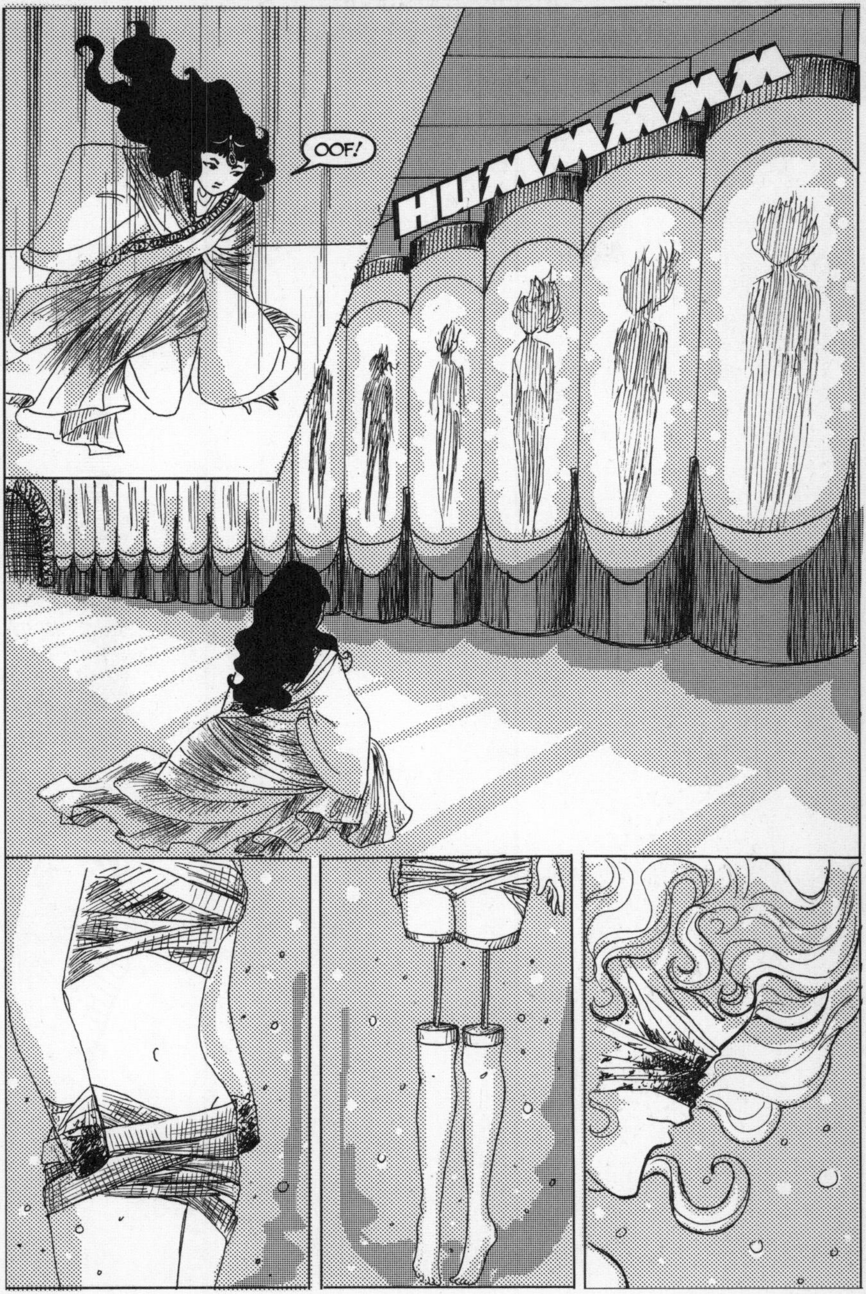
OOF!
HUMMMMMM

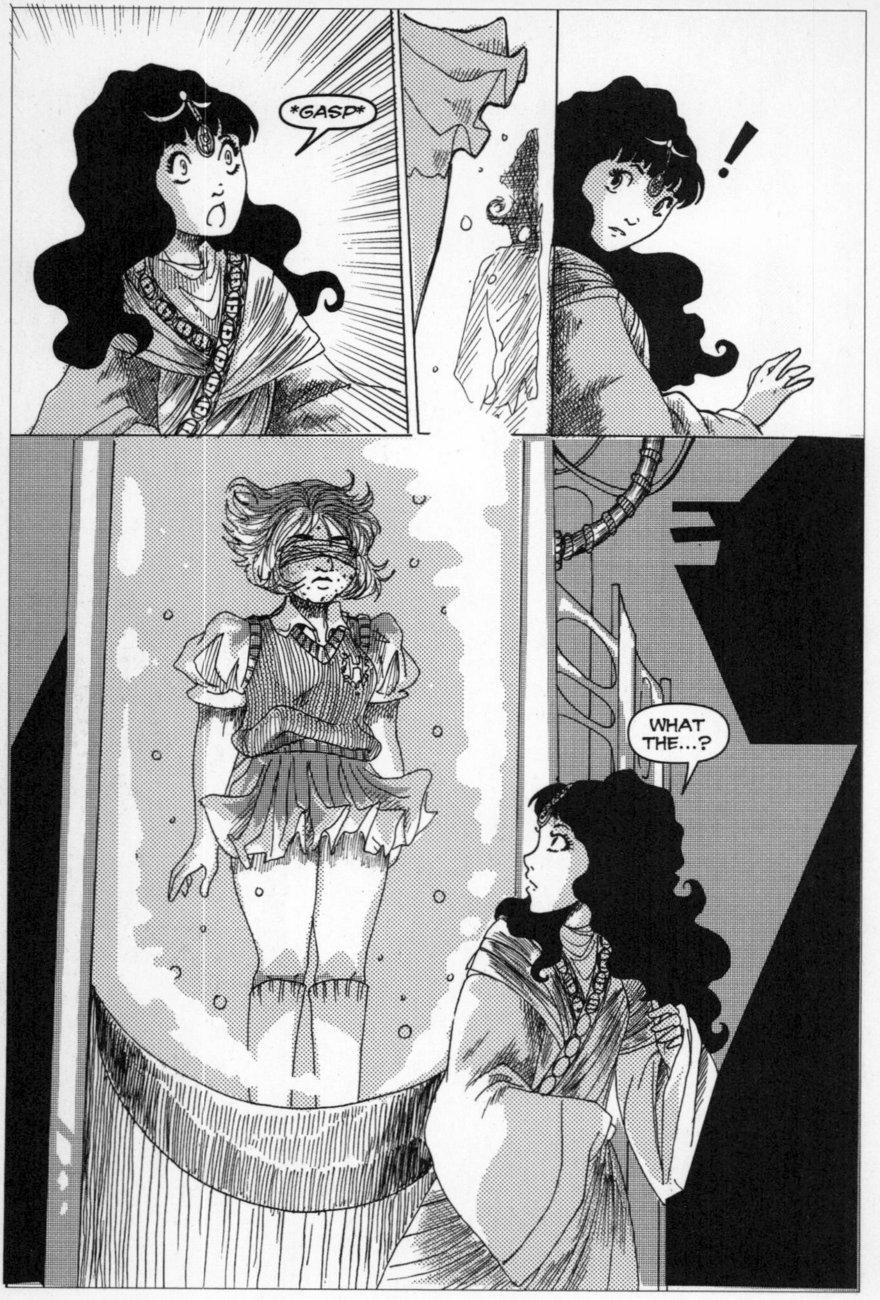
GASP
!
WHAT THE...?

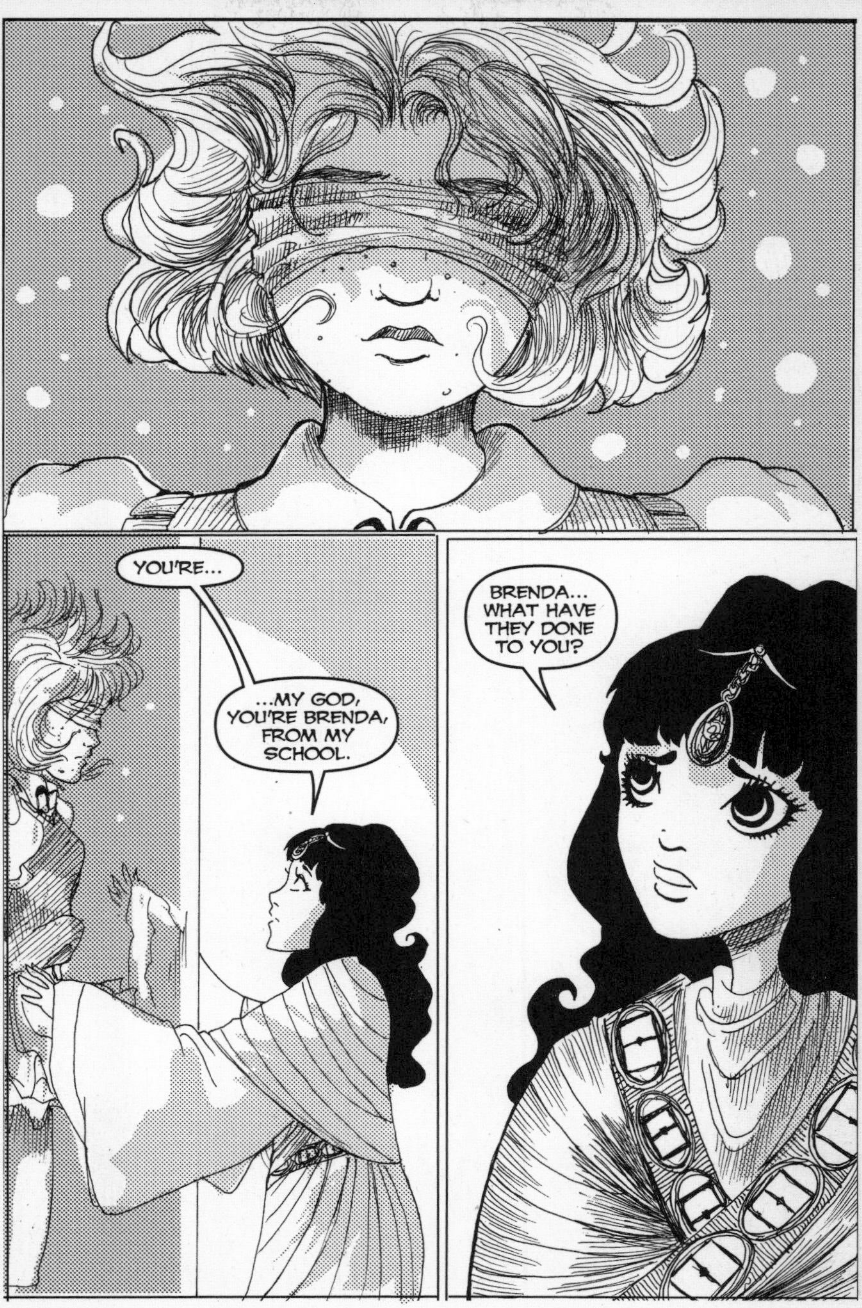
YOU'RE...
...MY GOD, YOU'RE BRENDA, FROM MY SCHOOL.
BRENDA... WHAT HAVE THEY DONE TO YOU?

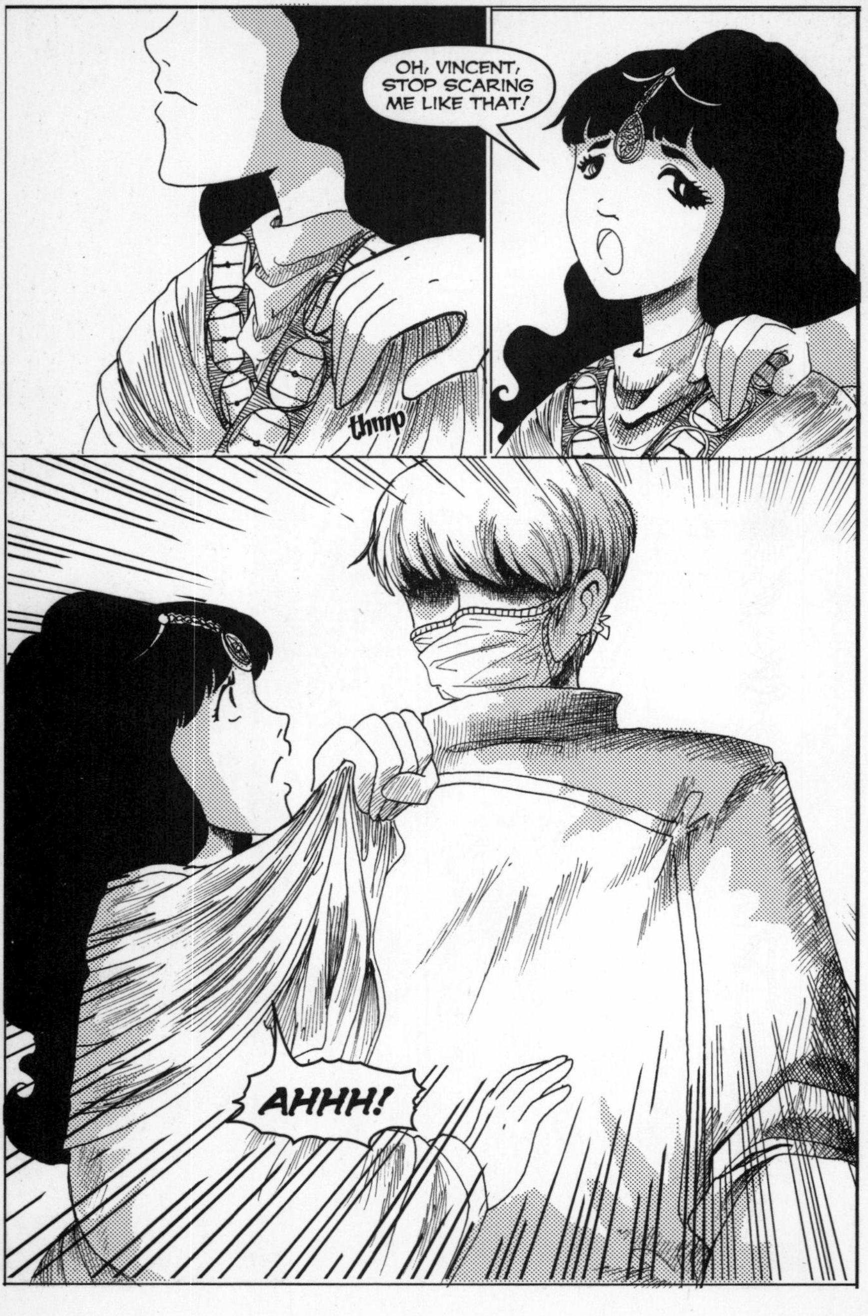
thmp
OH, VINCENT, STOP SCARING ME LIKE THAT!
AHHH!

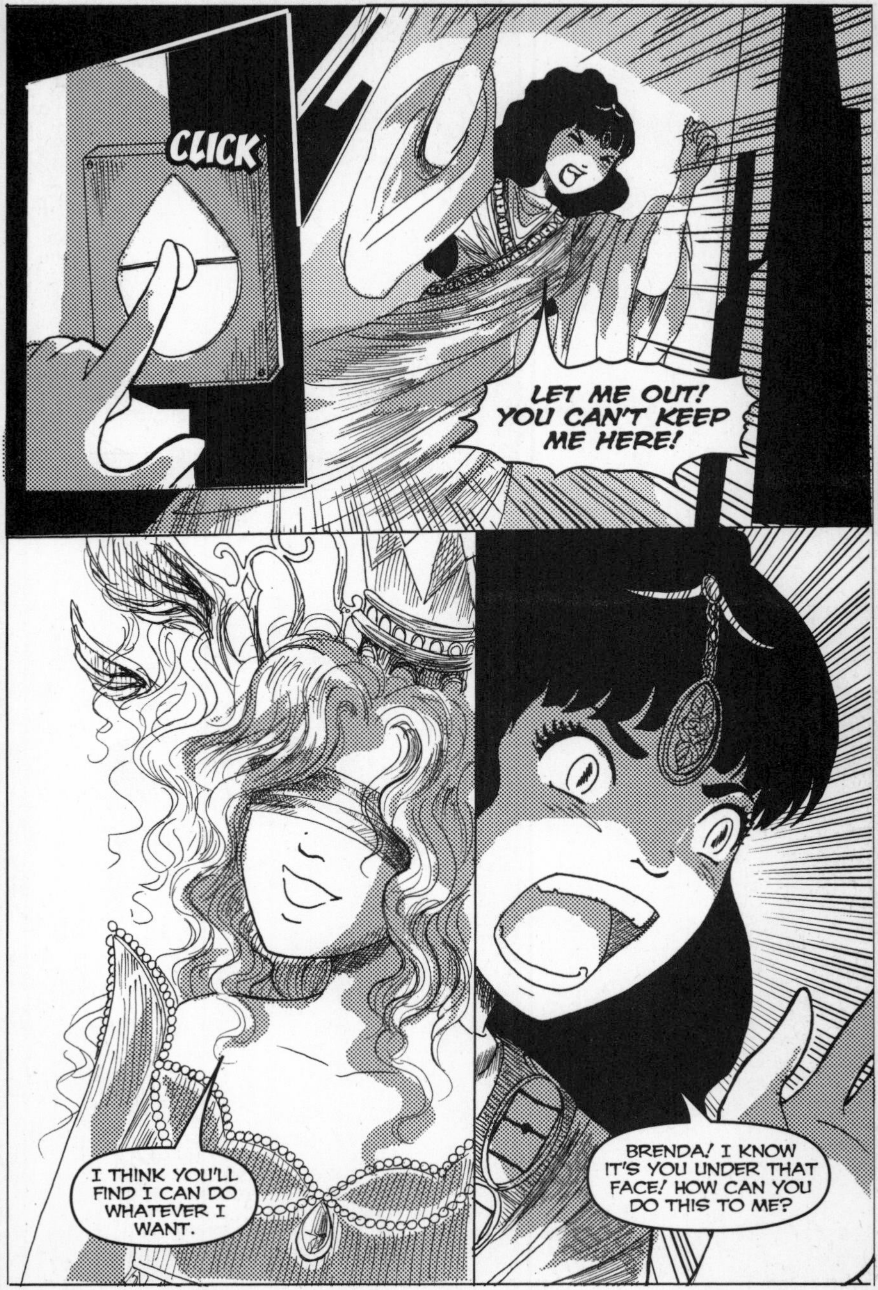
CLICK
LET ME OUT! YOU CAN'T KEEP ME HERE!
I THINK YOU'LL FIND I CAN DO WHATEVER I WANT.
BRENDA! I KNOW IT'S YOU UNDER THAT FACE! HOW CAN YOU DO THIS TO ME?

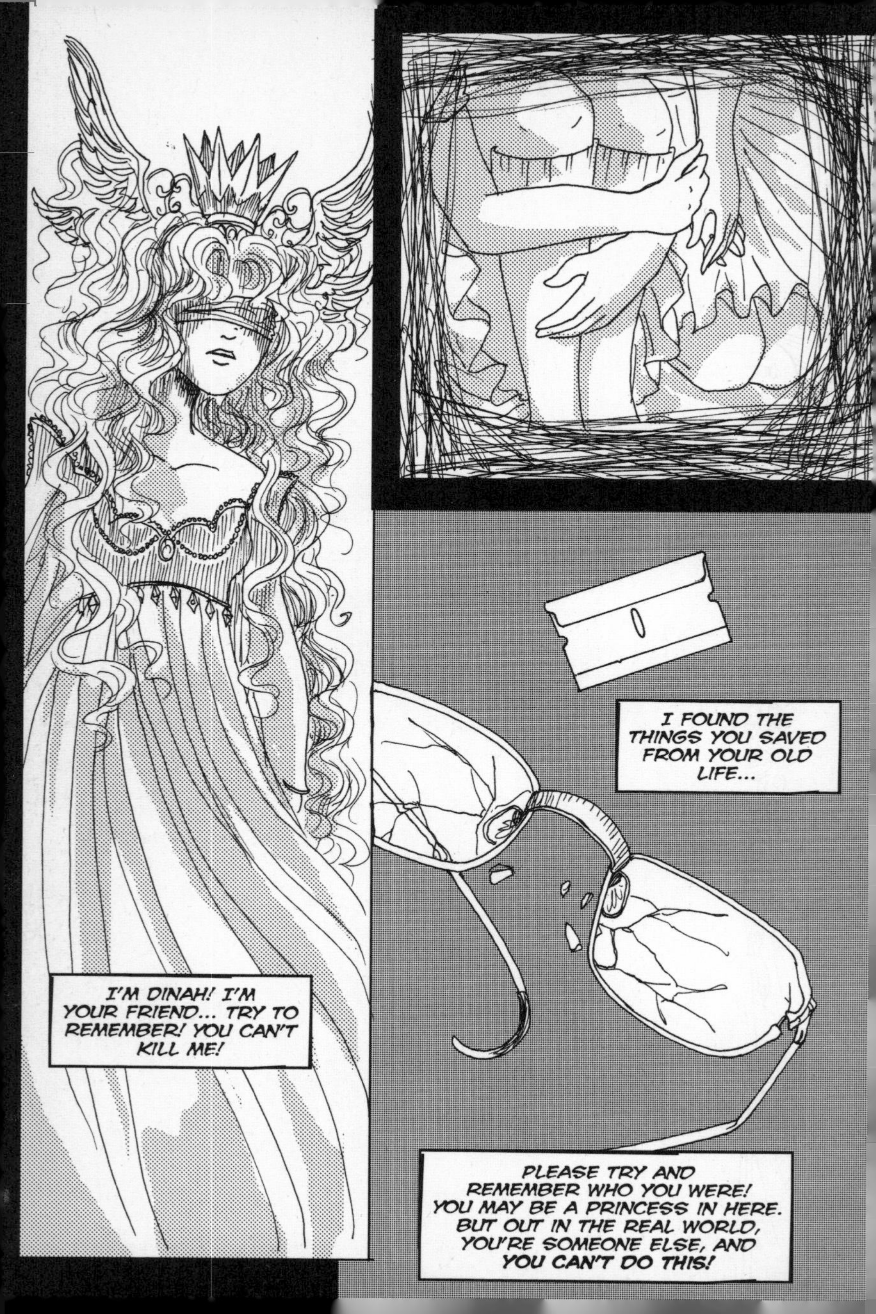
I'M DINAH! I'M YOUR FRIEND... TRY TO REMEMBER! YOU CAN'T KILL ME!
I FOUND THE THINGS YOU SAVED FROM YOUR OLD LIFE...
PLEASE TRY AND REMEMBER WHO YOU WERE! YOU MAY BE A PRINCESS IN HERE. BUT OUT IN THE REAL WORLD, YOU'RE SOMEONE ELSE, AND YOU CAN'T DO THIS!

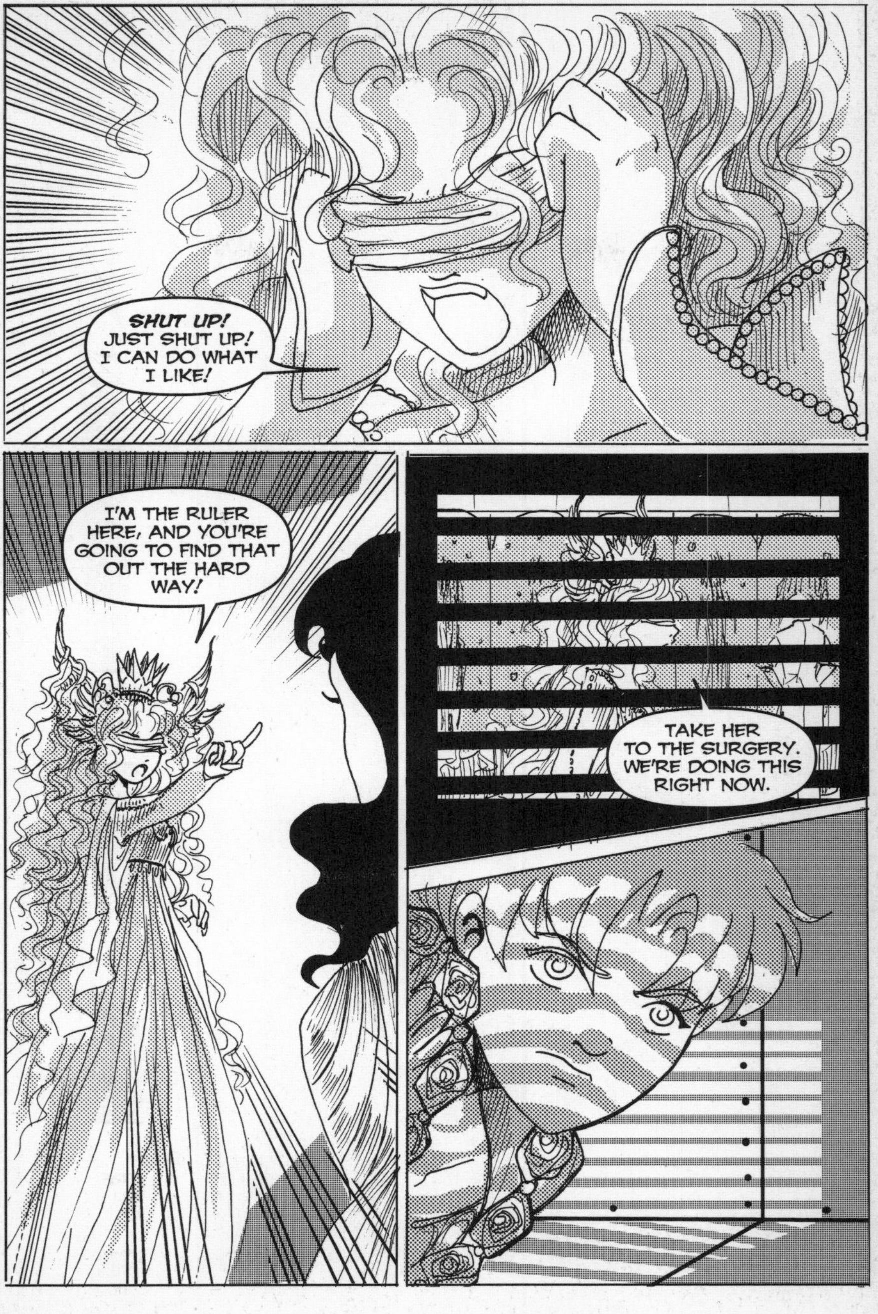
SHUT UP! JUST SHUT UP! I CAN DO WHAT I LIKE!
I'M THE RULER HERE, AND YOU'RE GOING TO FIND THAT OUT THE HARD WAY!
TAKE HER TO THE SURGERY. WE'RE DOING THIS RIGHT NOW.

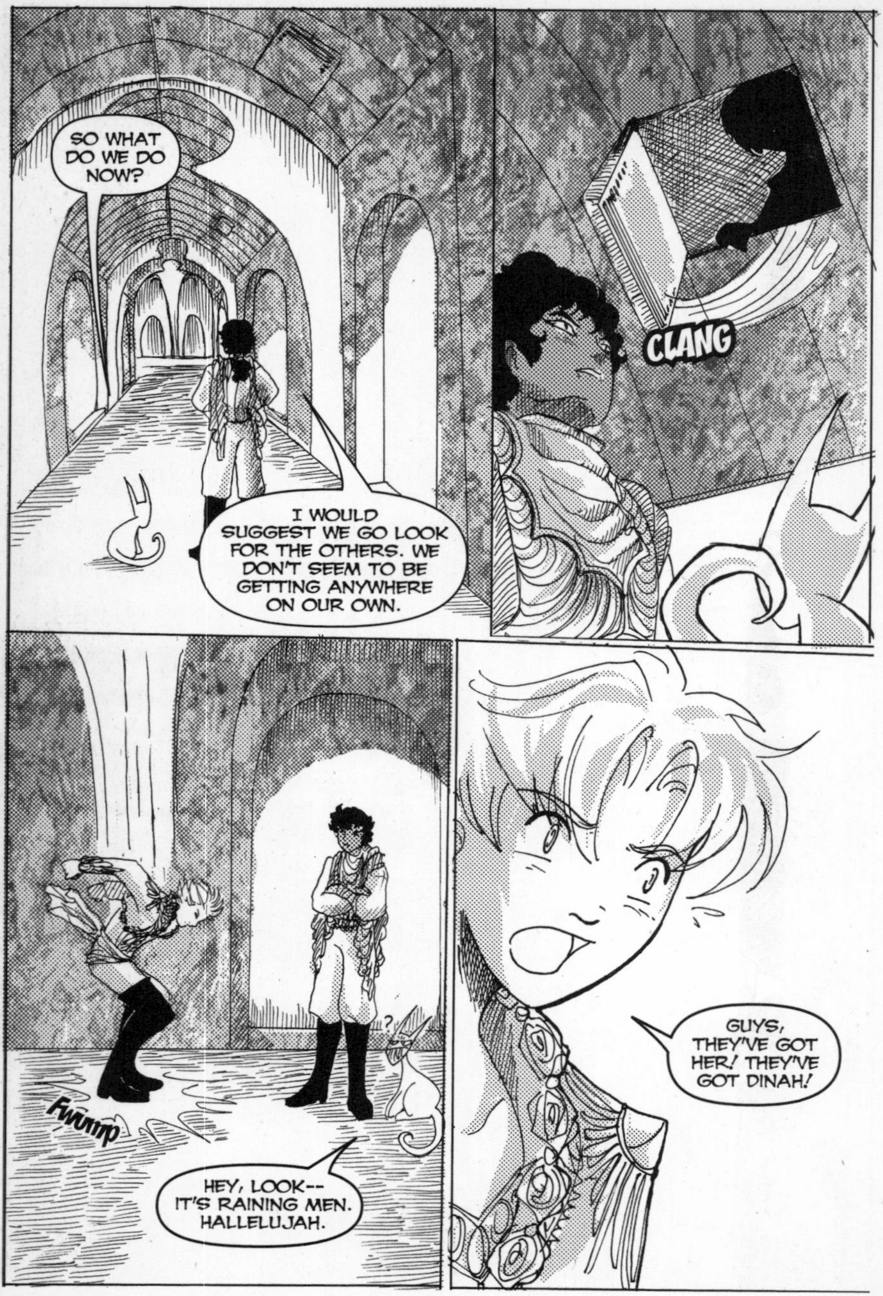
SO WHAT DO WE DO NOW?
I WOULD SUGGEST WE GO LOOK FOR THE OTHERS. WE DON'T SEEM TO BE GETTING ANYWHERE ON OUR OWN.
CLANG
Fwump
?
HEY, LOOK-- IT'S RAINING MEN. HALLELUJAH.
GUYS, THEY'VE GOT HER! THEY'VE GOT DINAH!

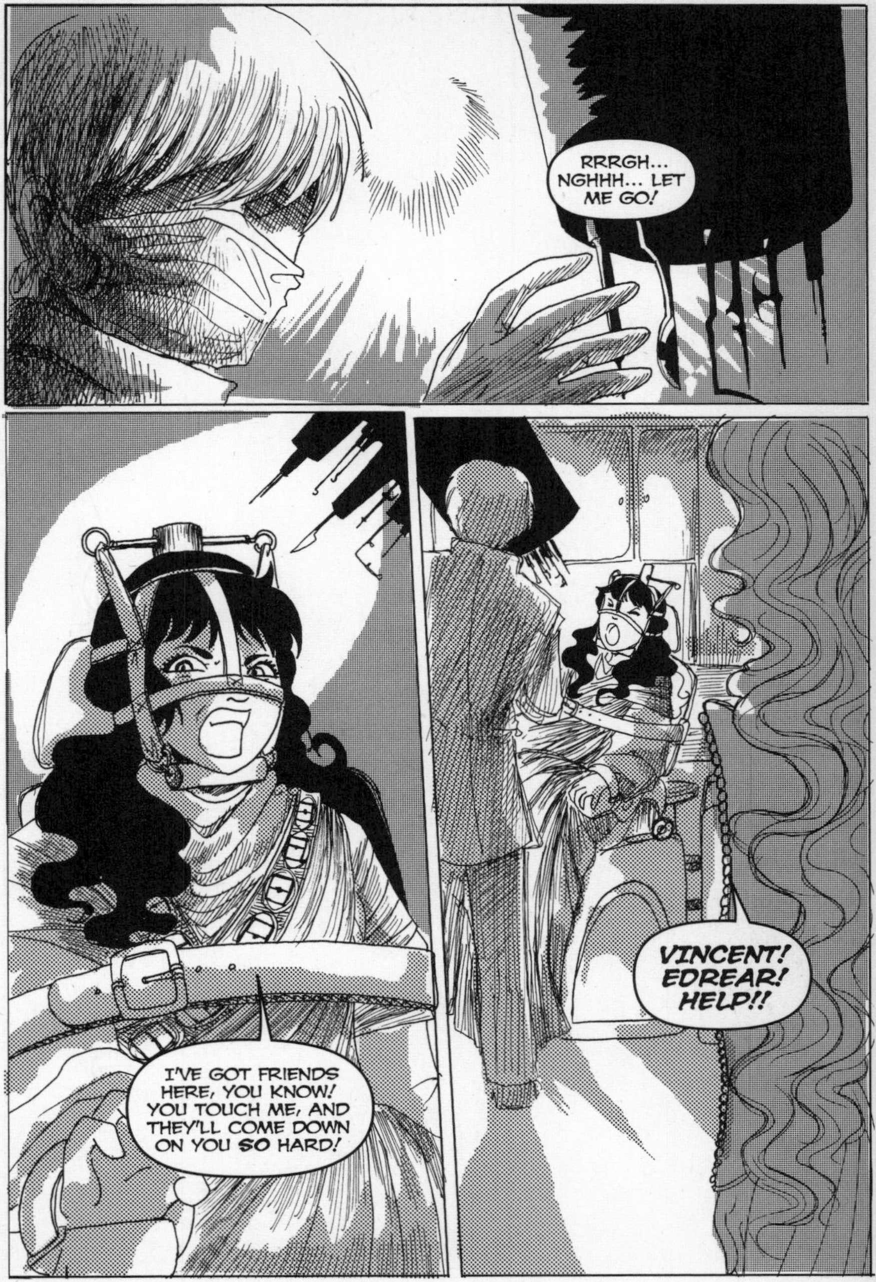
RRRGH... NGHHH... LET ME GO!
I'VE GOT FRIENDS HERE, YOU KNOW! YOU TOUCH ME, AND THEY'LL COME DOWN ON YOU SO HARD!
VINCENT! EDREAR! HELP!!

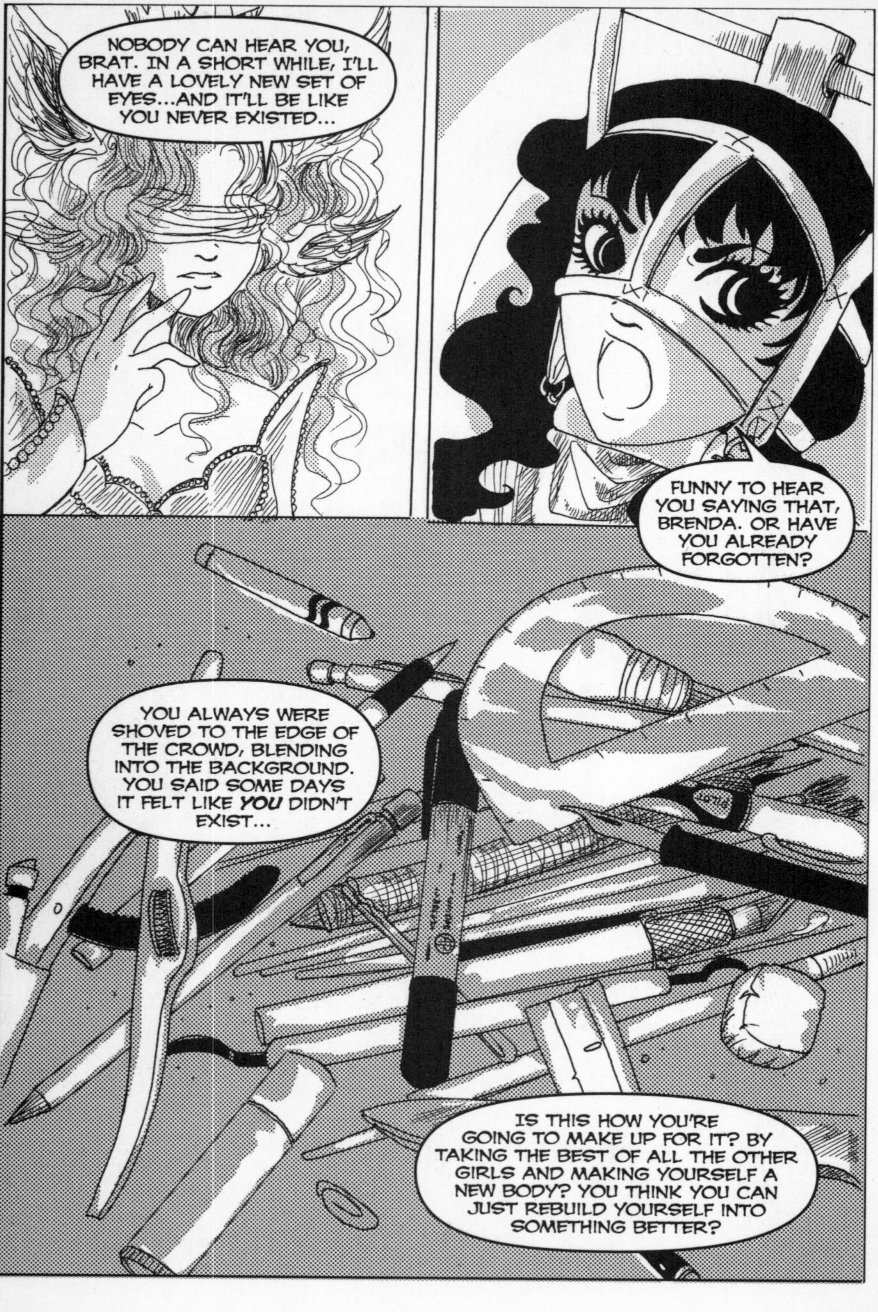
NOBODY CAN HEAR YOU, BRAT. IN A SHORT WHILE, I'LL HAVE A LOVELY NEW SET OF EYES...AND IT'LL BE LIKE YOU NEVER EXISTED...
FUNNY TO HEAR YOU SAYING THAT, BRENDA. OR HAVE YOU ALREADY FORGOTTEN?
YOU ALWAYS WERE SHOVED TO THE EDGE OF THE CROWD, BLENDING INTO THE BACKGROUND. YOU SAID SOME DAYS IT FELT LIKE *YOU* DIDN'T EXIST...
IS THIS HOW YOU'RE GOING TO MAKE UP FOR IT? BY TAKING THE BEST OF ALL THE OTHER GIRLS AND MAKING YOURSELF A NEW BODY? YOU THINK YOU CAN JUST REBUILD YOURSELF INTO SOMETHING BETTER?

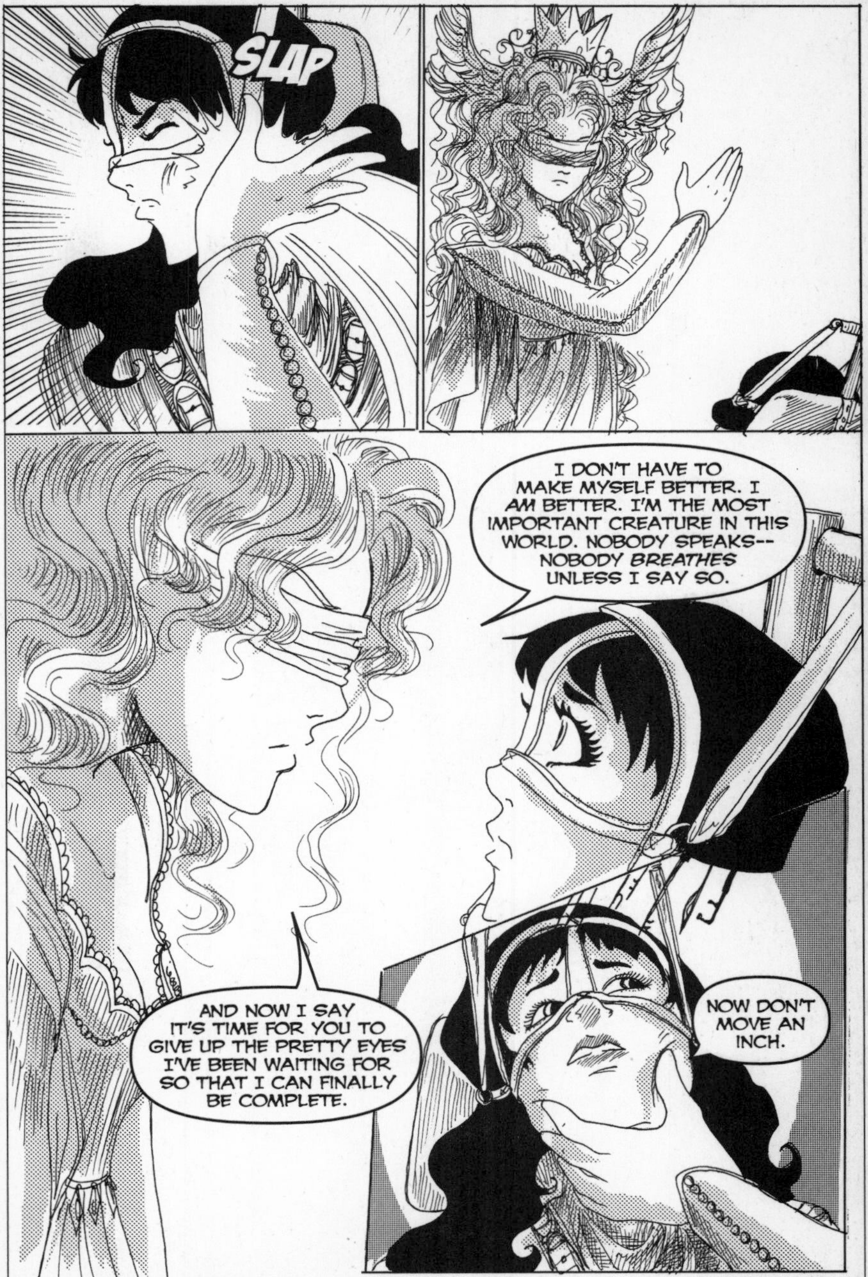
SLAP
I DON'T HAVE TO MAKE MYSELF BETTER. I *AM* BETTER. I'M THE MOST IMPORTANT CREATURE IN THIS WORLD. NOBODY SPEAKS-- NOBODY *BREATHES* UNLESS I SAY SO.
AND NOW I SAY IT'S TIME FOR YOU TO GIVE UP THE PRETTY EYES I'VE BEEN WAITING FOR SO THAT I CAN FINALLY BE COMPLETE.
NOW DON'T MOVE AN INCH.

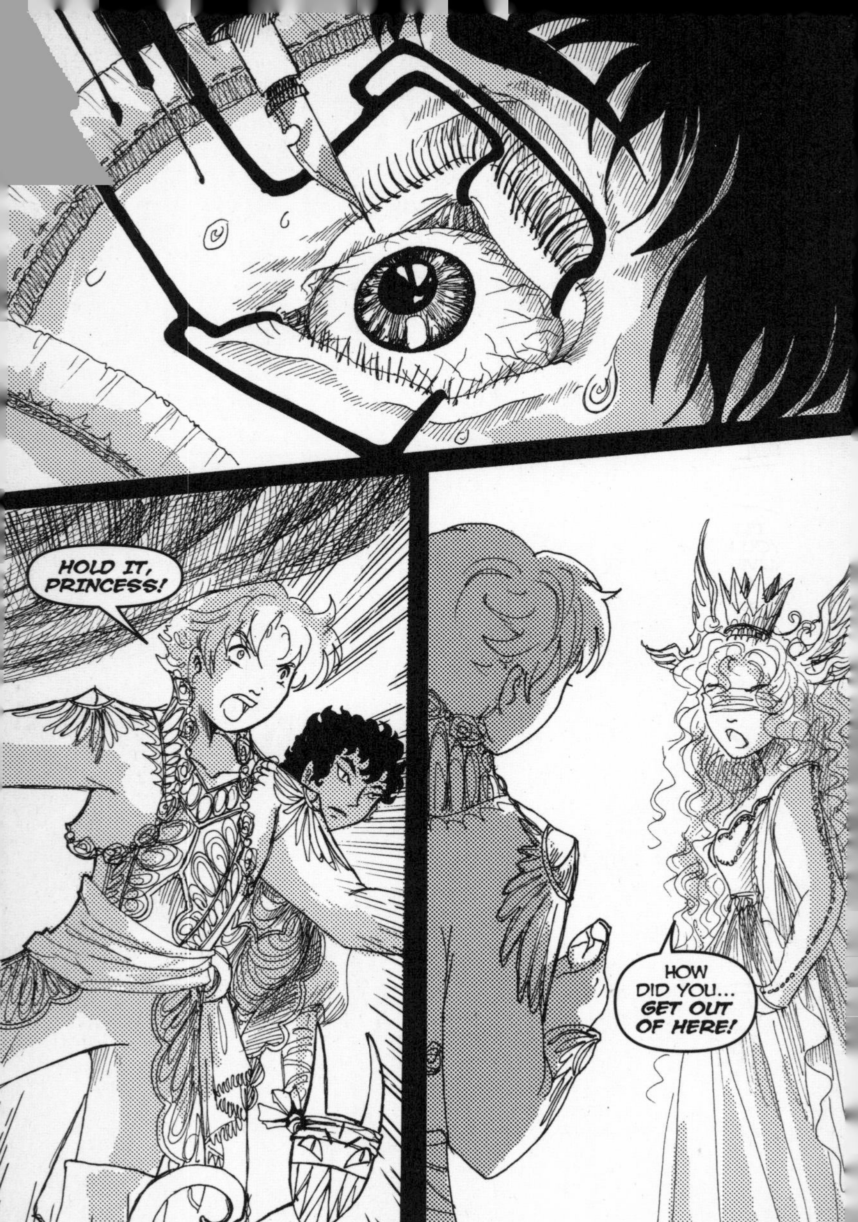
HOLD IT, PRINCESS!
HOW DID YOU... GET OUT OF HERE!

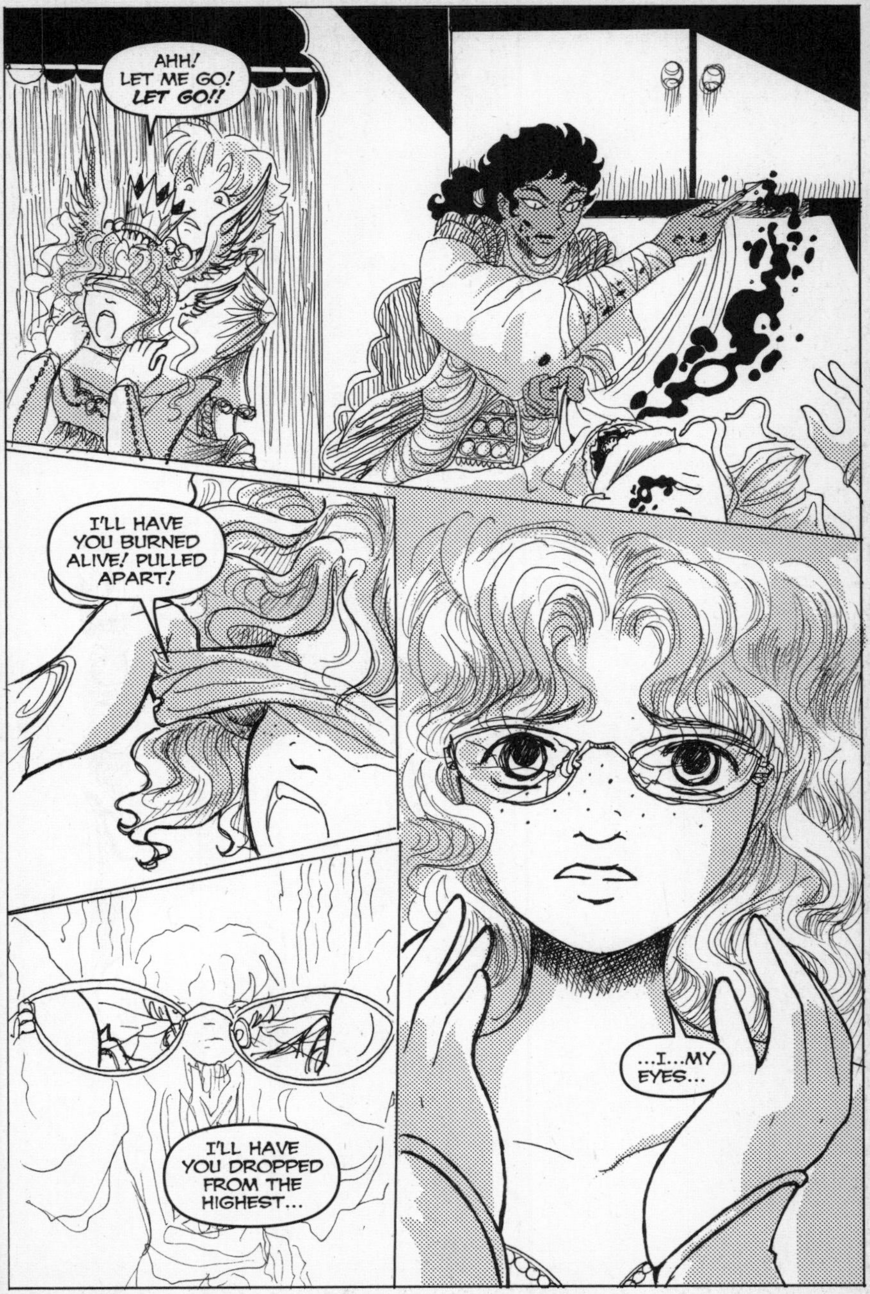
AHH! LET ME GO! LET GO!!
I'LL HAVE YOU BURNED ALIVE! PULLED APART!
I'LL HAVE YOU DROPPED FROM THE HIGHEST...
...I...MY EYES...

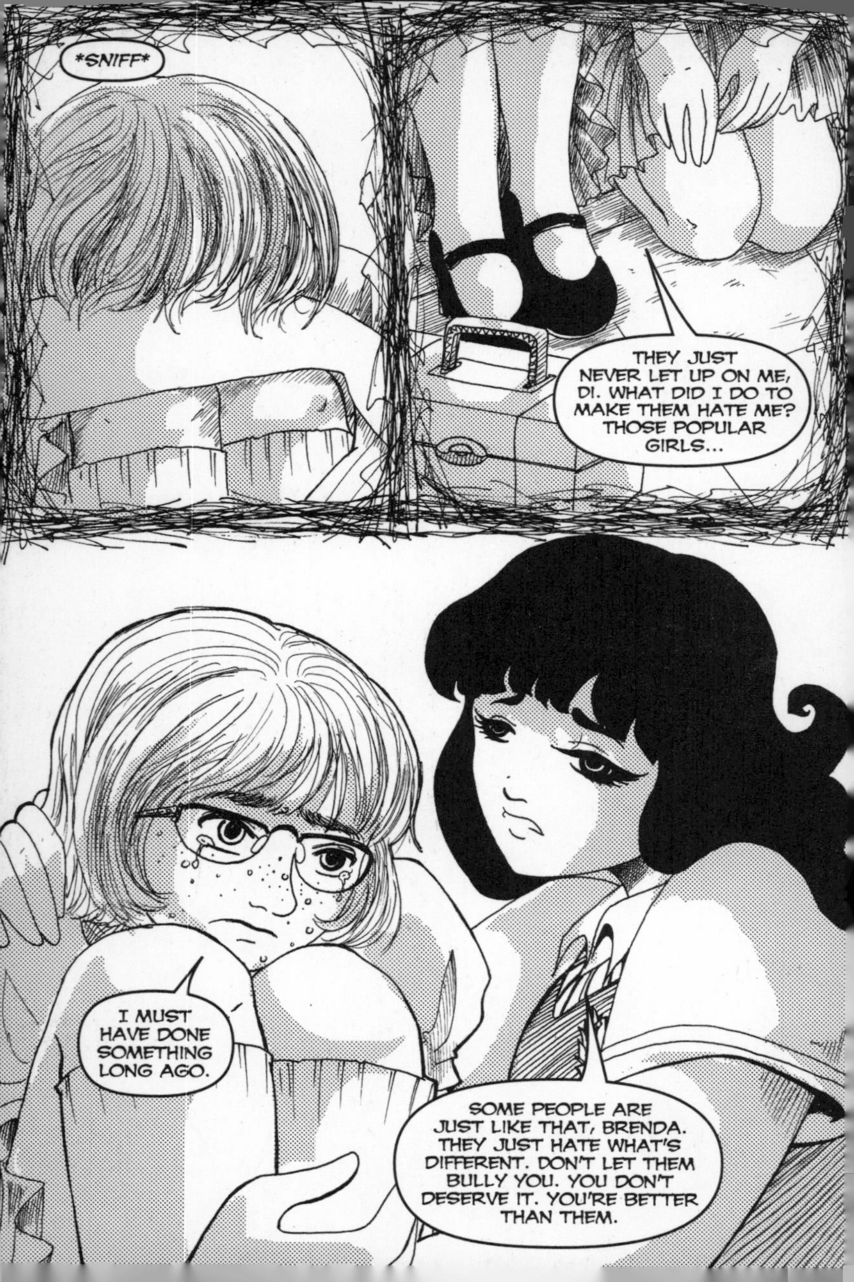
SNIFF
THEY JUST NEVER LET UP ON ME, DI. WHAT DID I DO TO MAKE THEM HATE ME? THOSE POPULAR GIRLS...
I MUST HAVE DONE SOMETHING LONG AGO.
SOME PEOPLE ARE JUST LIKE THAT, BRENDA. THEY JUST HATE WHAT'S DIFFERENT. DON'T LET THEM BULLY YOU. YOU DON'T DESERVE IT. YOU'RE BETTER THAN THEM.

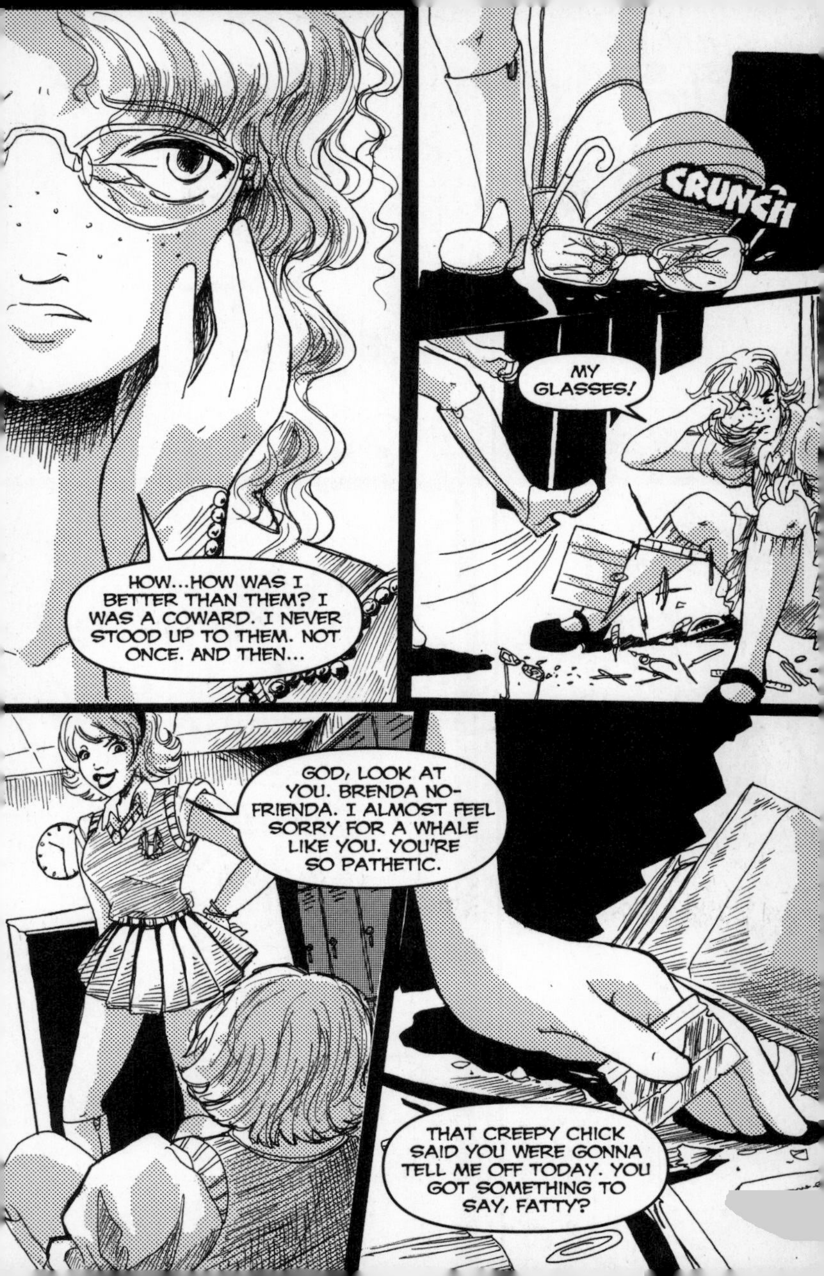
HOW...HOW WAS I BETTER THAN THEM? I WAS A COWARD. I NEVER STOOD UP TO THEM. NOT ONCE. AND THEN...
CRUNCH
MY GLASSES!
GOD, LOOK AT YOU. BRENDA NO-FRIENDA. I ALMOST FEEL SORRY FOR A WHALE LIKE YOU. YOU'RE SO PATHETIC.
THAT CREEPY CHICK SAID YOU WERE GONNA TELL ME OFF TODAY. YOU GOT SOMETHING TO SAY, FATTY?

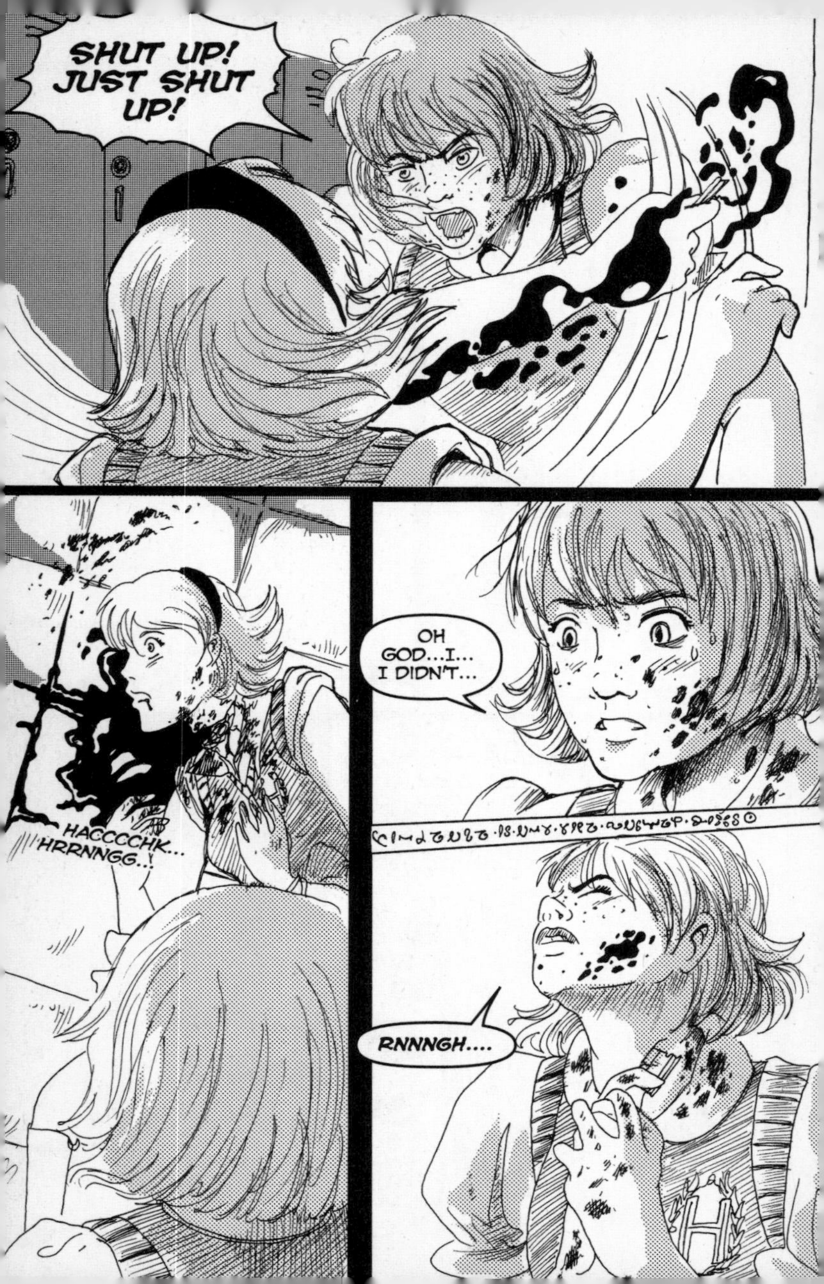
SHUT UP! JUST SHUT UP!
HACCCCHK... HRRNNGG...
OH GOD...I... I DIDN'T...
RNNNGH....

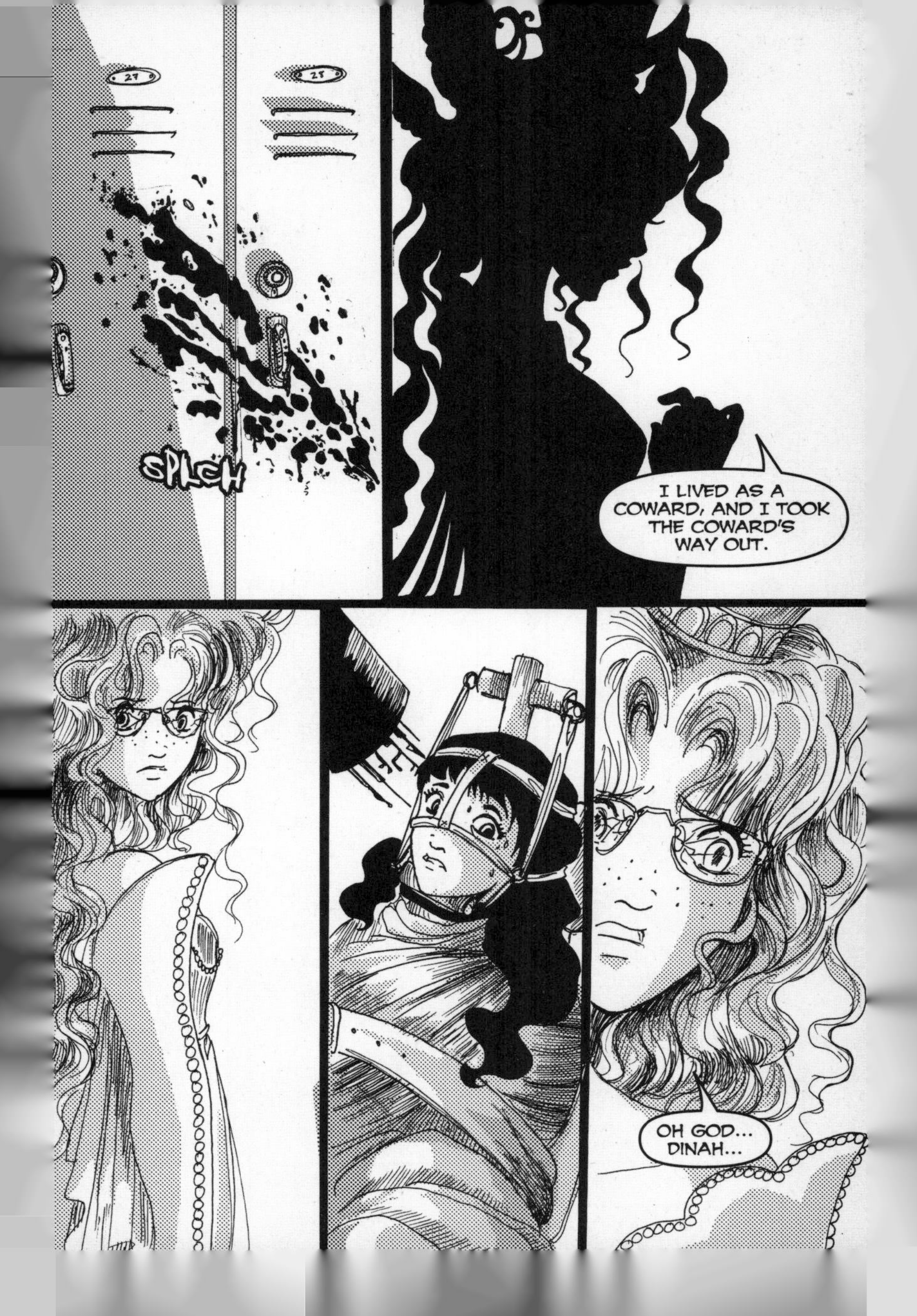
27
28
SPLCH
I LIVED AS A COWARD, AND I TOOK THE COWARD'S WAY OUT.
OH GOD... DINAH...

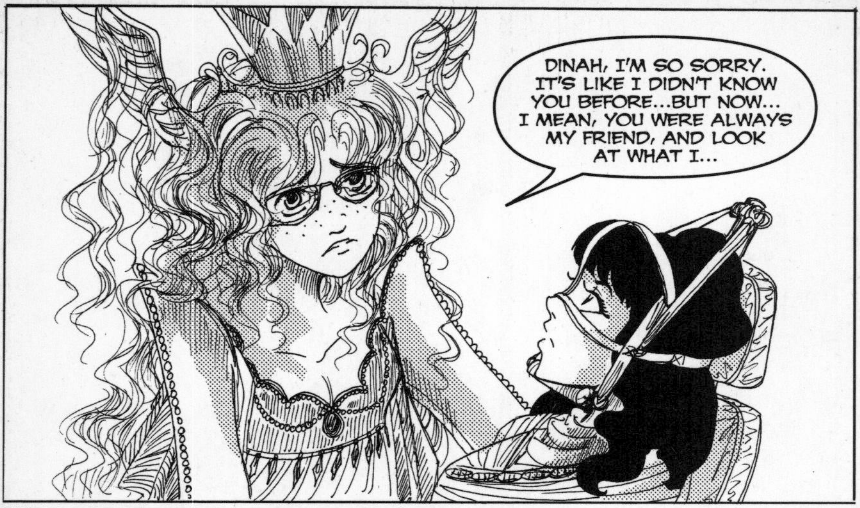
DINAH, I'M SO SORRY. IT'S LIKE I DIDN'T KNOW YOU BEFORE...BUT NOW... I MEAN, YOU WERE ALWAYS MY FRIEND, AND LOOK AT WHAT I...
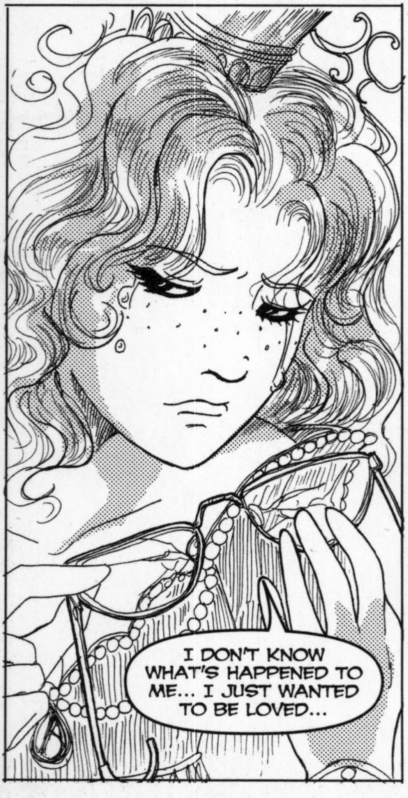
I DON'T KNOW WHAT'S HAPPENED TO ME... I JUST WANTED TO BE LOVED...
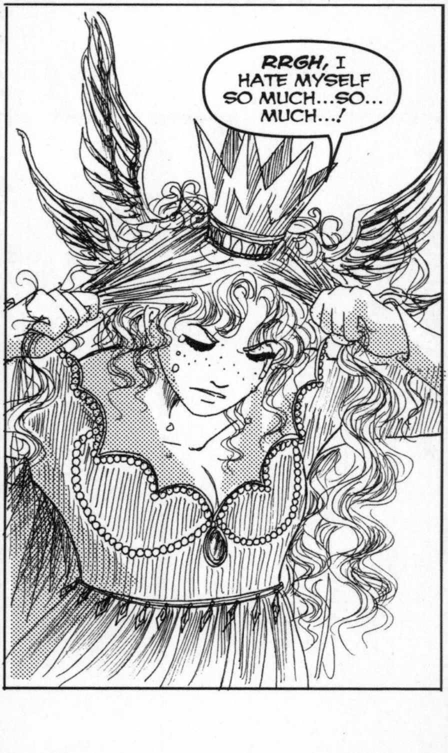
RRGH, I HATE MYSELF SO MUCH...SO... MUCH...!

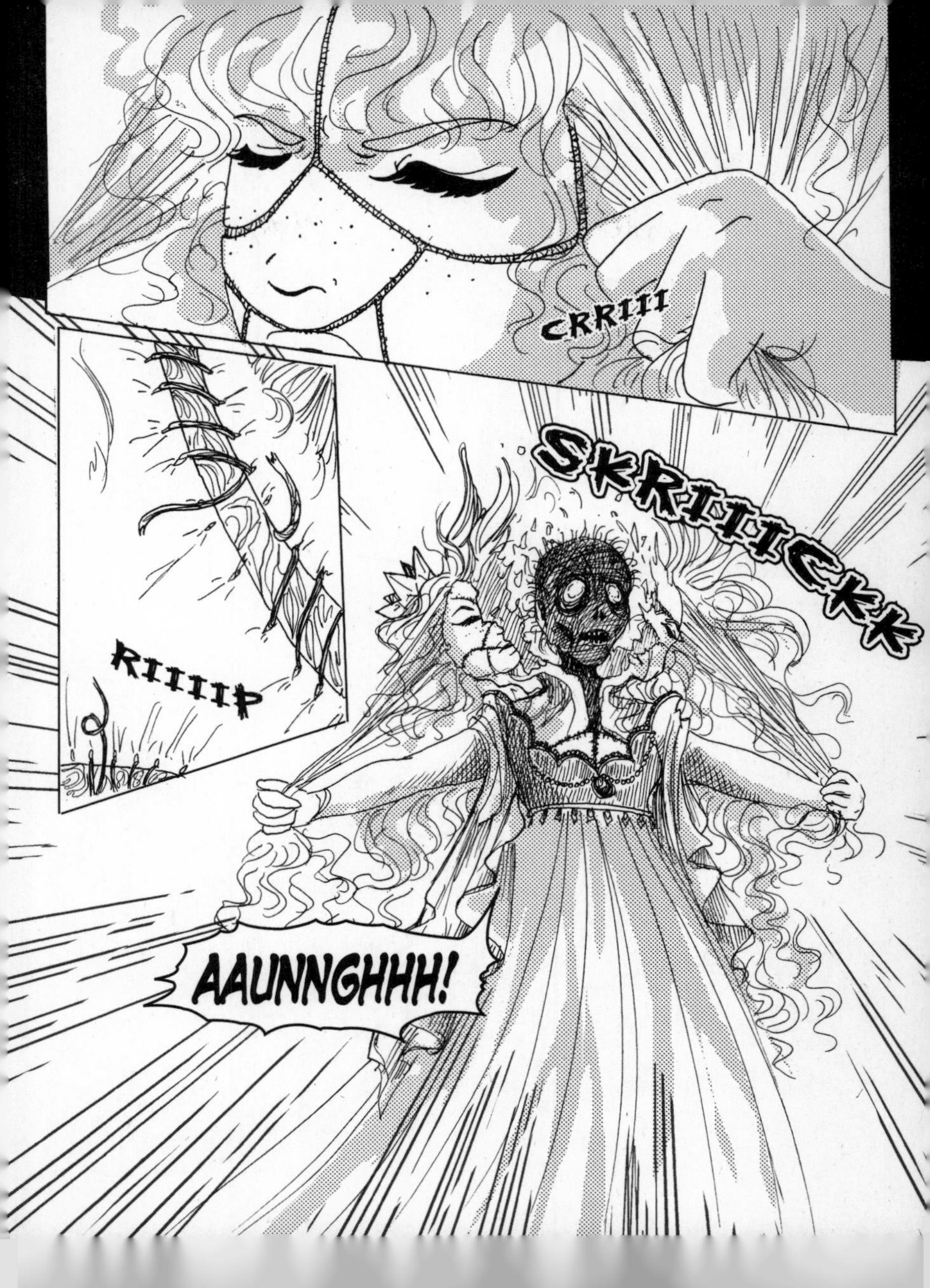
CRRIII
RIIIIIP
SKRIIIICKK
AAUNNGHHH!

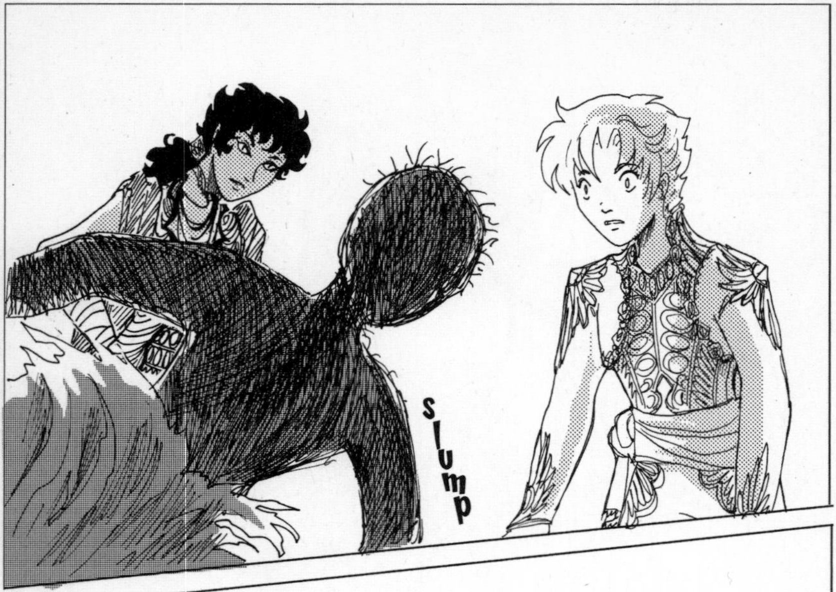
slump

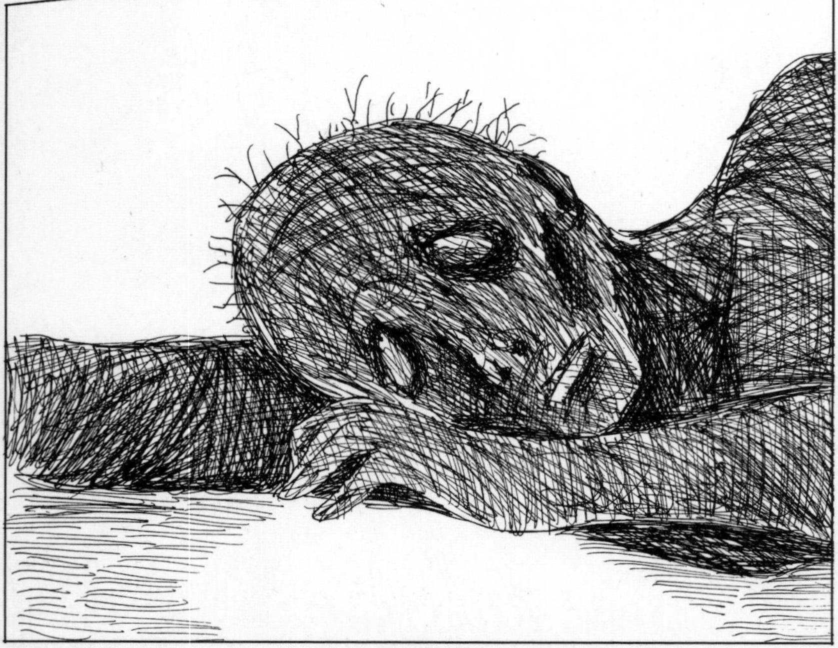

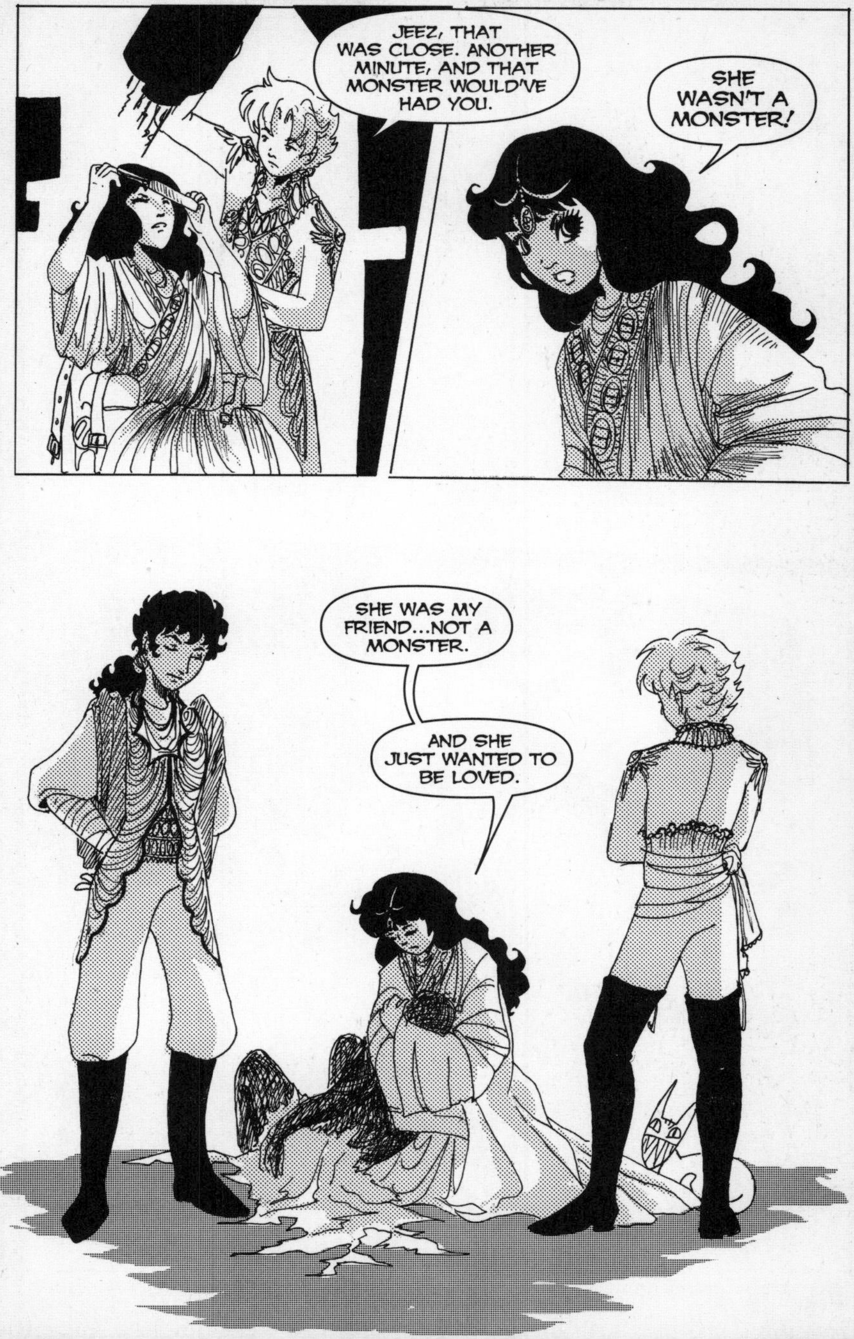
JEEZ, THAT WAS CLOSE. ANOTHER MINUTE, AND THAT MONSTER WOULD'VE HAD YOU.
SHE WASN'T A MONSTER!
SHE WAS MY FRIEND...NOT A MONSTER.
AND SHE JUST WANTED TO BE LOVED.

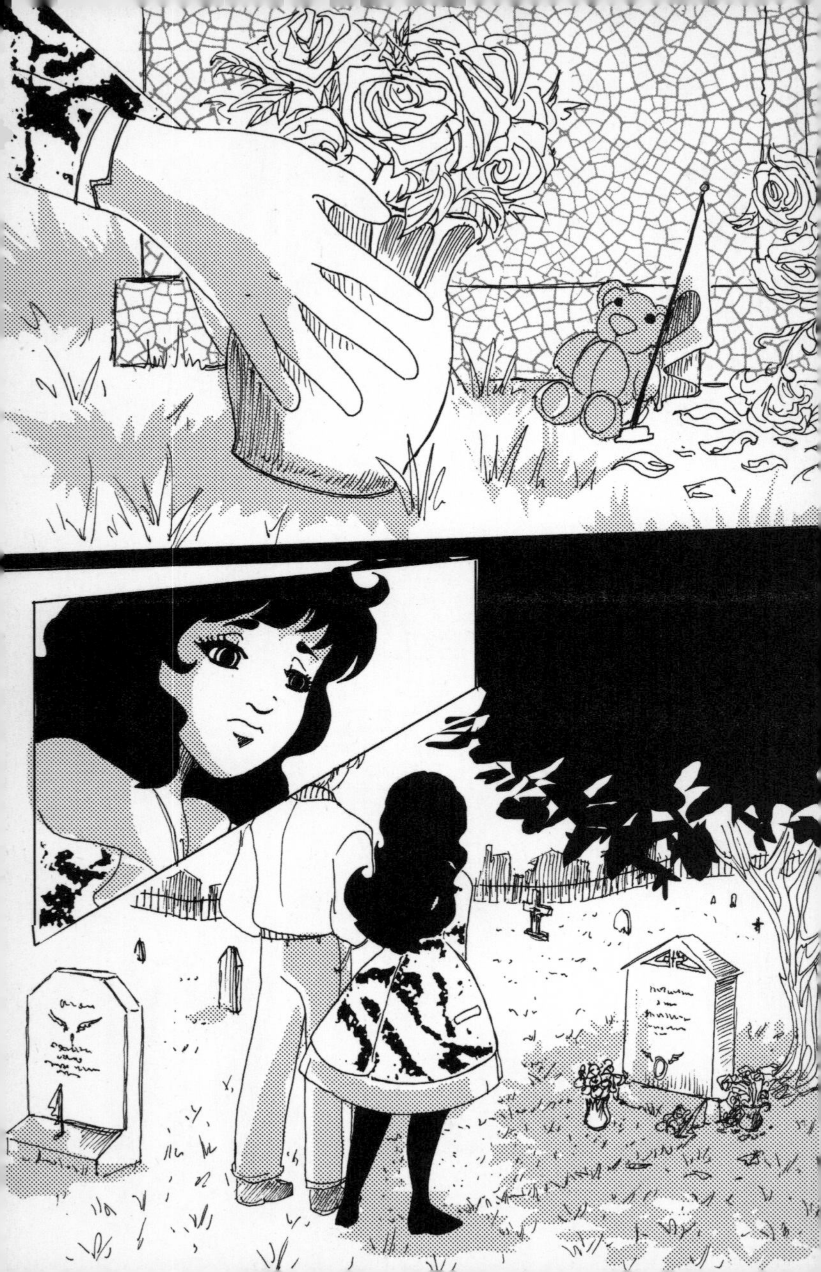

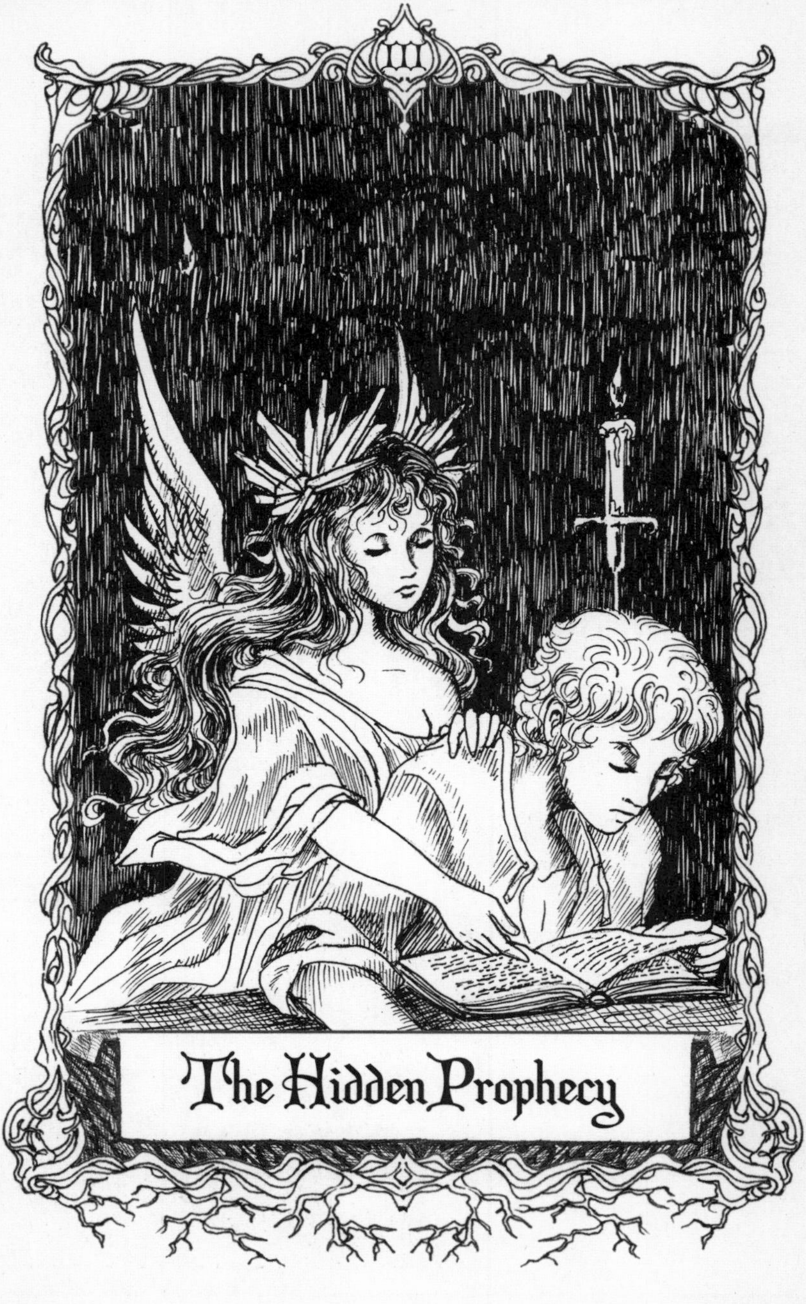
III
The Hidden Prophecy

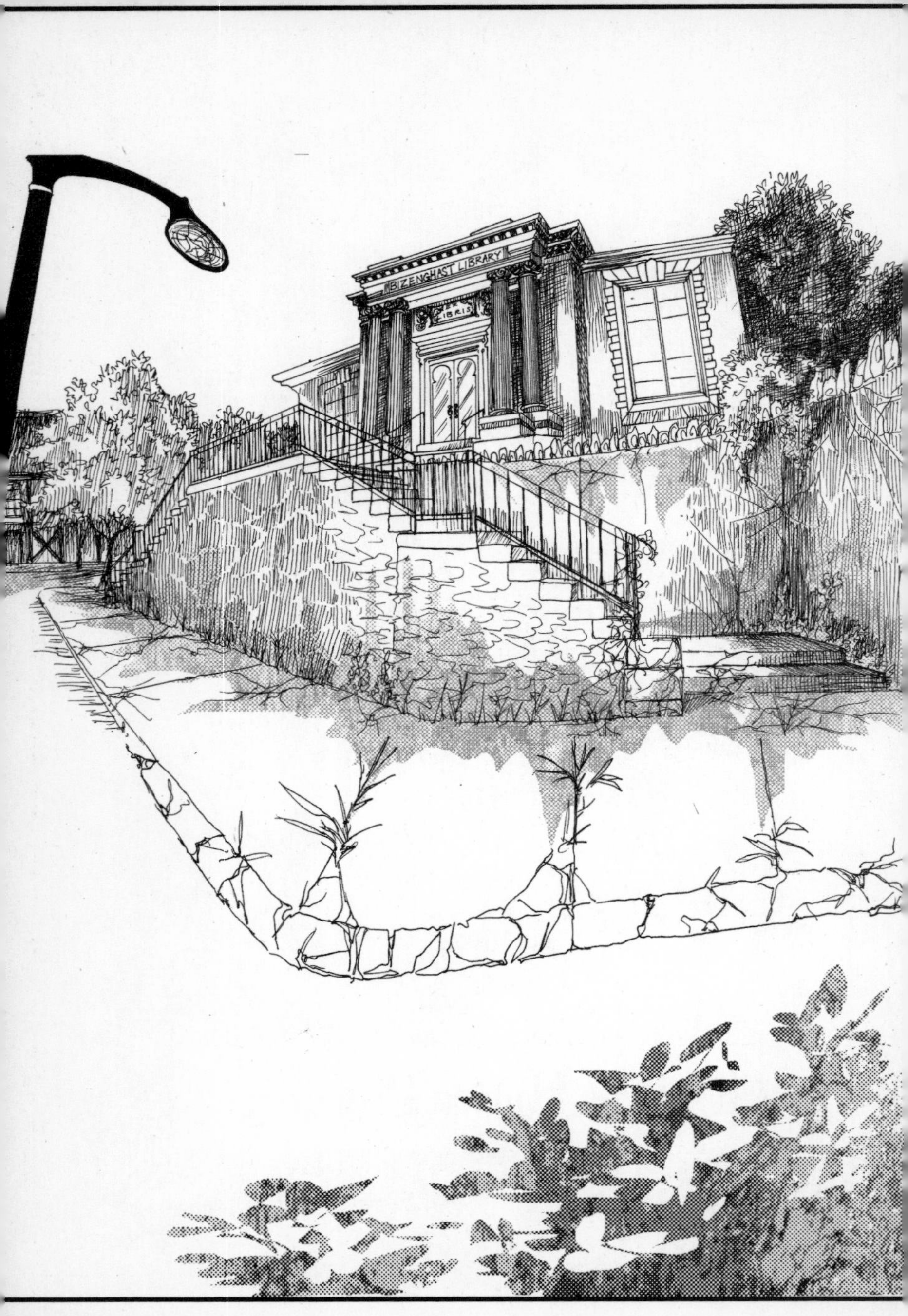
BIZENGHAST LIBRARY
EX LIBRIS

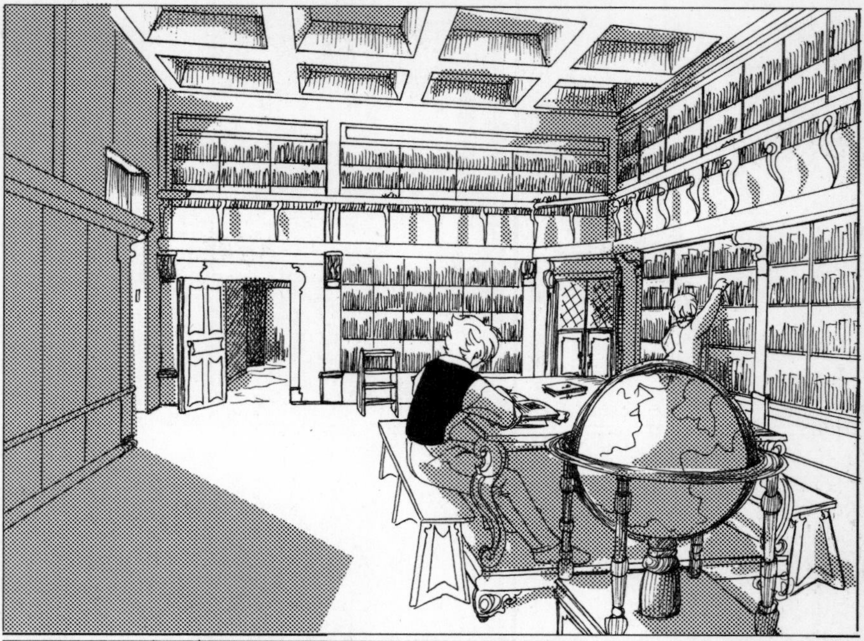
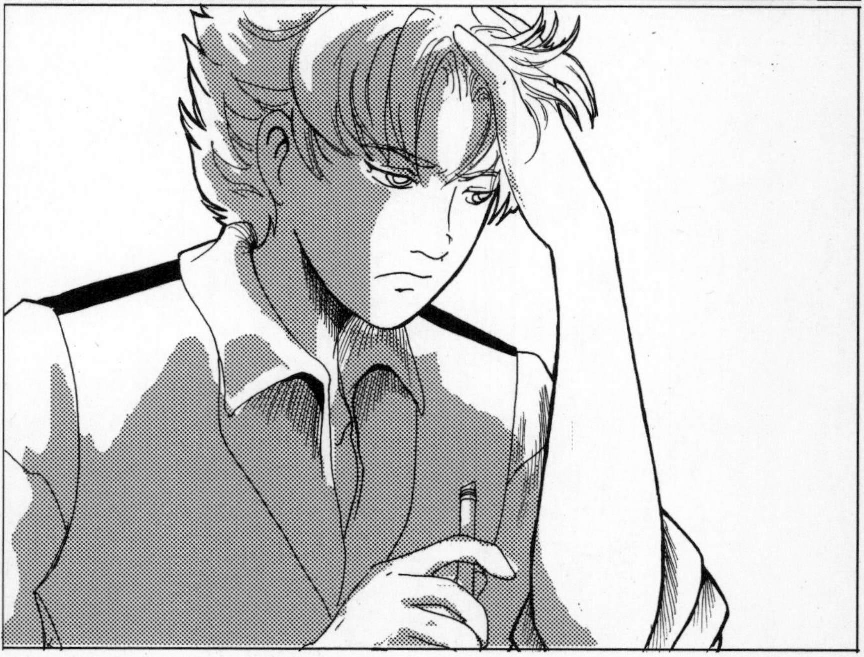

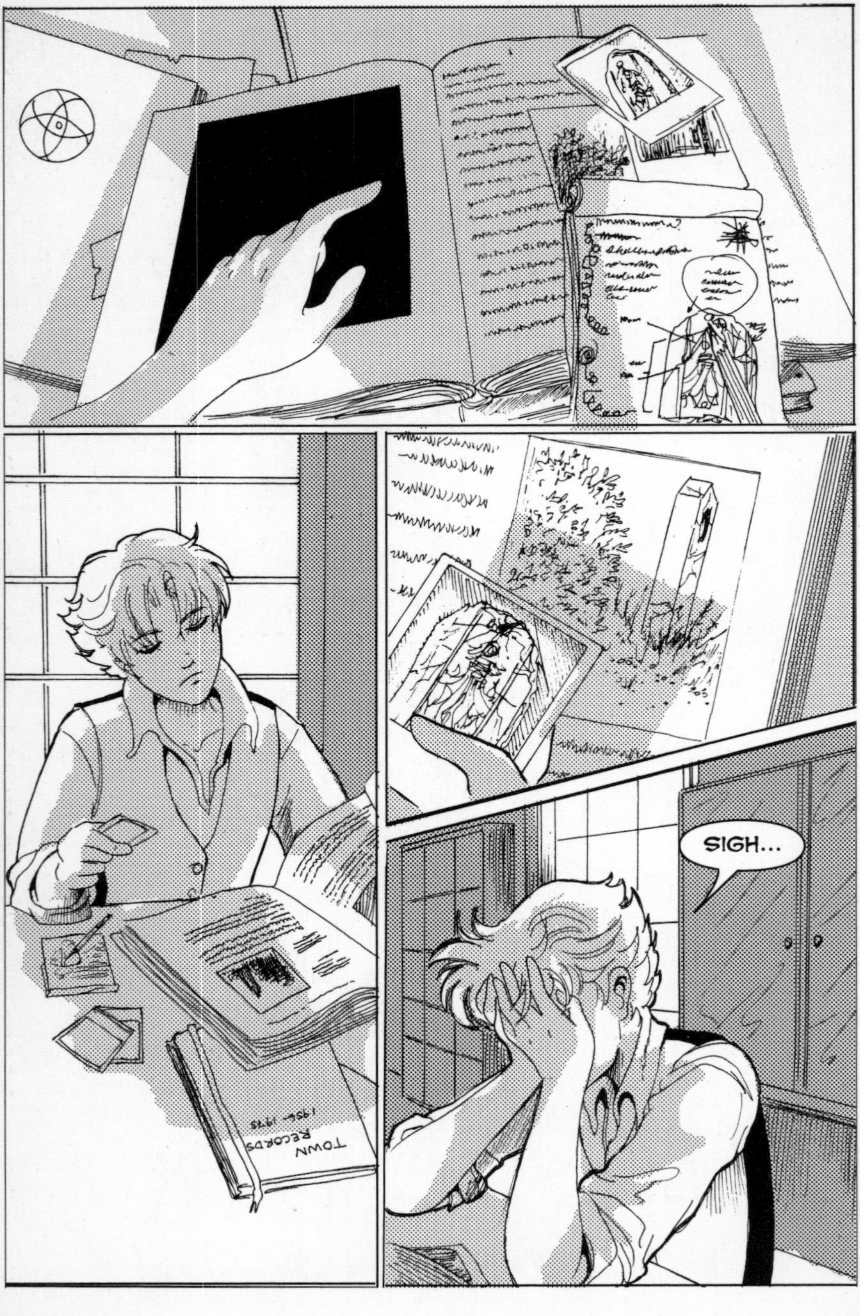
TOWN RECORDS 1956-1975
SIGH...

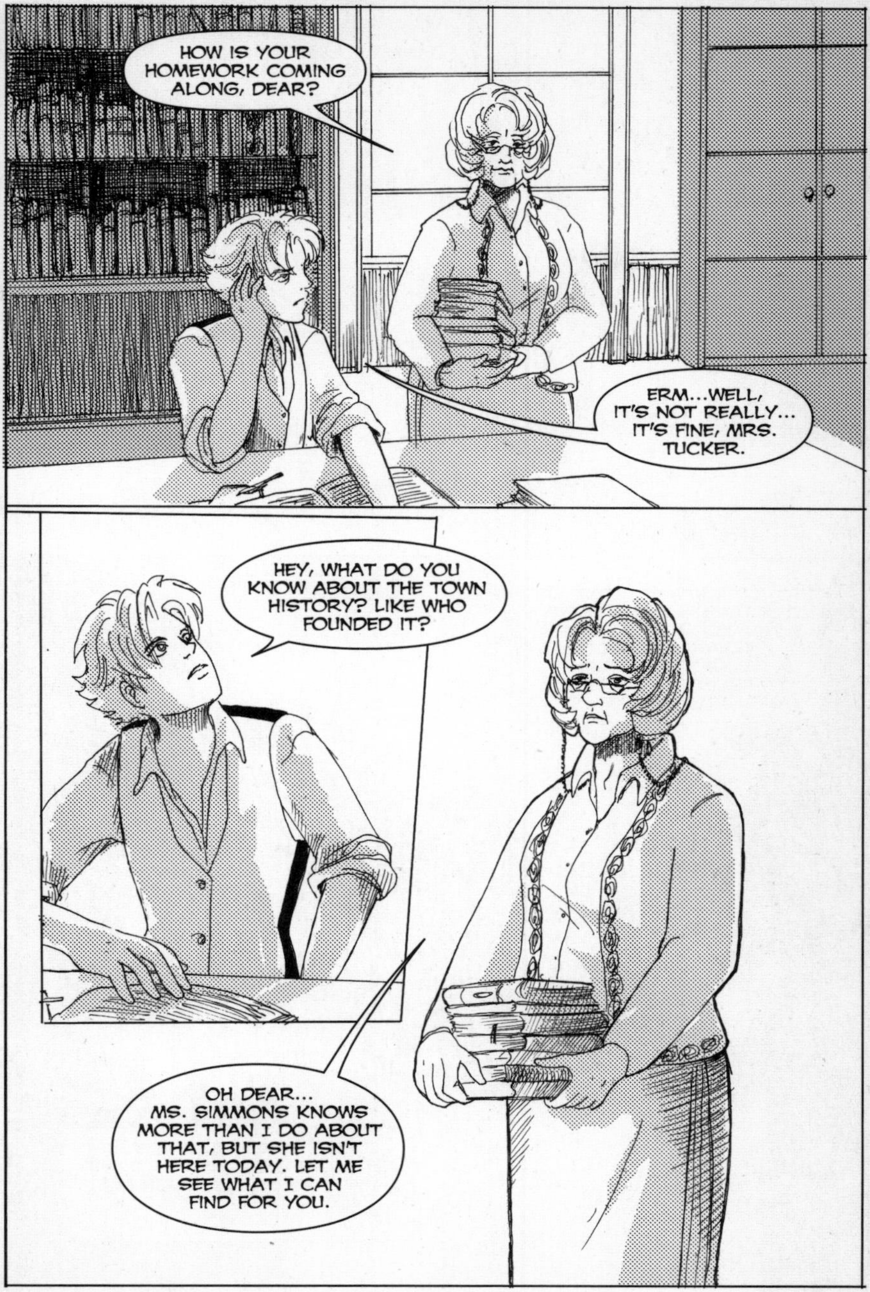
HOW IS YOUR HOMEWORK COMING ALONG, DEAR?
ERM...WELL, IT'S NOT REALLY... IT'S FINE, MRS. TUCKER.
HEY, WHAT DO YOU KNOW ABOUT THE TOWN HISTORY? LIKE WHO FOUNDED IT?
OH DEAR... MS. SIMMONS KNOWS MORE THAN I DO ABOUT THAT, BUT SHE ISN'T HERE TODAY. LET ME SEE WHAT I CAN FIND FOR YOU.

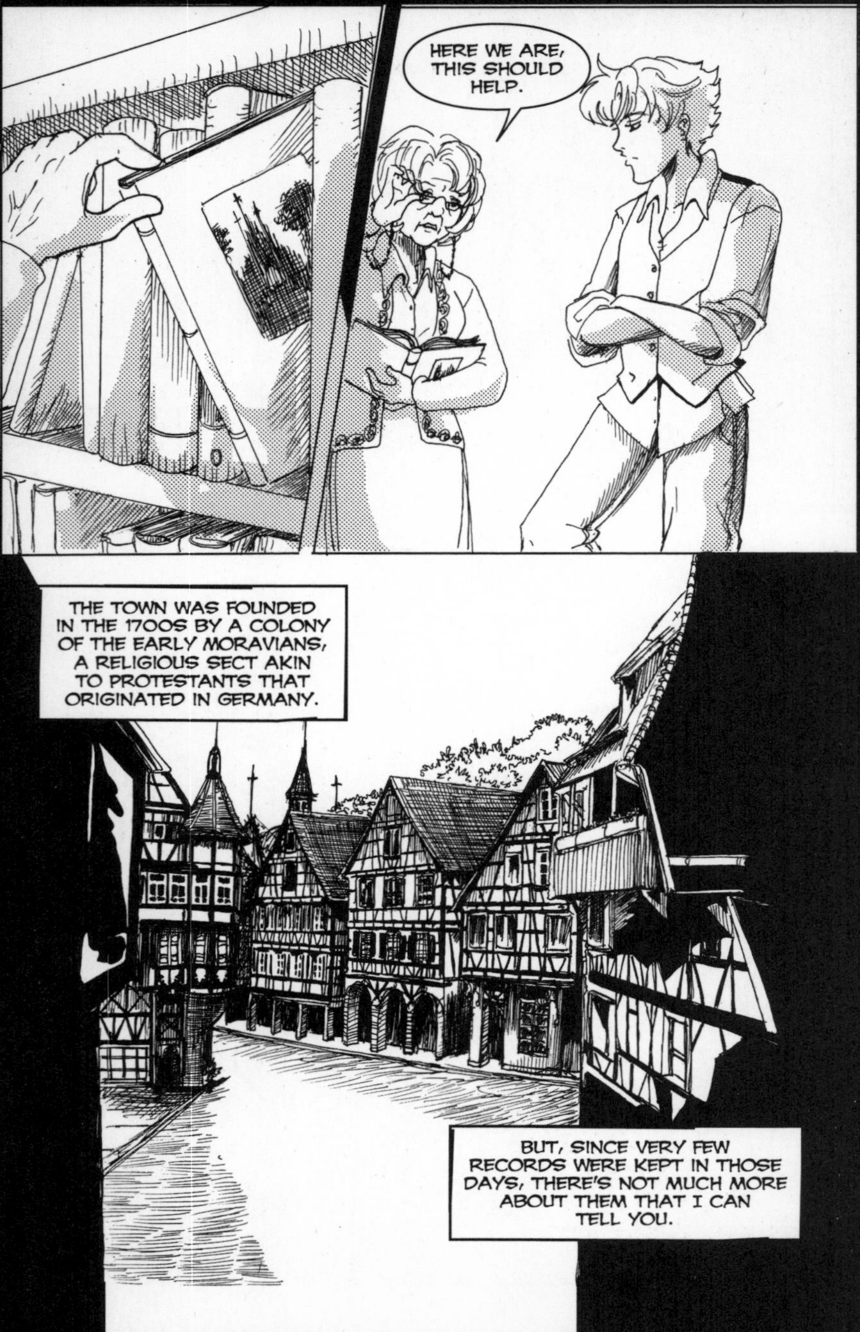
HERE WE ARE, THIS SHOULD HELP.
THE TOWN WAS FOUNDED IN THE 1700S BY A COLONY OF THE EARLY MORAVIANS, A RELIGIOUS SECT AKIN TO PROTESTANTS THAT ORIGINATED IN GERMANY.
BUT, SINCE VERY FEW RECORDS WERE KEPT IN THOSE DAYS, THERE'S NOT MUCH MORE ABOUT THEM THAT I CAN TELL YOU.

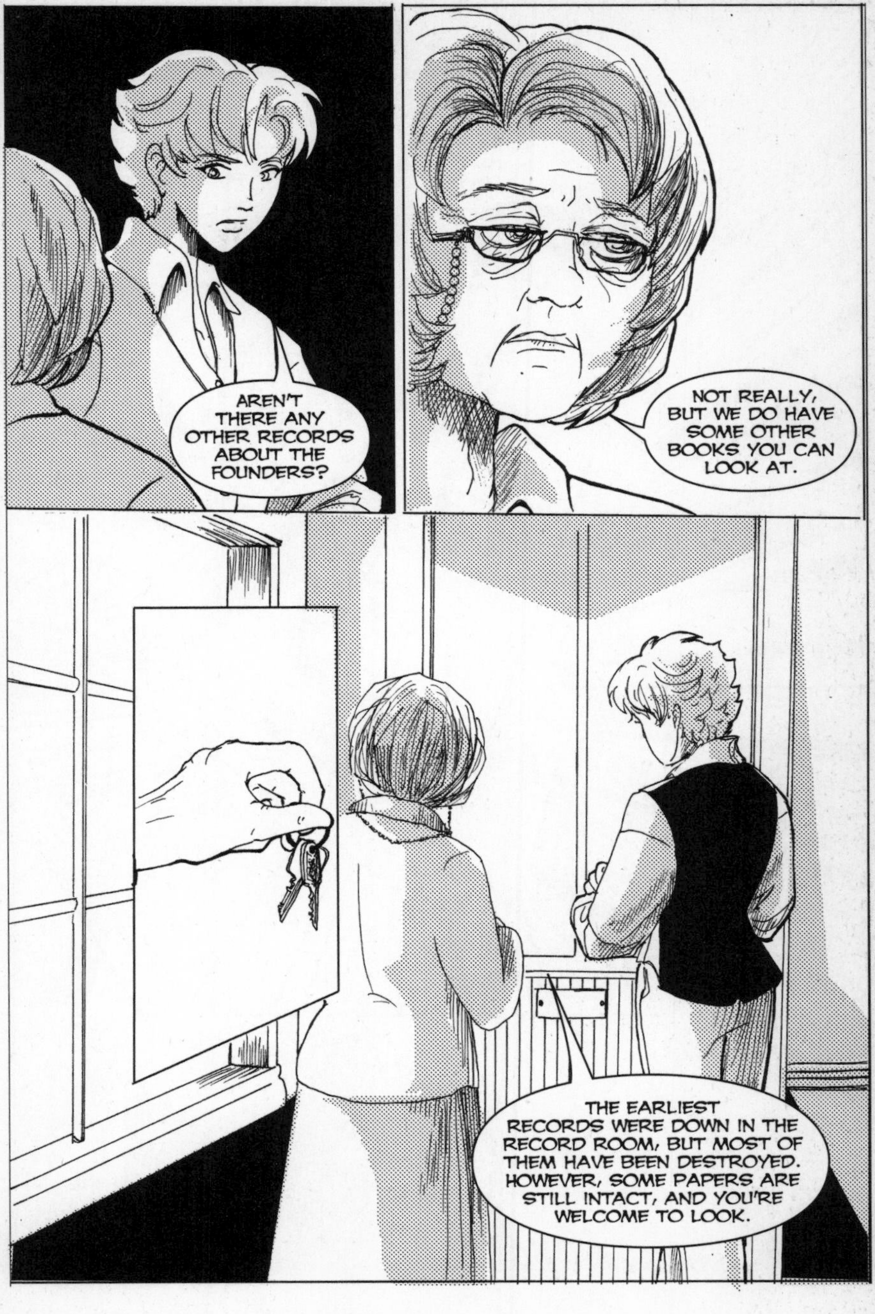
AREN'T THERE ANY OTHER RECORDS ABOUT THE FOUNDERS?
NOT REALLY, BUT WE DO HAVE SOME OTHER BOOKS YOU CAN LOOK AT.
THE EARLIEST RECORDS WERE DOWN IN THE RECORD ROOM, BUT MOST OF THEM HAVE BEEN DESTROYED. HOWEVER, SOME PAPERS ARE STILL INTACT, AND YOU'RE WELCOME TO LOOK.

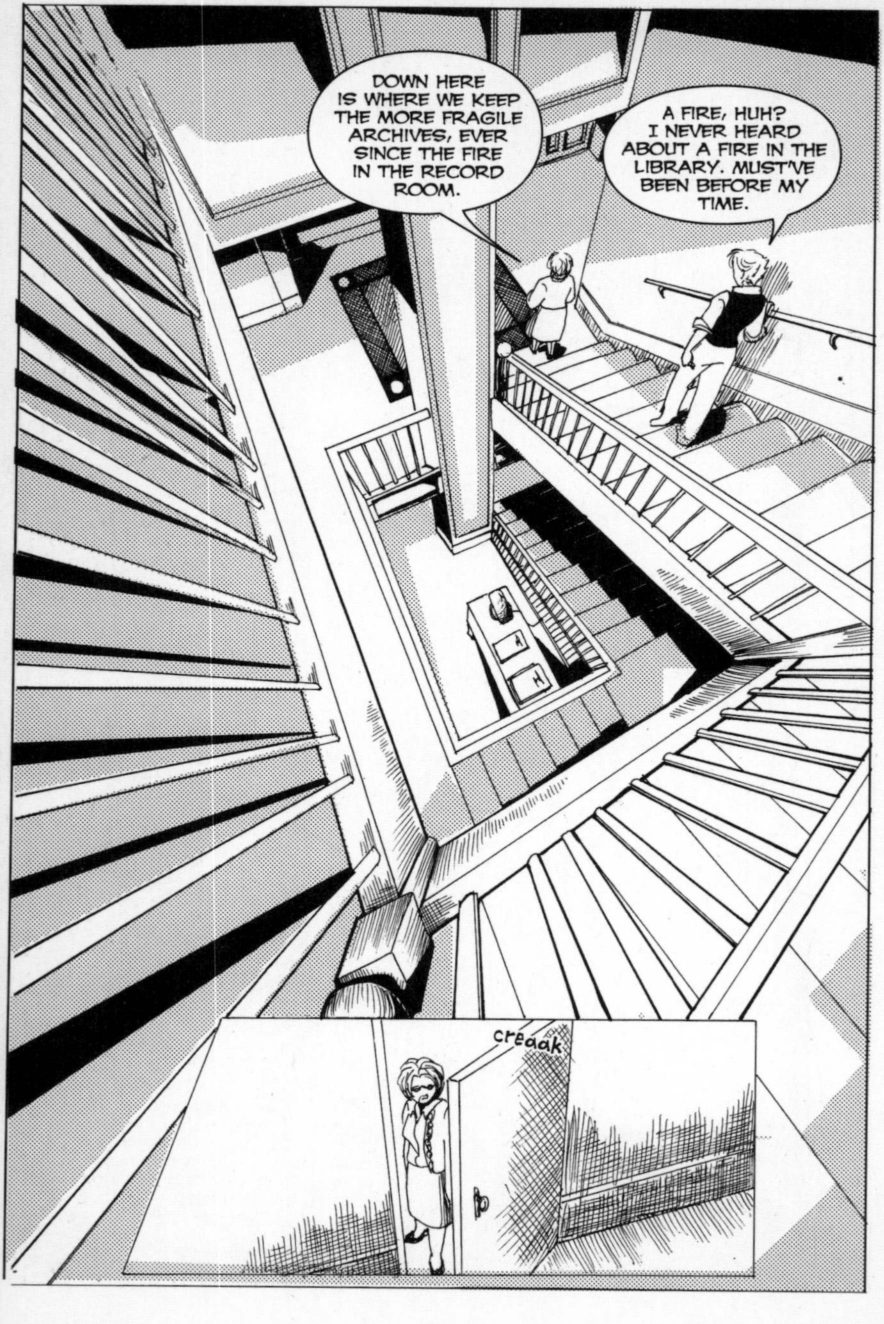
DOWN HERE IS WHERE WE KEEP THE MORE FRAGILE ARCHIVES, EVER SINCE THE FIRE IN THE RECORD ROOM.
A FIRE, HUH? I NEVER HEARD ABOUT A FIRE IN THE LIBRARY. MUST'VE BEEN BEFORE MY TIME.
creaak

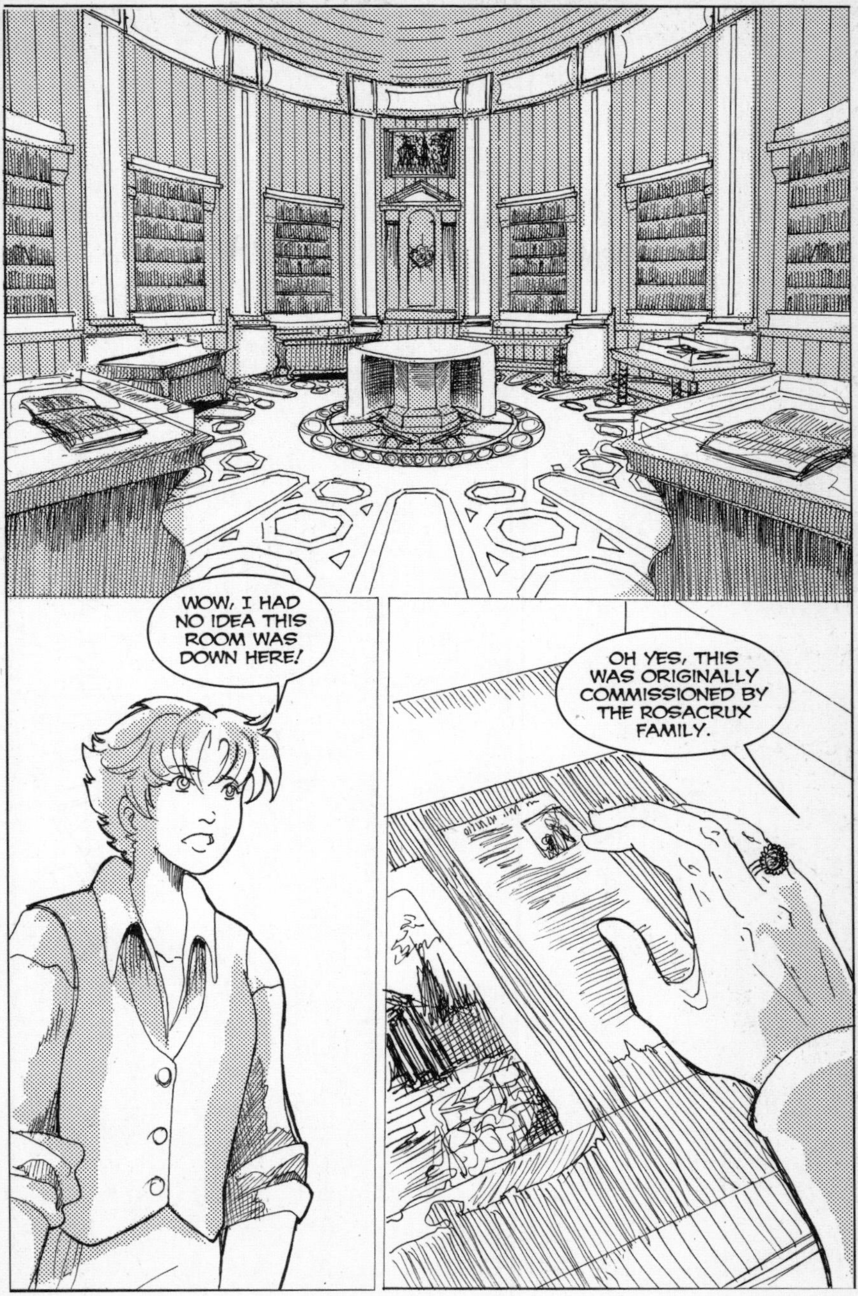
WOW, I HAD NO IDEA THIS ROOM WAS DOWN HERE!
OH YES, THIS WAS ORIGINALLY COMMISSIONED BY THE ROSACRUX FAMILY.

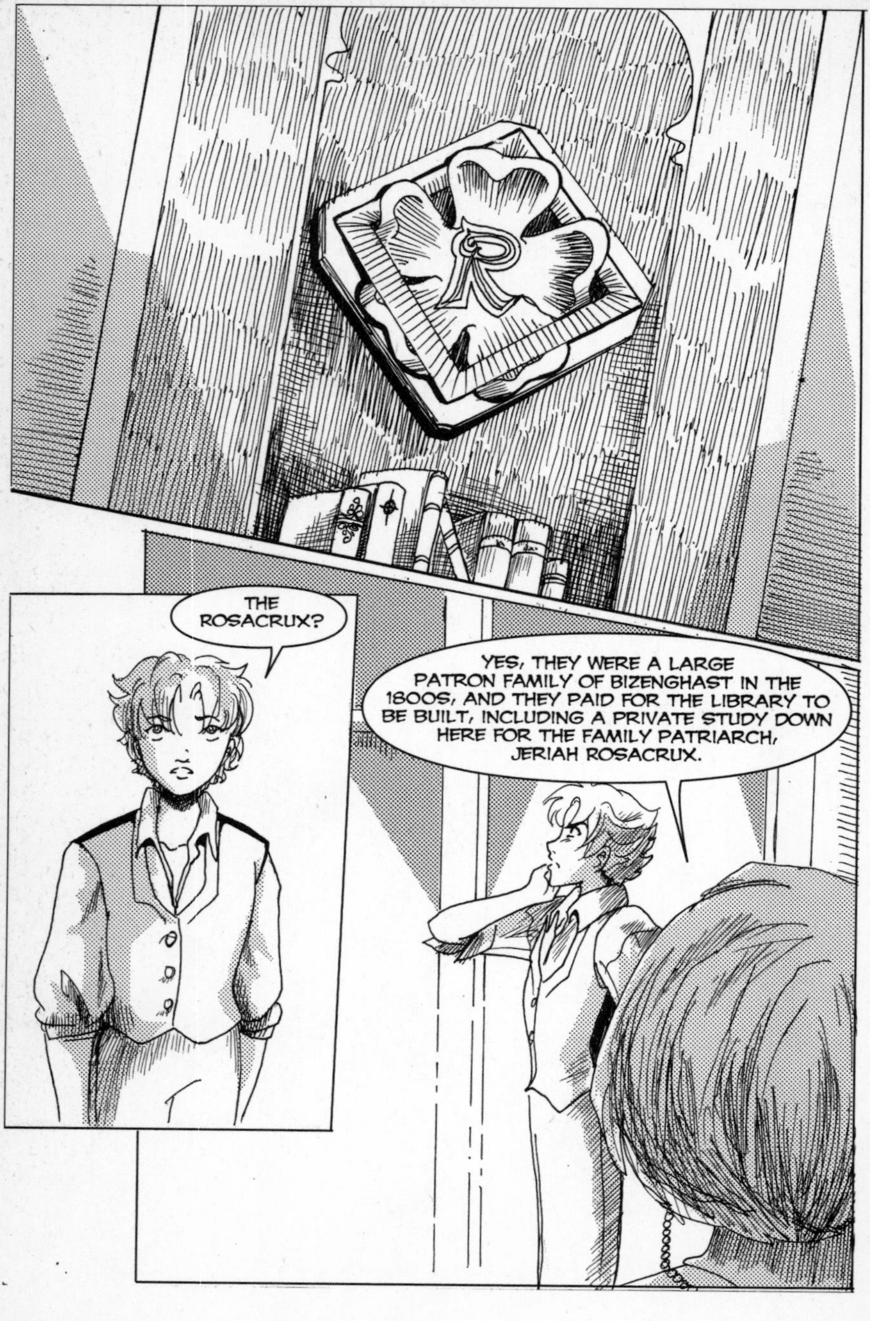
THE ROSACRUX?
YES, THEY WERE A LARGE PATRON FAMILY OF BIZENGHAST IN THE 1800S, AND THEY PAID FOR THE LIBRARY TO BE BUILT, INCLUDING A PRIVATE STUDY DOWN HERE FOR THE FAMILY PATRIARCH, JERIAH ROSACRUX.

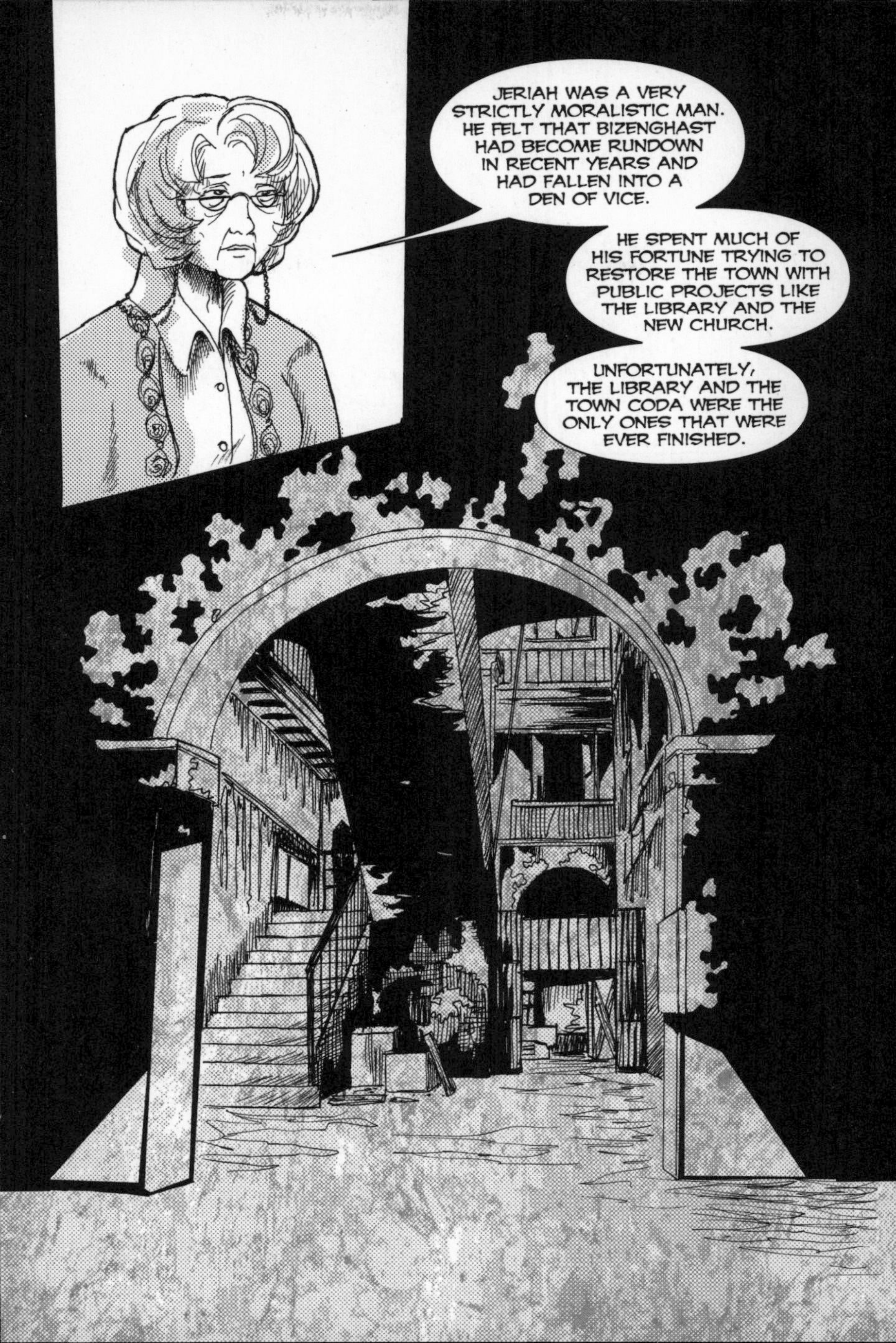
JERIAH WAS A VERY STRICTLY MORALISTIC MAN. HE FELT THAT BIZENGHAST HAD BECOME RUNDOWN IN RECENT YEARS AND HAD FALLEN INTO A DEN OF VICE.
HE SPENT MUCH OF HIS FORTUNE TRYING TO RESTORE THE TOWN WITH PUBLIC PROJECTS LIKE THE LIBRARY AND THE NEW CHURCH.
UNFORTUNATELY, THE LIBRARY AND THE TOWN CODA WERE THE ONLY ONES THAT WERE EVER FINISHED.

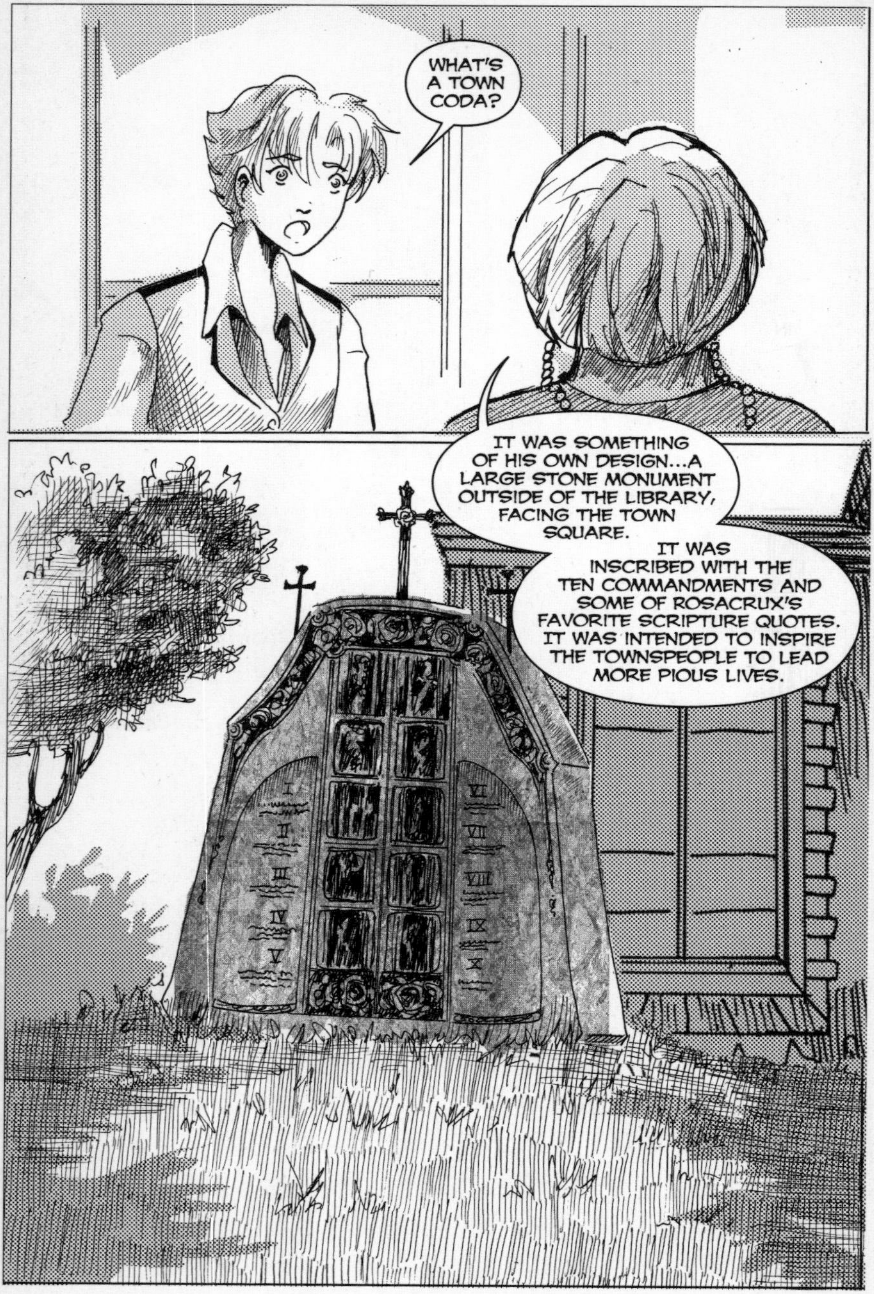
WHAT'S A TOWN CODA?
IT WAS SOMETHING OF HIS OWN DESIGN...A LARGE STONE MONUMENT OUTSIDE OF THE LIBRARY, FACING THE TOWN SQUARE.
IT WAS INSCRIBED WITH THE TEN COMMANDMENTS AND SOME OF ROSACRUX'S FAVORITE SCRIPTURE QUOTES. IT WAS INTENDED TO INSPIRE THE TOWNSPEOPLE TO LEAD MORE PIOUS LIVES.

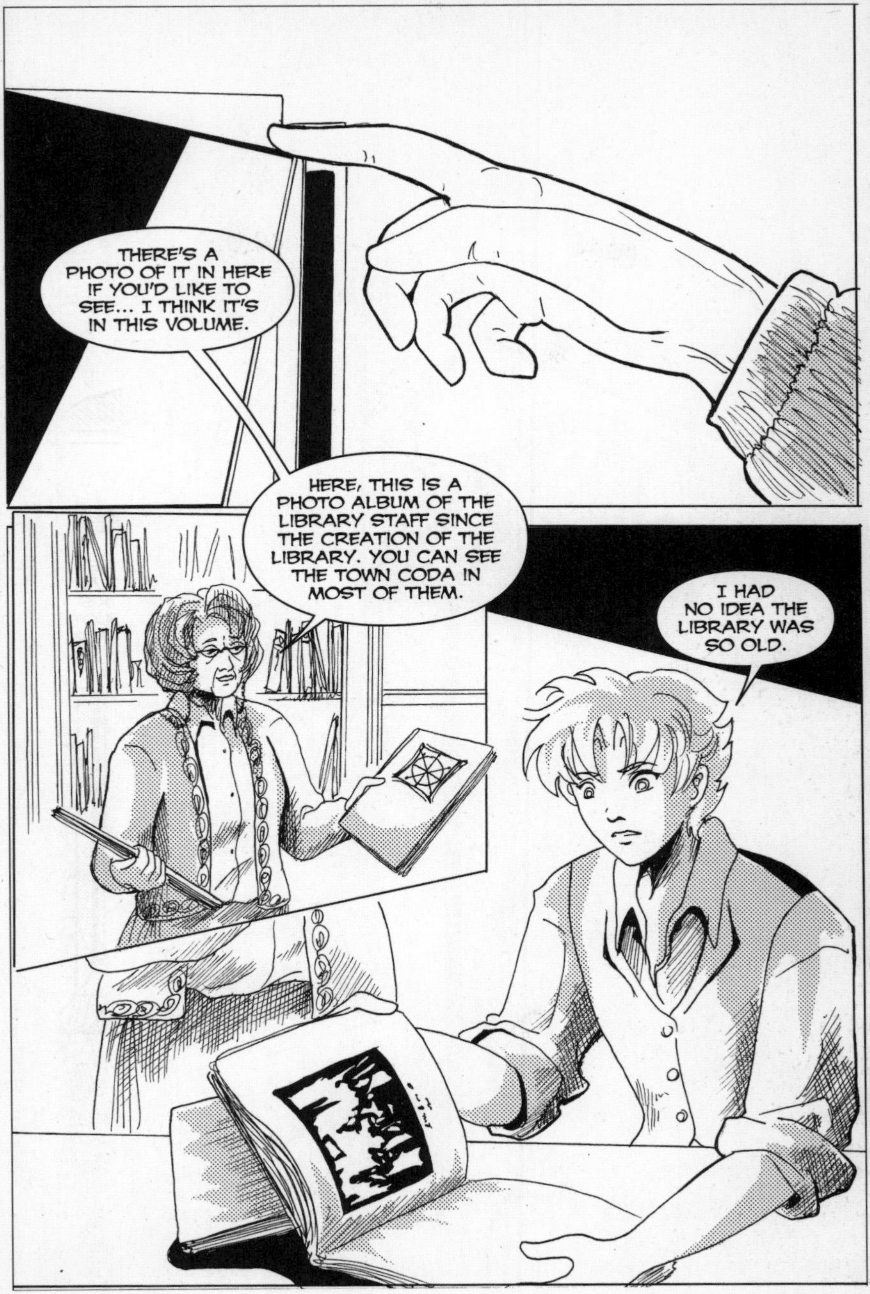
THERE'S A PHOTO OF IT IN HERE IF YOU'D LIKE TO SEE... I THINK IT'S IN THIS VOLUME.
HERE, THIS IS A PHOTO ALBUM OF THE LIBRARY STAFF SINCE THE CREATION OF THE LIBRARY. YOU CAN SEE THE TOWN CODA IN MOST OF THEM.
I HAD NO IDEA THE LIBRARY WAS SO OLD.

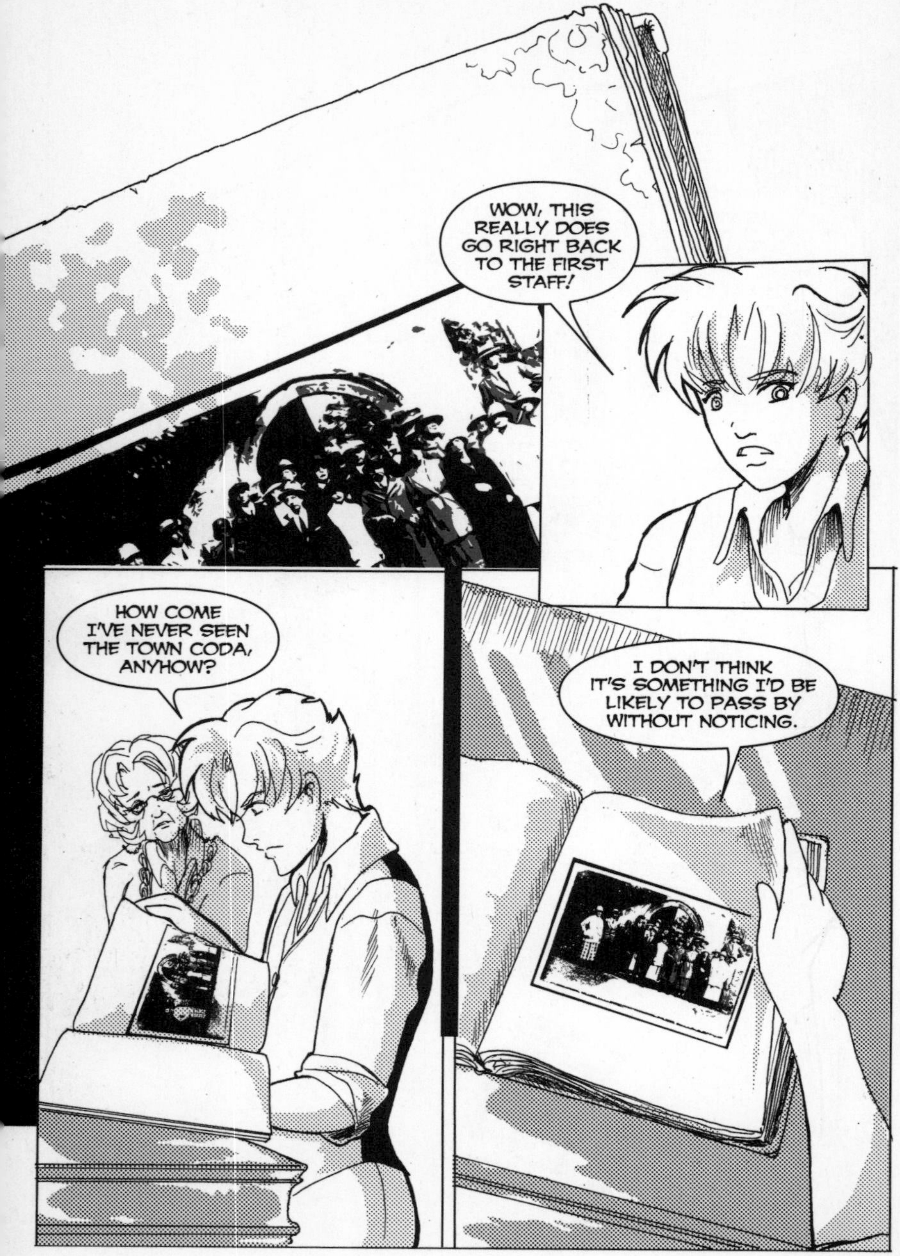
WOW, THIS REALLY DOES GO RIGHT BACK TO THE FIRST STAFF!
HOW COME I'VE NEVER SEEN THE TOWN CODA, ANYHOW?
I DON'T THINK IT'S SOMETHING I'D BE LIKELY TO PASS BY WITHOUT NOTICING.

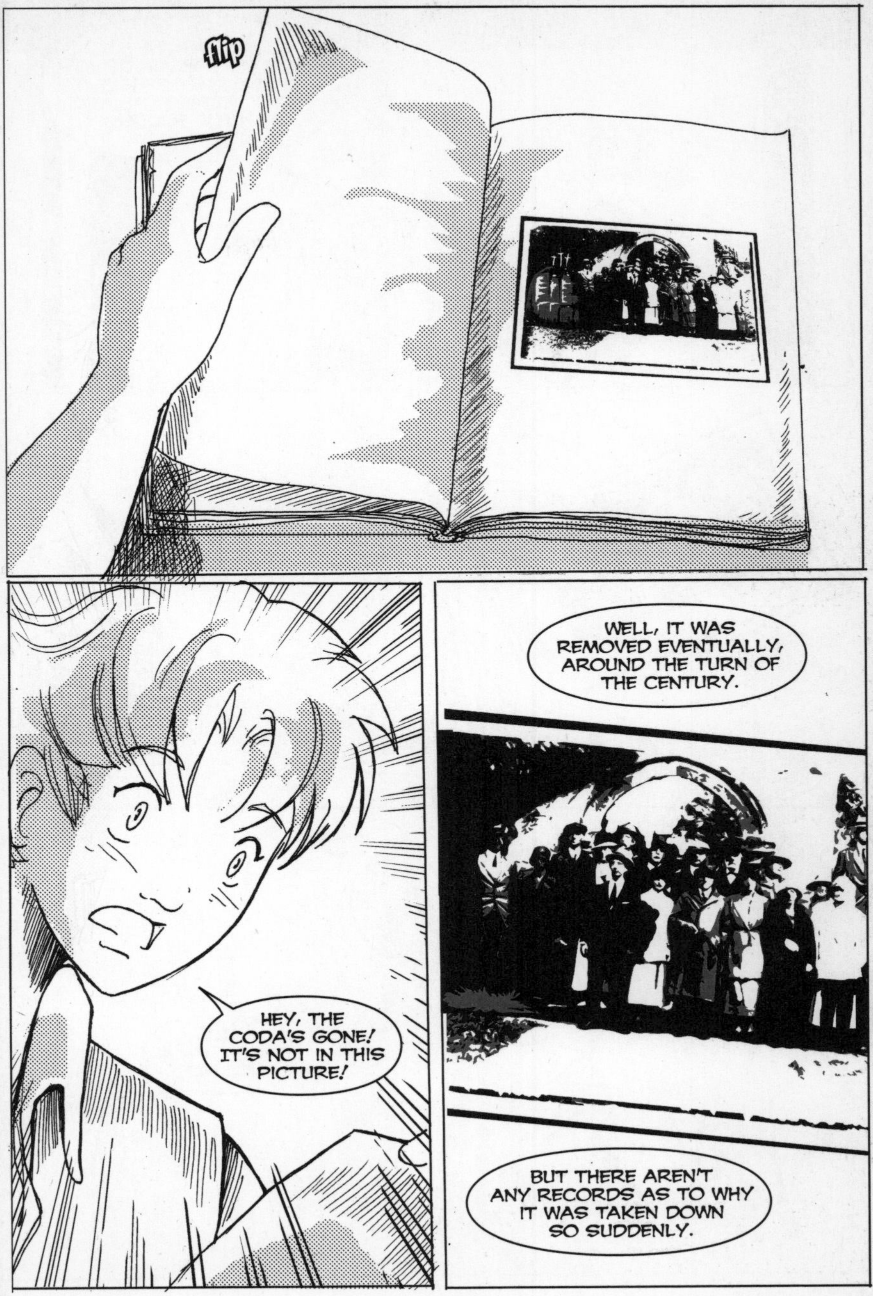
flip
HEY, THE CODA'S GONE! IT'S NOT IN THIS PICTURE!
WELL, IT WAS REMOVED EVENTUALLY, AROUND THE TURN OF THE CENTURY.
BUT THERE AREN'T ANY RECORDS AS TO WHY IT WAS TAKEN DOWN SO SUDDENLY.

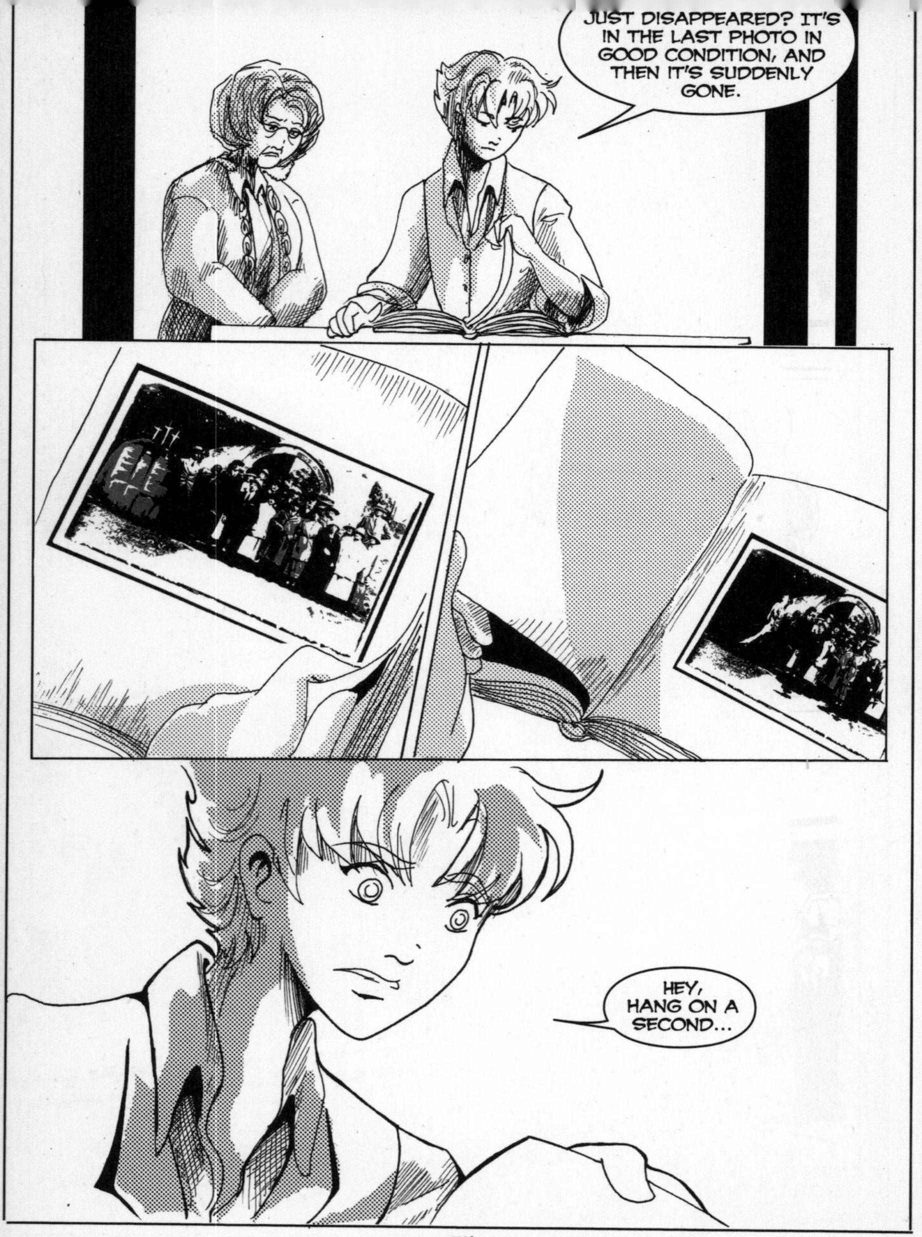
JUST DISAPPEARED? IT'S IN THE LAST PHOTO IN GOOD CONDITION, AND THEN IT'S SUDDENLY GONE.
HEY, HANG ON A SECOND...

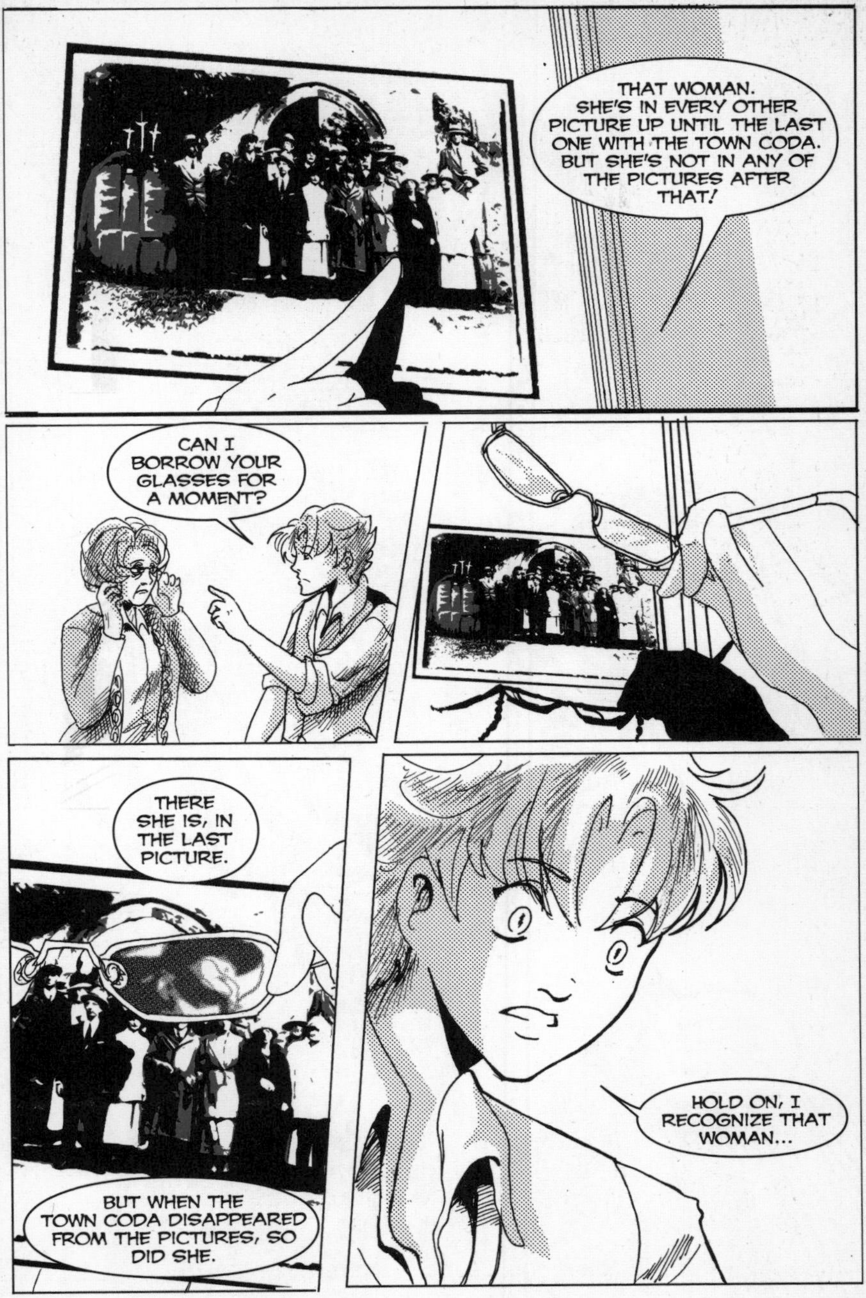
THAT WOMAN. SHE'S IN EVERY OTHER PICTURE UP UNTIL THE LAST ONE WITH THE TOWN CODA. BUT SHE'S NOT IN ANY OF THE PICTURES AFTER THAT!
CAN I BORROW YOUR GLASSES FOR A MOMENT?
THERE SHE IS, IN THE LAST PICTURE.
BUT WHEN THE TOWN CODA DISAPPEARED FROM THE PICTURES, SO DID SHE.
HOLD ON, I RECOGNIZE THAT WOMAN...

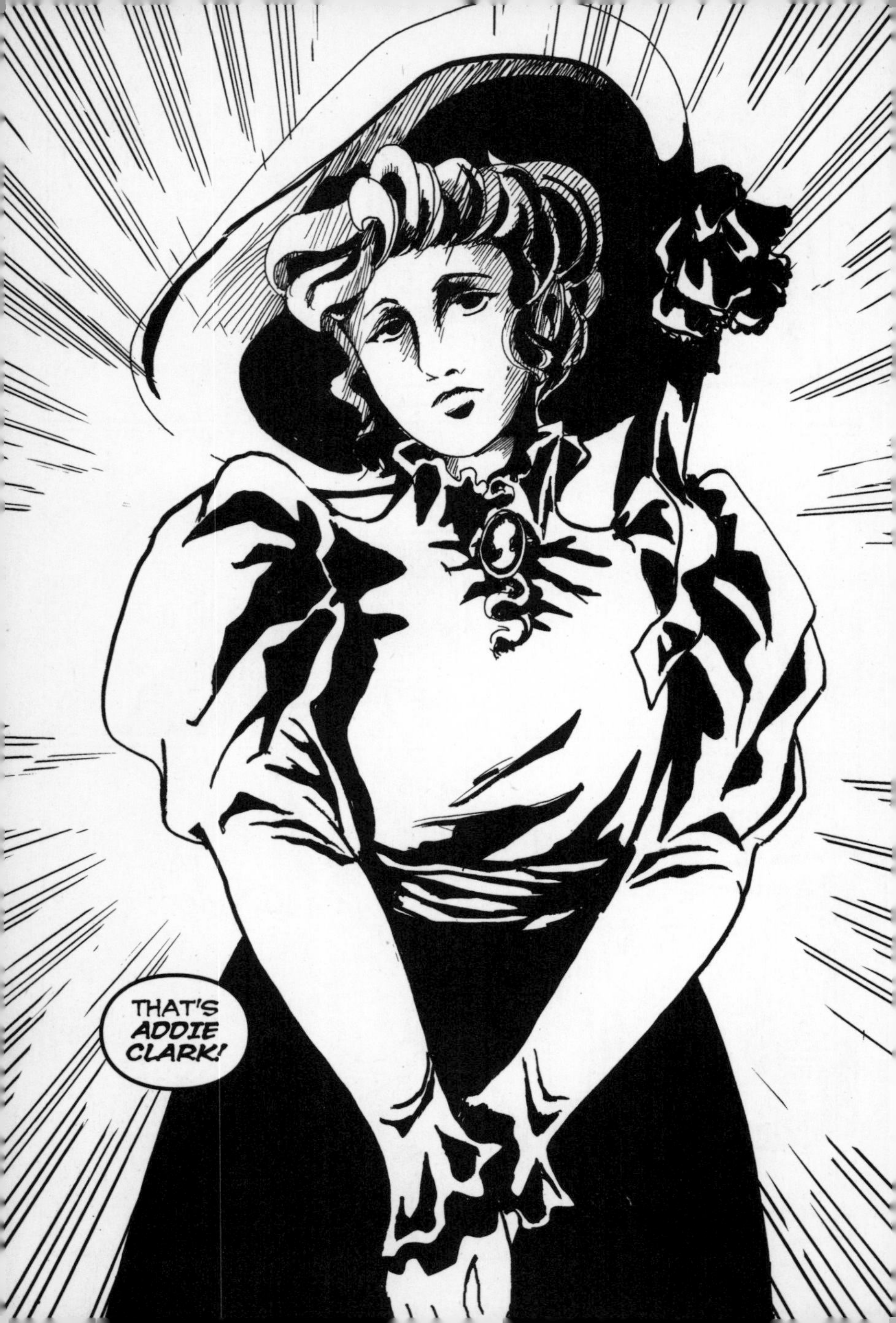
THAT'S ADDIE CLARK!

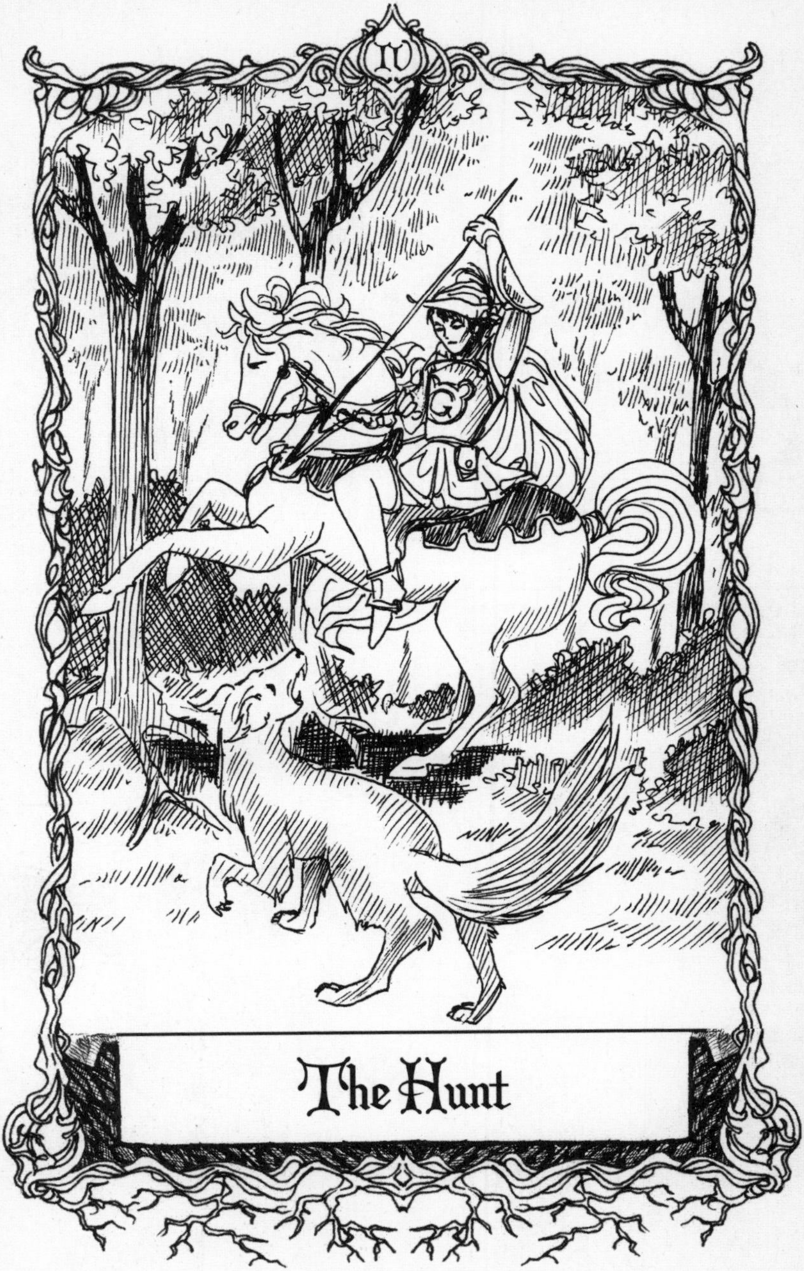
IV
The Hunt

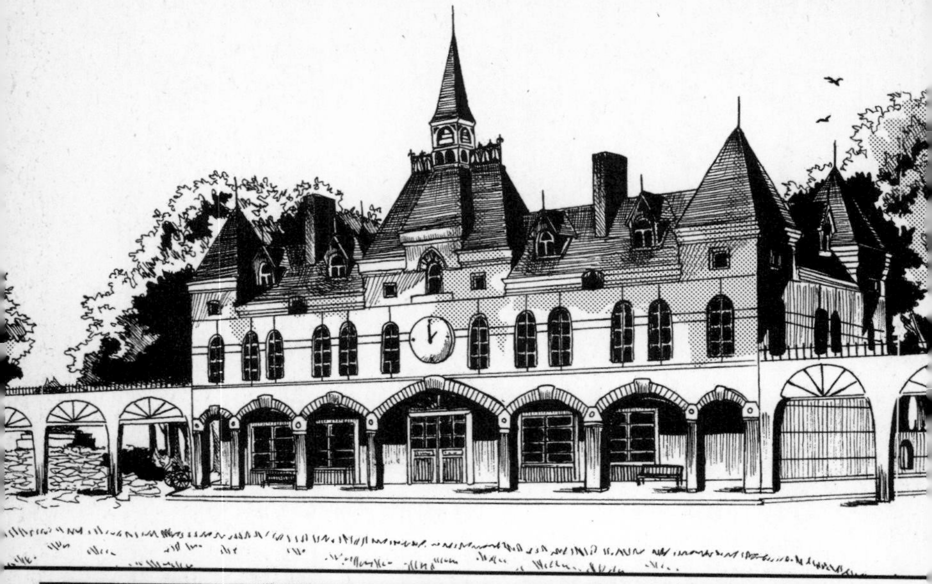

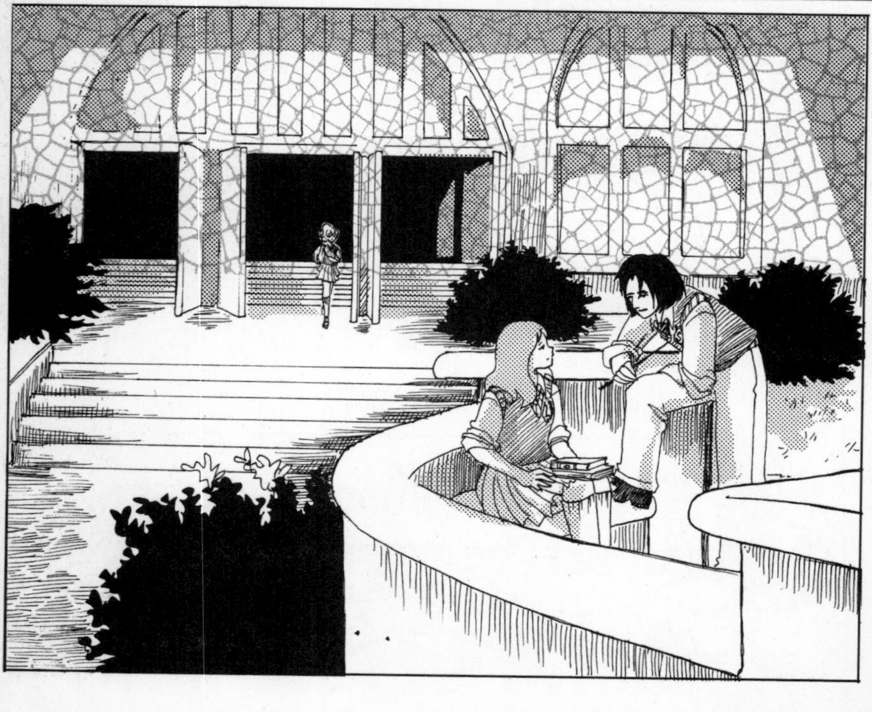

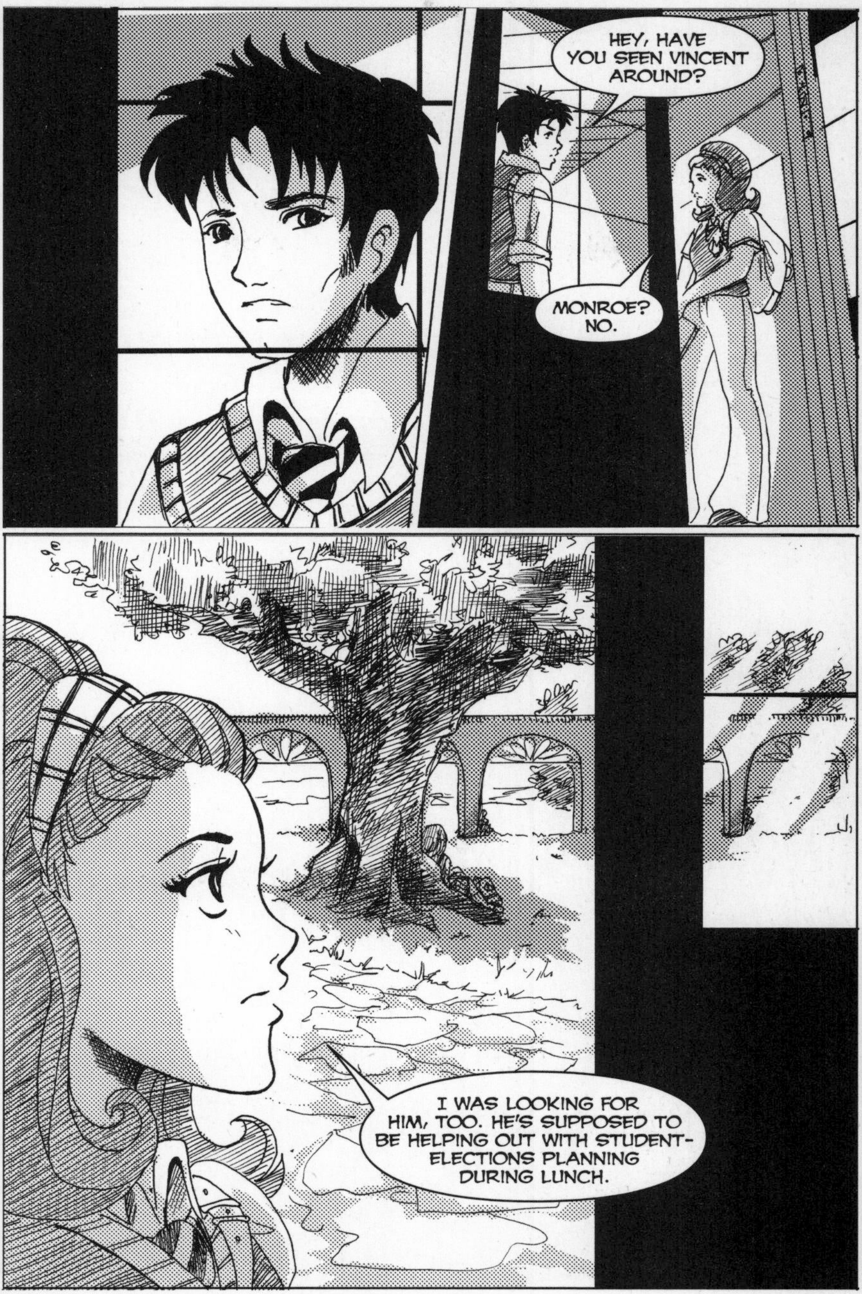
HEY, HAVE YOU SEEN VINCENT AROUND?
MONROE? NO.
I WAS LOOKING FOR HIM, TOO. HE'S SUPPOSED TO BE HELPING OUT WITH STUDENT-ELECTIONS PLANNING DURING LUNCH.

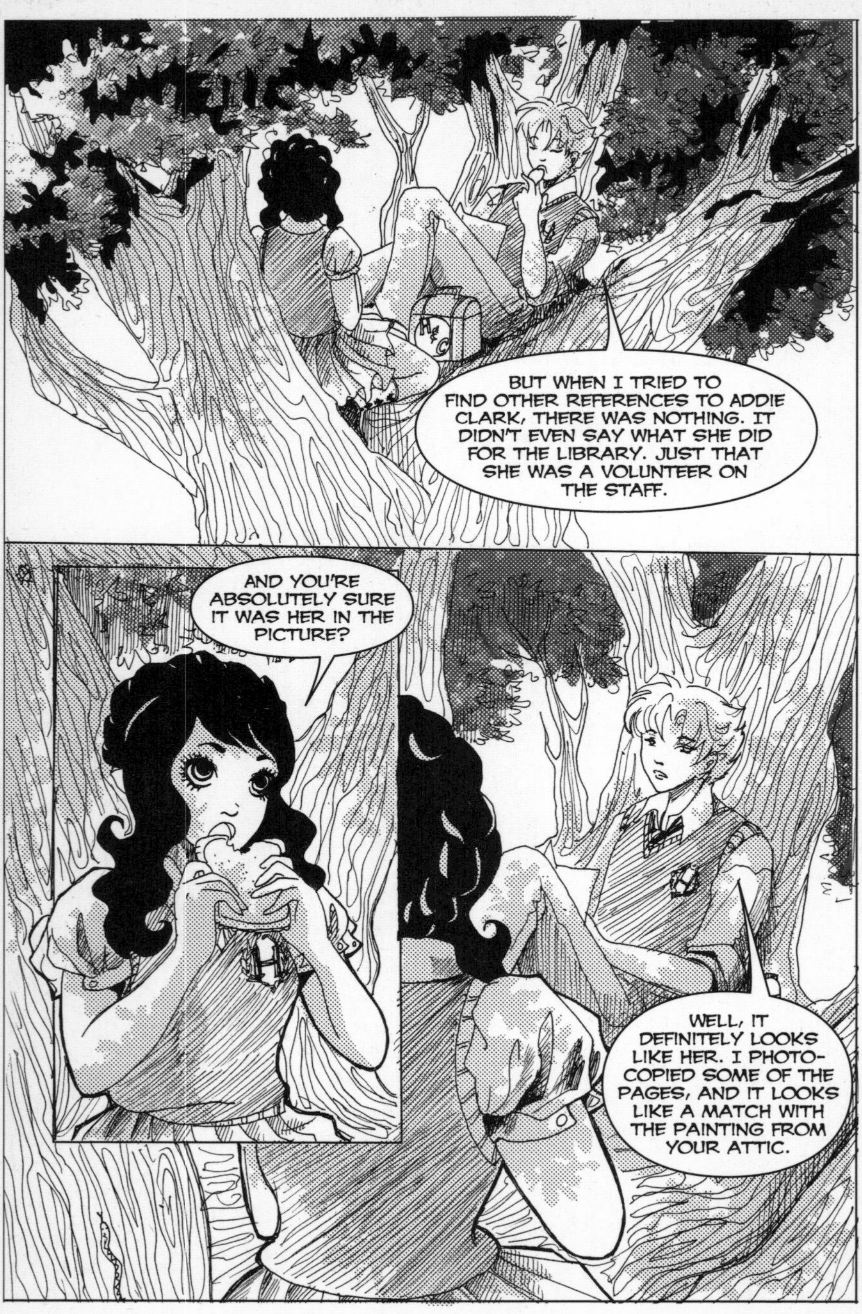
BUT WHEN I TRIED TO FIND OTHER REFERENCES TO ADDIE CLARK, THERE WAS NOTHING. IT DIDN'T EVEN SAY WHAT SHE DID FOR THE LIBRARY. JUST THAT SHE WAS A VOLUNTEER ON THE STAFF.
AND YOU'RE ABSOLUTELY SURE IT WAS HER IN THE PICTURE?
WELL, IT DEFINITELY LOOKS LIKE HER. I PHOTO-COPIED SOME OF THE PAGES, AND IT LOOKS LIKE A MATCH WITH THE PAINTING FROM YOUR ATTIC.

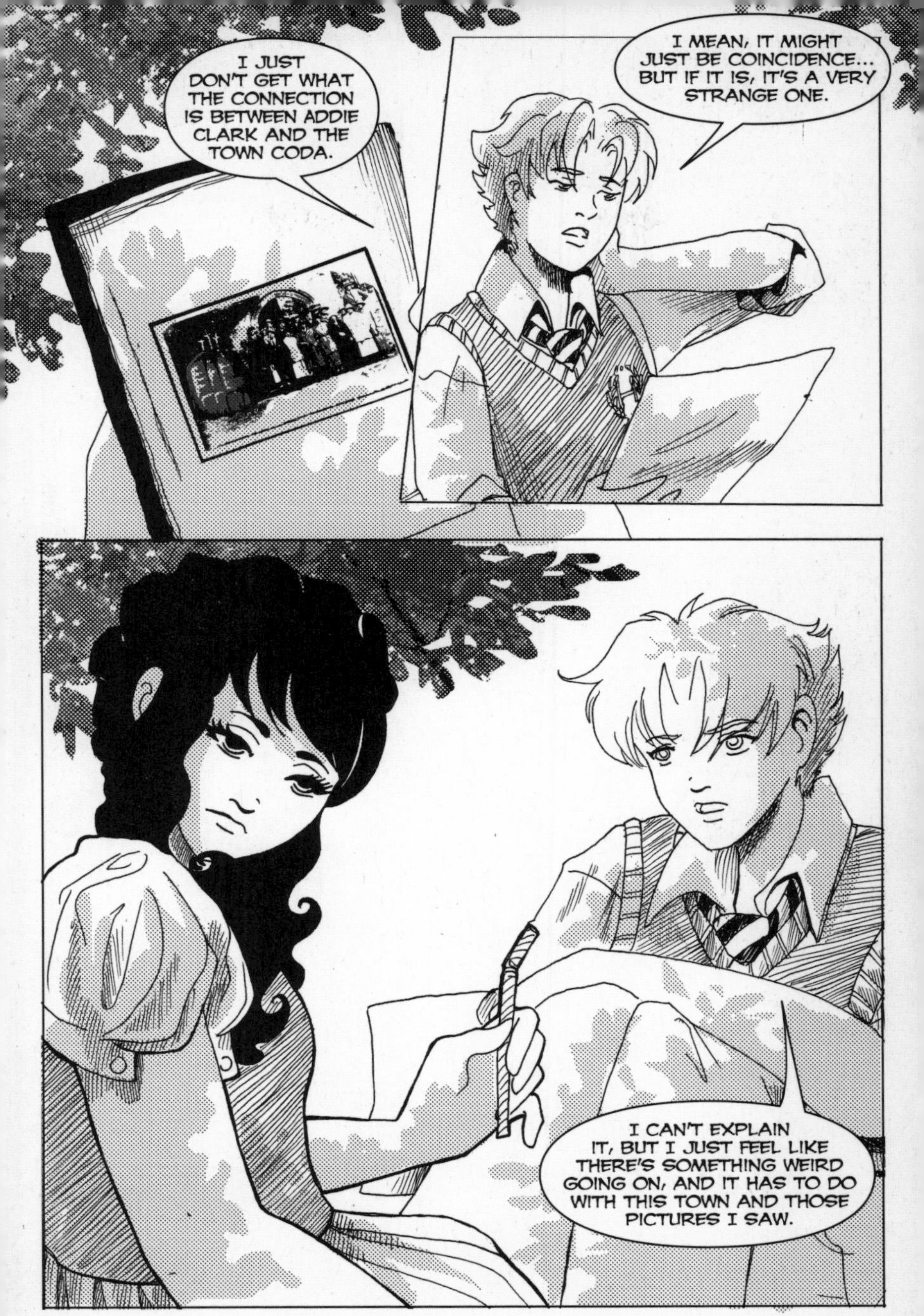
I JUST DON'T GET WHAT THE CONNECTION IS BETWEEN ADDIE CLARK AND THE TOWN CODA.
I MEAN, IT MIGHT JUST BE COINCIDENCE... BUT IF IT IS, IT'S A VERY STRANGE ONE.
I CAN'T EXPLAIN IT, BUT I JUST FEEL LIKE THERE'S SOMETHING WEIRD GOING ON, AND IT HAS TO DO WITH THIS TOWN AND THOSE PICTURES I SAW.

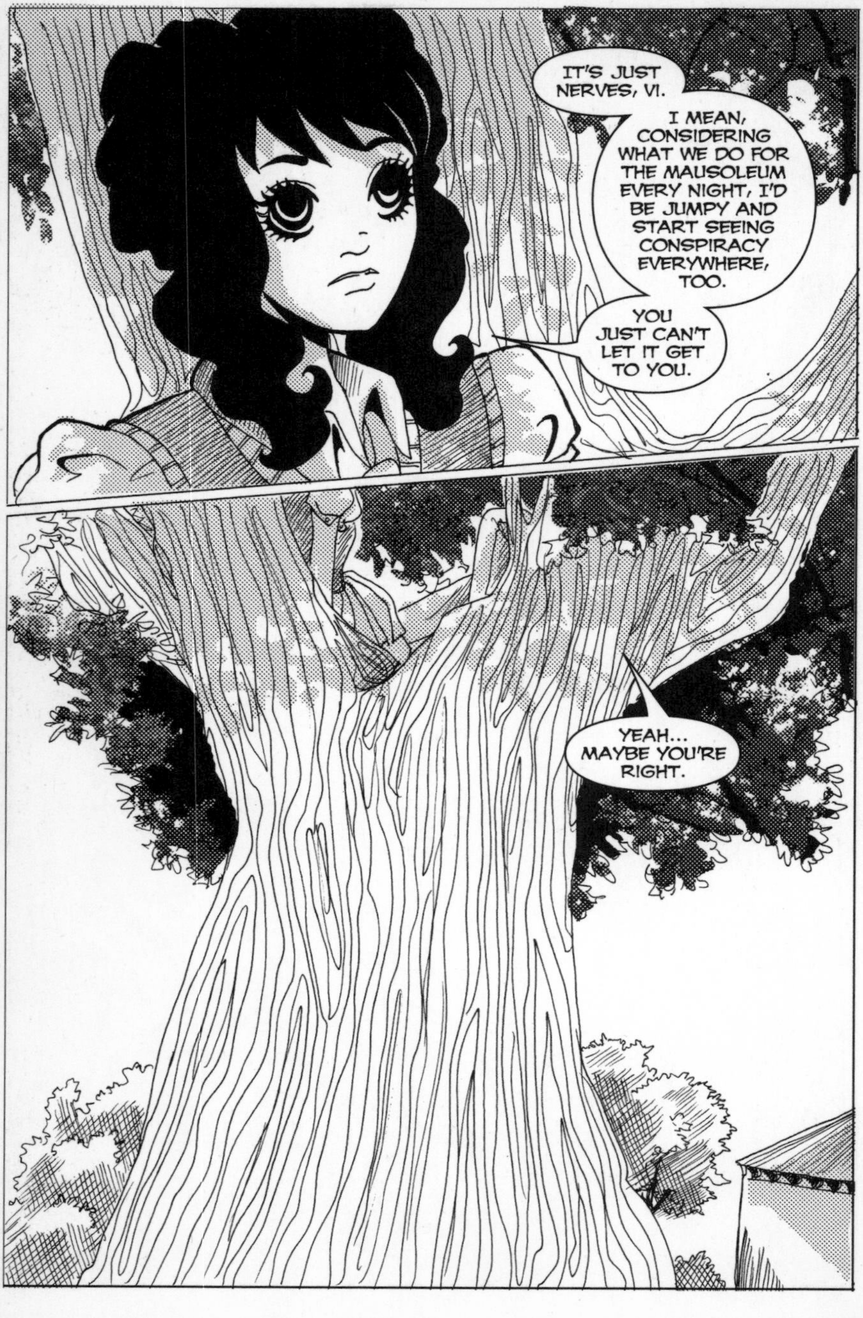
IT'S JUST NERVES, VI.
I MEAN, CONSIDERING WHAT WE DO FOR THE MAUSOLEUM EVERY NIGHT, I'D BE JUMPY AND START SEEING CONSPIRACY EVERYWHERE, TOO.
YOU JUST CAN'T LET IT GET TO YOU.
YEAH... MAYBE YOU'RE RIGHT.

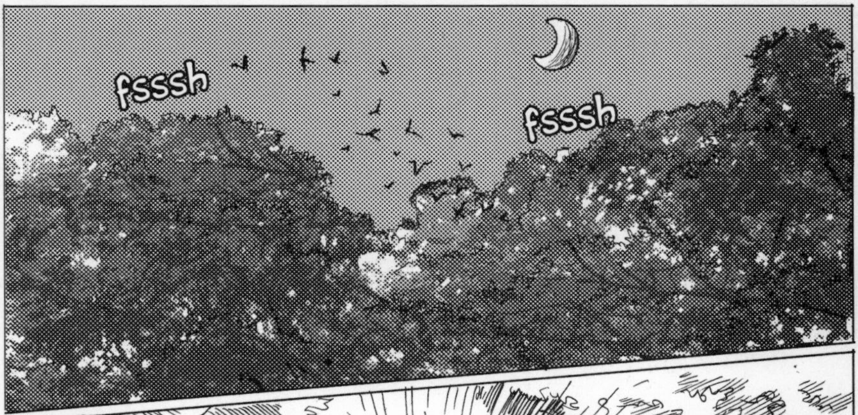
fsssh
fsssh
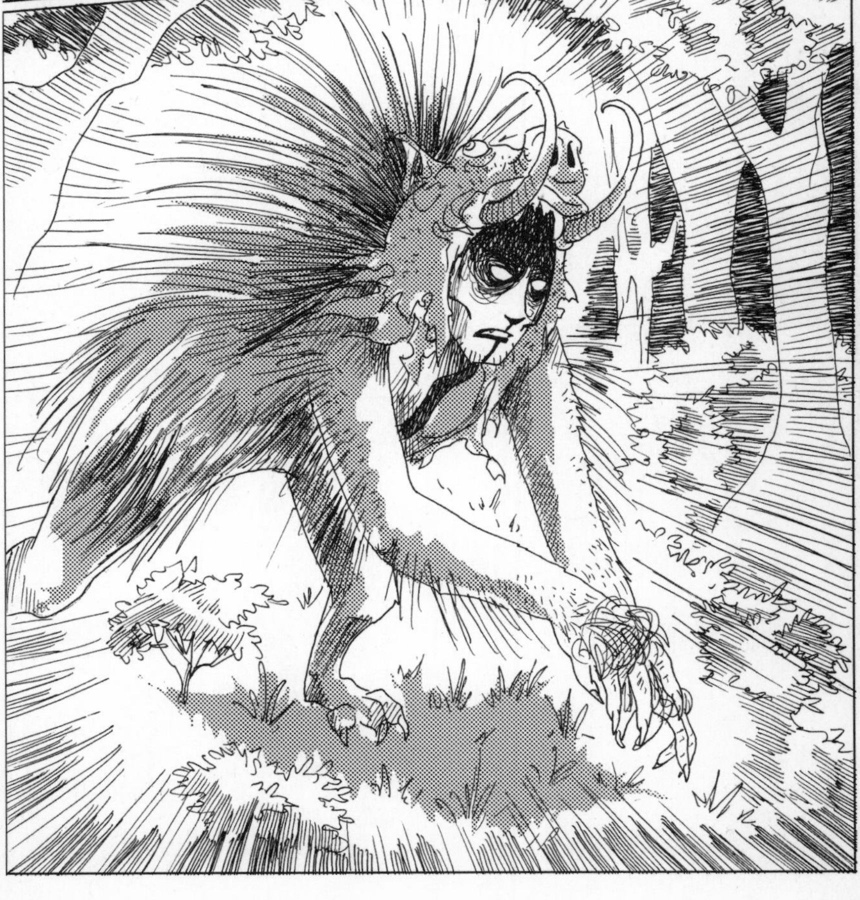

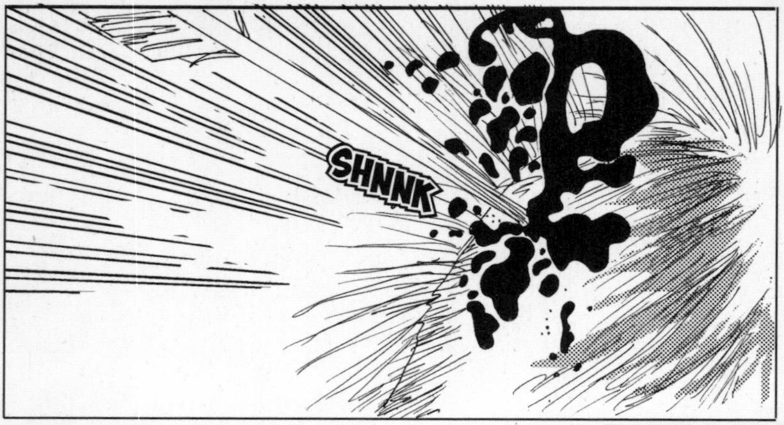
SHNNK

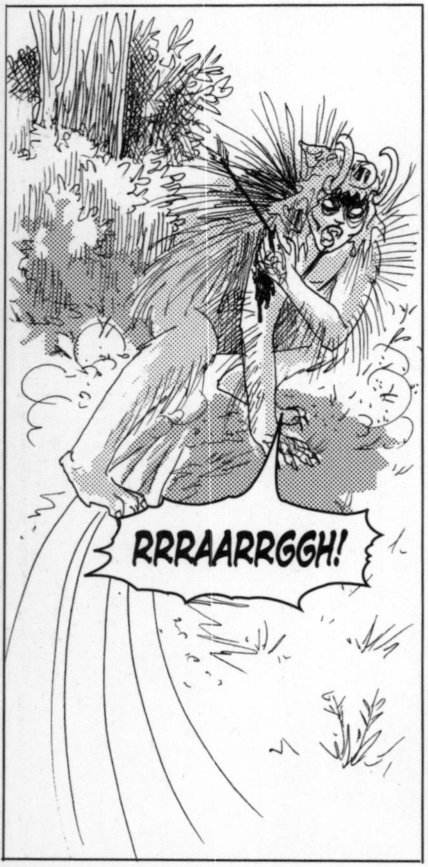
RRRAARRGGH!

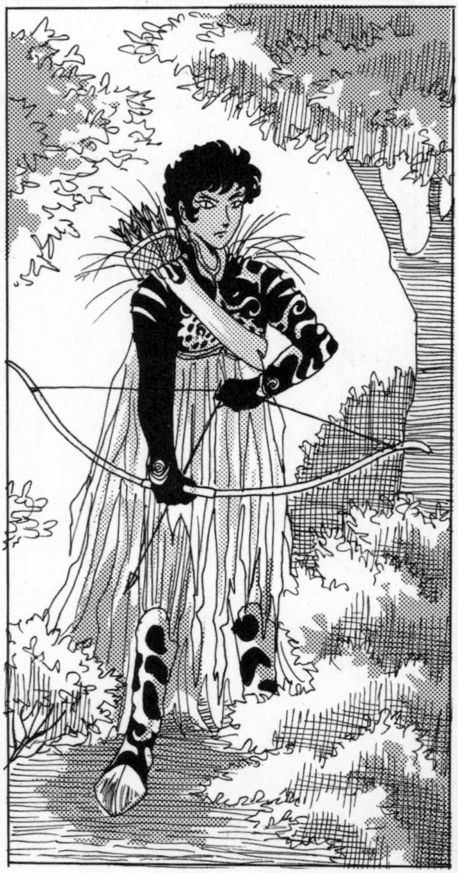

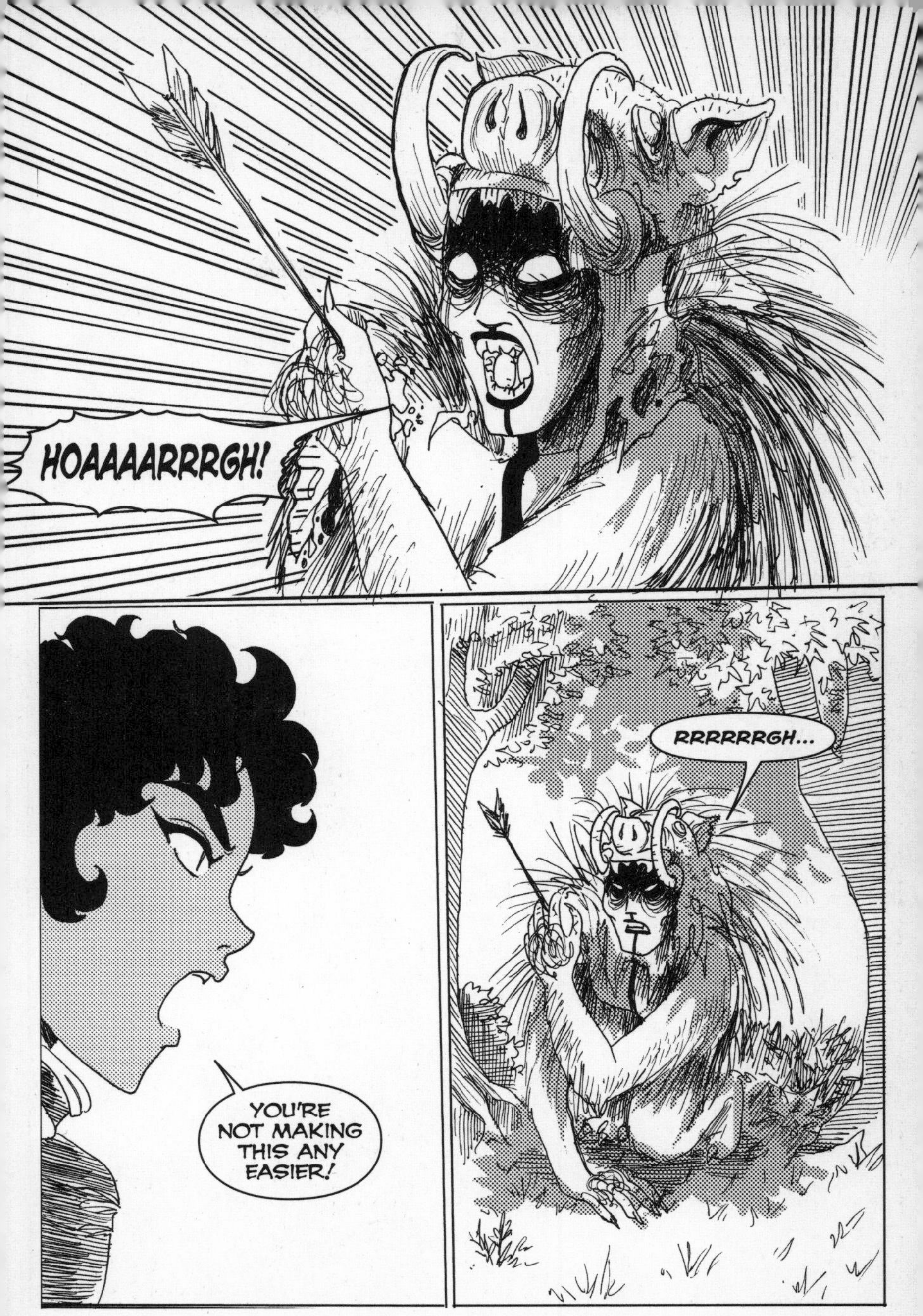
HOAAAARRRGH!
YOU'RE NOT MAKING THIS ANY EASIER!
RRRRRRGH...

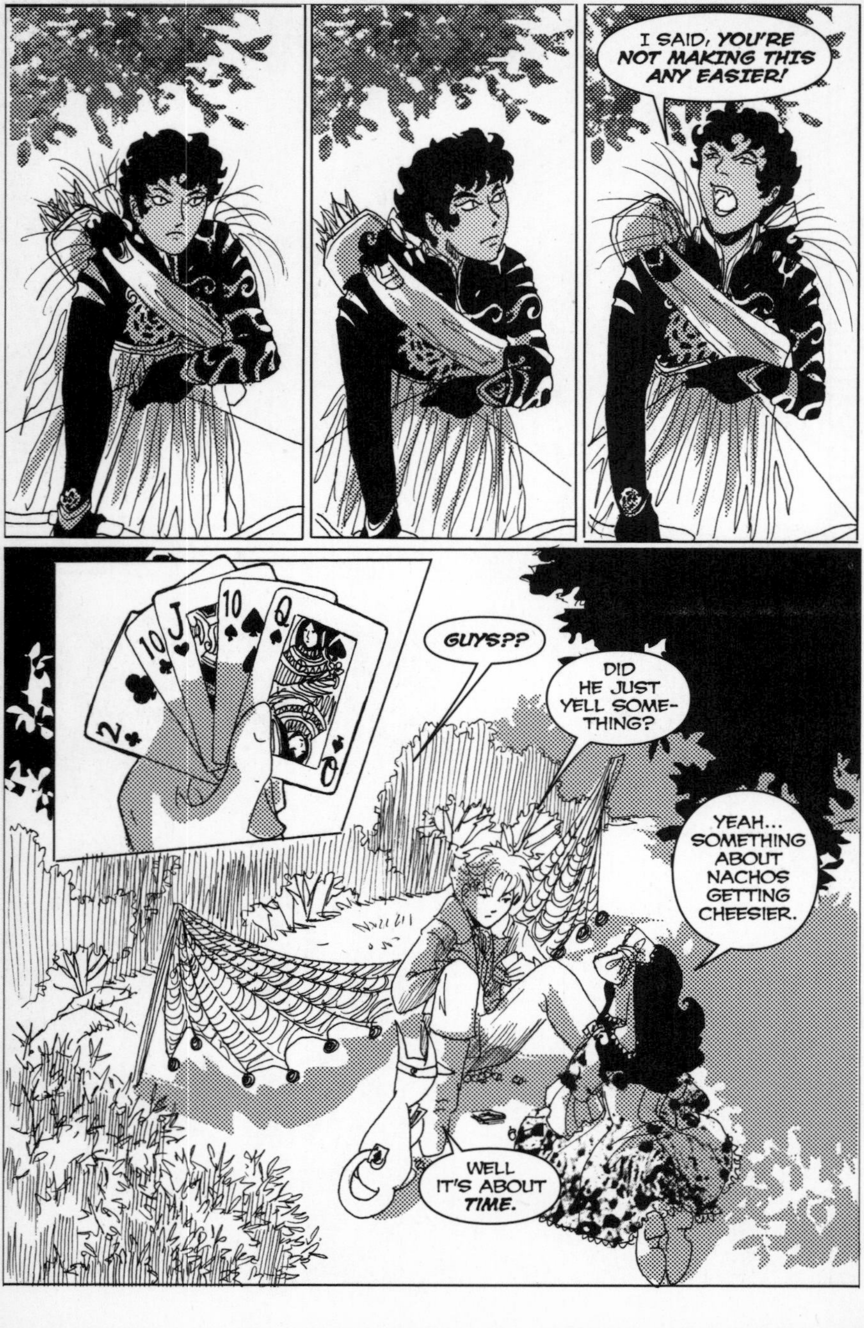
I SAID, *YOU'RE NOT MAKING THIS ANY EASIER!*
GUYS??
DID HE JUST YELL SOME-THING?
YEAH... SOMETHING ABOUT NACHOS GETTING CHEESIER.
WELL IT'S ABOUT *TIME.*

GOSH, EDREAR, I'M SORRY. WE SORTA FORGOT THE SIGNAL WORDS.

THAT'S QUITE ALL RIGHT, MISS DINAH. AT LEAST I WAS ABLE TO BRING THE SPIRIT DOWN MYSELF.

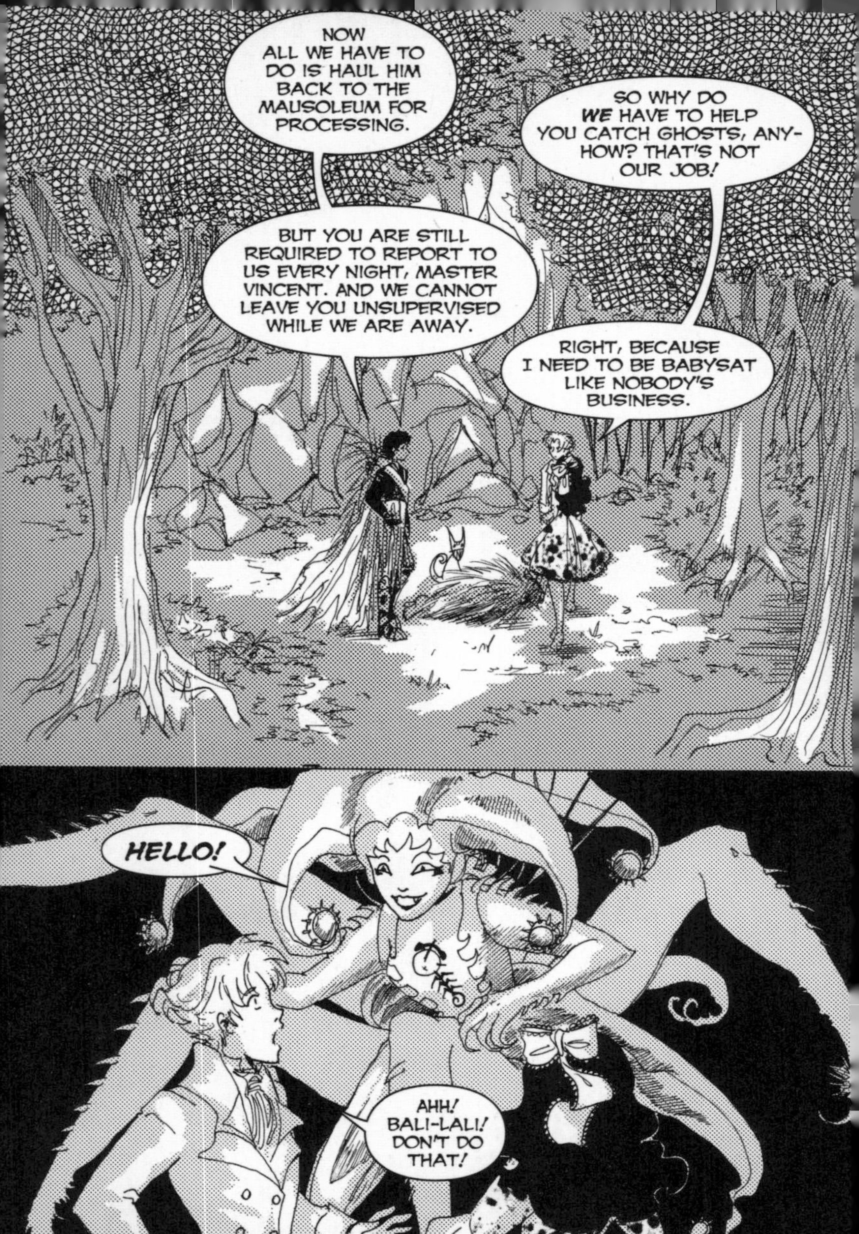
NOW ALL WE HAVE TO DO IS HAUL HIM BACK TO THE MAUSOLEUM FOR PROCESSING.
SO WHY DO WE HAVE TO HELP YOU CATCH GHOSTS, ANY-HOW? THAT'S NOT OUR JOB!
BUT YOU ARE STILL REQUIRED TO REPORT TO US EVERY NIGHT, MASTER VINCENT. AND WE CANNOT LEAVE YOU UNSUPERVISED WHILE WE ARE AWAY.
RIGHT, BECAUSE I NEED TO BE BABYSAT LIKE NOBODY'S BUSINESS.
HELLO!
AHH! BALI-LALI! DON'T DO THAT!

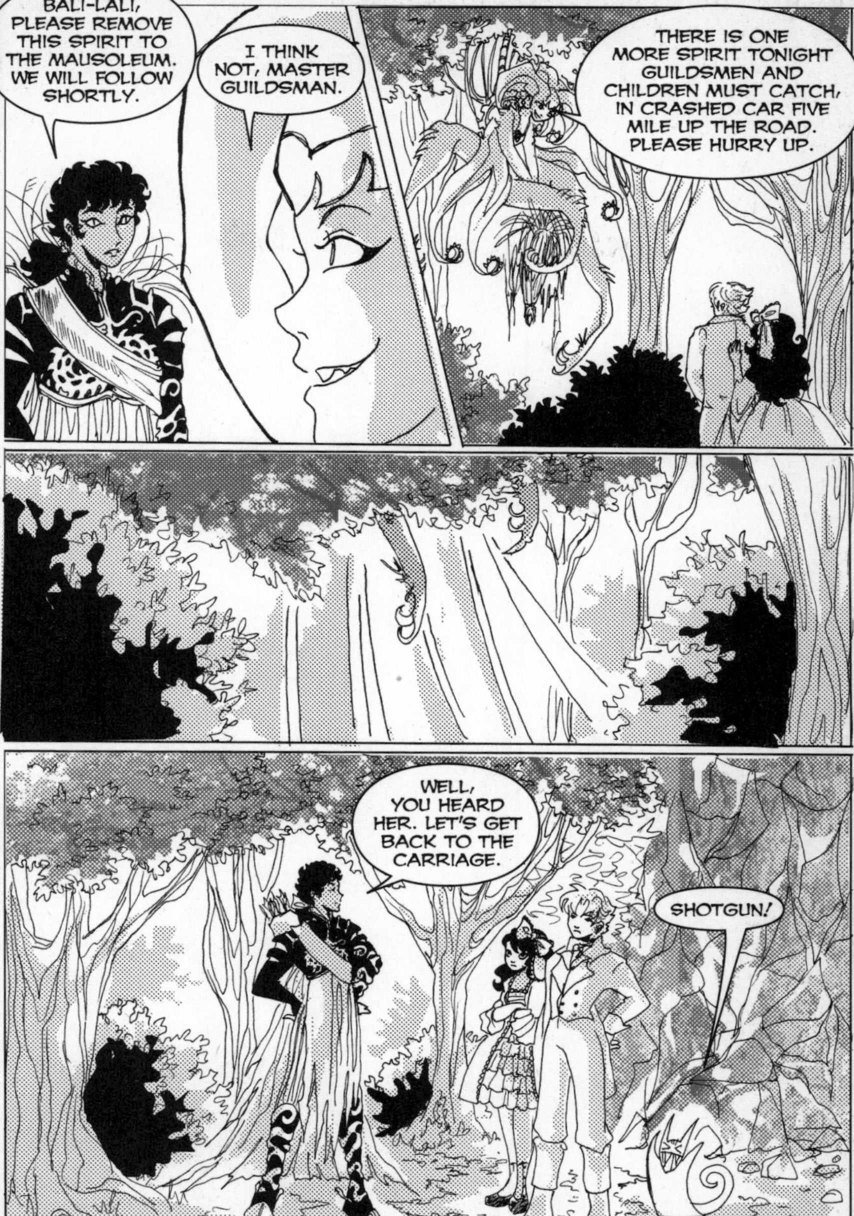
BALI-LALI, PLEASE REMOVE THIS SPIRIT TO THE MAUSOLEUM. WE WILL FOLLOW SHORTLY.
I THINK NOT, MASTER GUILDSMAN.
THERE IS ONE MORE SPIRIT TONIGHT GUILDSMEN AND CHILDREN MUST CATCH, IN CRASHED CAR FIVE MILE UP THE ROAD. PLEASE HURRY UP.
WELL, YOU HEARD HER. LET'S GET BACK TO THE CARRIAGE.
SHOTGUN!

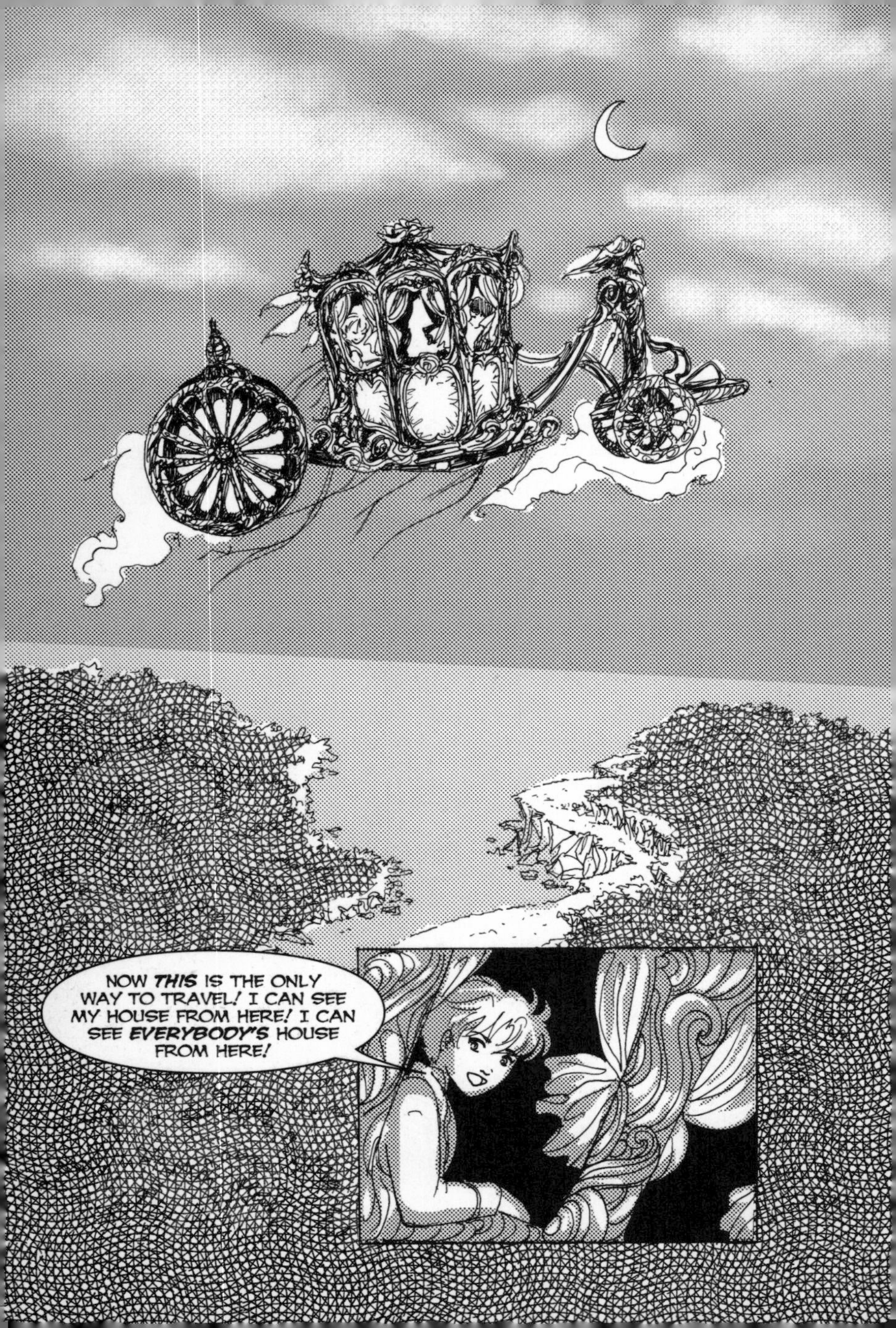
NOW **THIS** IS THE ONLY WAY TO TRAVEL! I CAN SEE MY HOUSE FROM HERE! I CAN SEE **EVERYBODY'S** HOUSE FROM HERE!

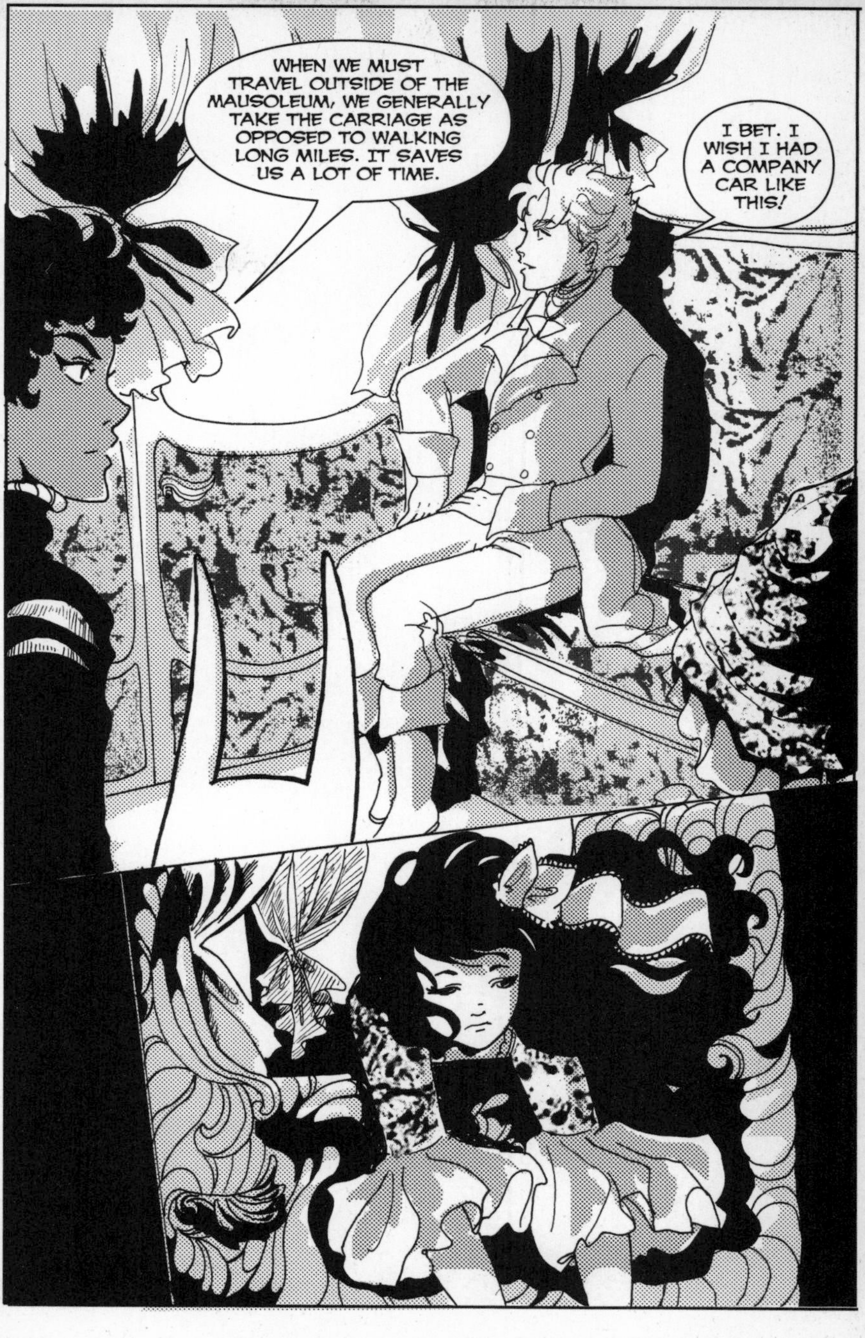
WHEN WE MUST TRAVEL OUTSIDE OF THE MAUSOLEUM, WE GENERALLY TAKE THE CARRIAGE AS OPPOSED TO WALKING LONG MILES. IT SAVES US A LOT OF TIME.
I BET. I WISH I HAD A COMPANY CAR LIKE THIS!

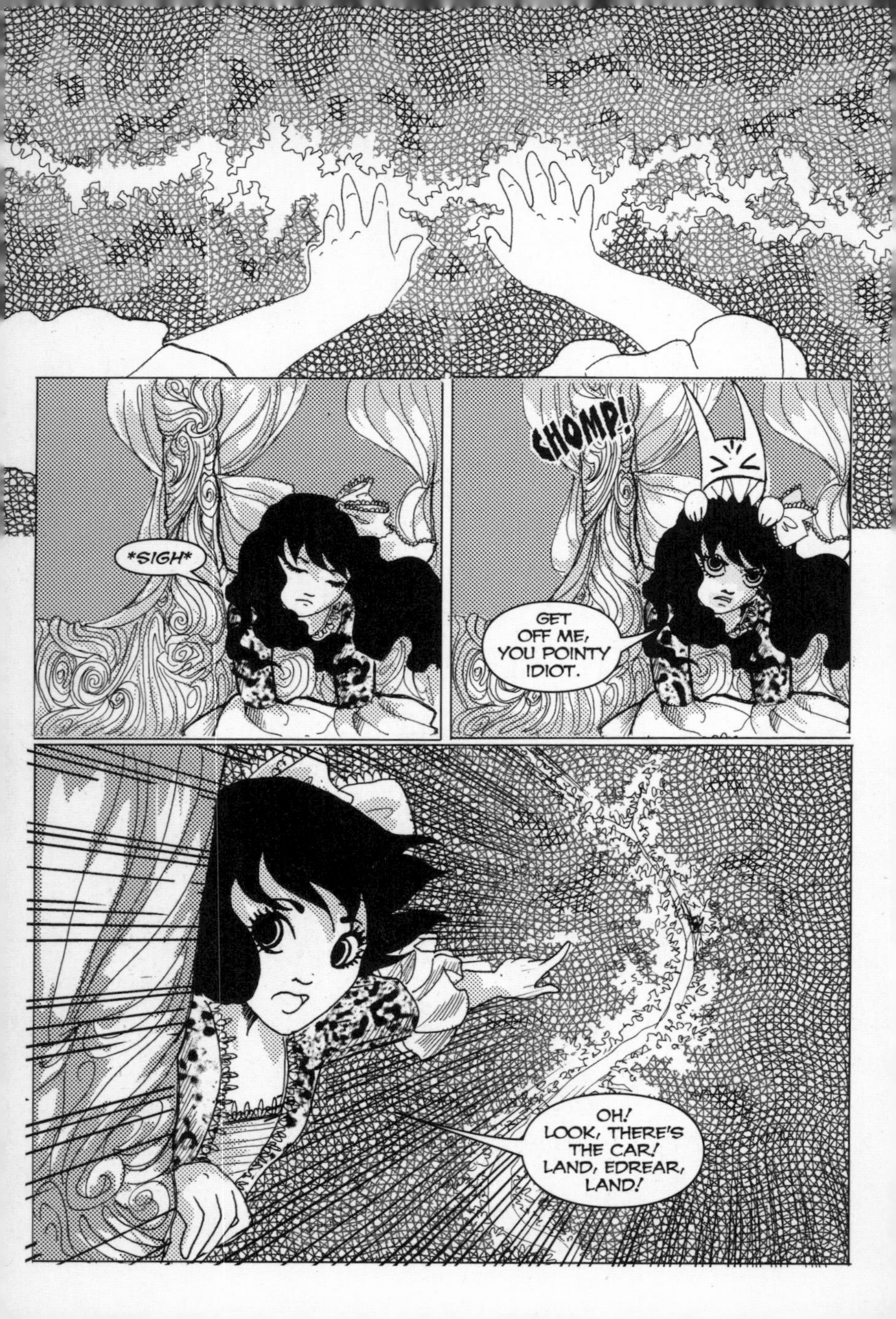
SIGH
CHOMP!
GET OFF ME, YOU POINTY IDIOT.
OH! LOOK, THERE'S THE CAR! LAND, EDREAR, LAND!

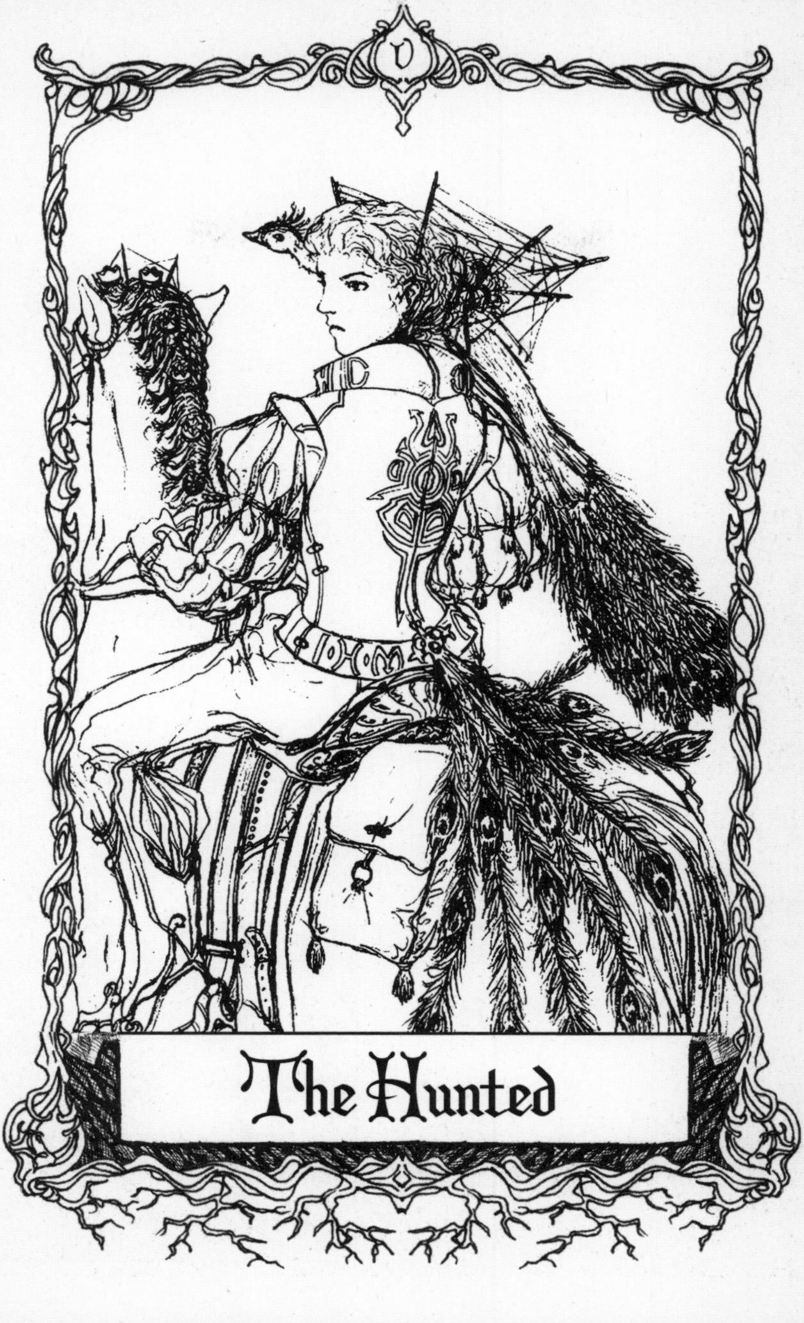
V
The Hunted

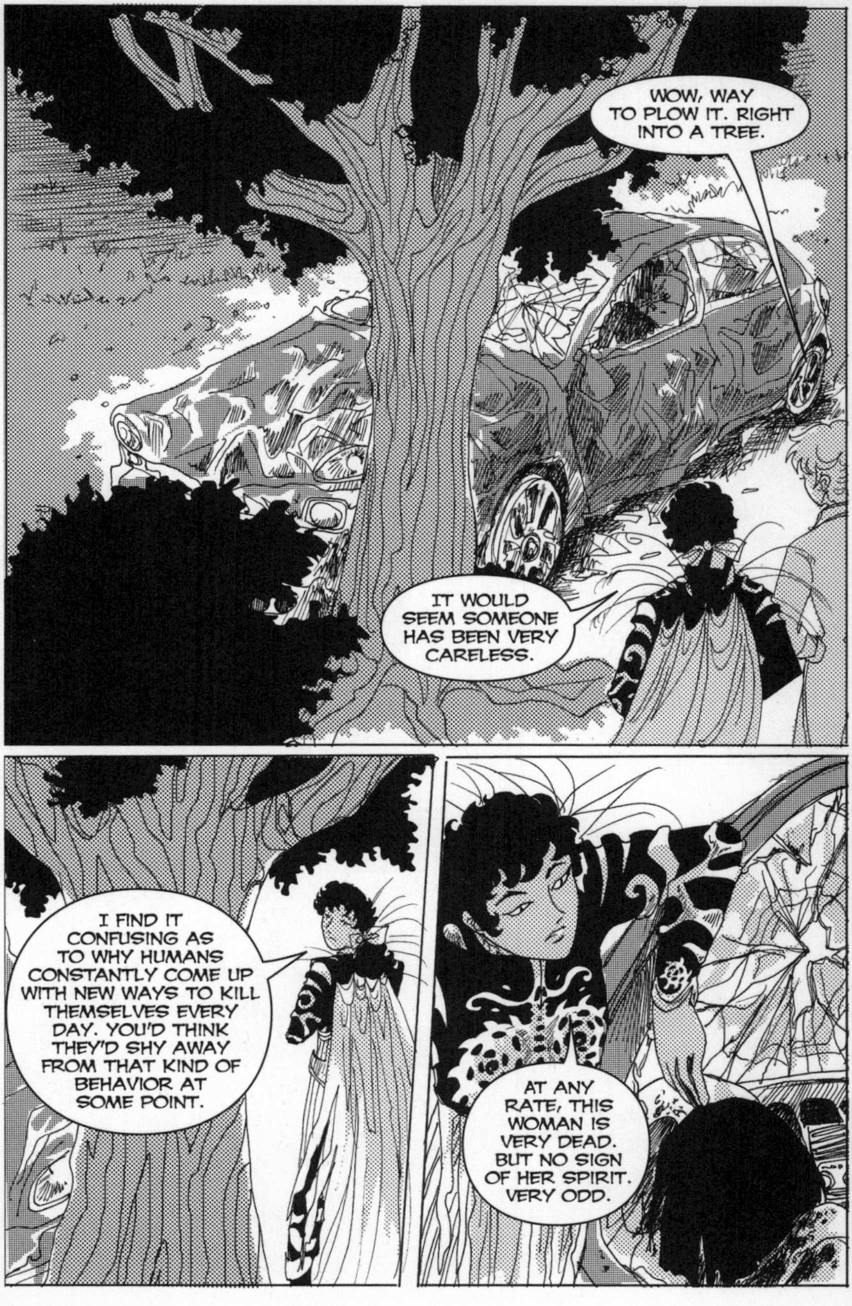
WOW, WAY TO PLOW IT. RIGHT INTO A TREE.
IT WOULD SEEM SOMEONE HAS BEEN VERY CARELESS.
I FIND IT CONFUSING AS TO WHY HUMANS CONSTANTLY COME UP WITH NEW WAYS TO KILL THEMSELVES EVERY DAY. YOU'D THINK THEY'D SHY AWAY FROM THAT KIND OF BEHAVIOR AT SOME POINT.
AT ANY RATE, THIS WOMAN IS VERY DEAD. BUT NO SIGN OF HER SPIRIT. VERY ODD.

SO WHAT DO WE DO NOW? SHE'S OBVIOUSLY NOT HERE. I MEAN SHE'S *HERE*, BUT NOT *HERE* HERE.

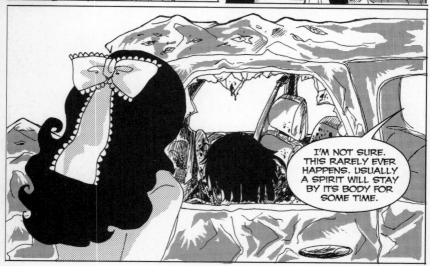

I'M NOT SURE. THIS RARELY EVER HAPPENS. USUALLY A SPIRIT WILL STAY BY ITS BODY FOR SOME TIME.

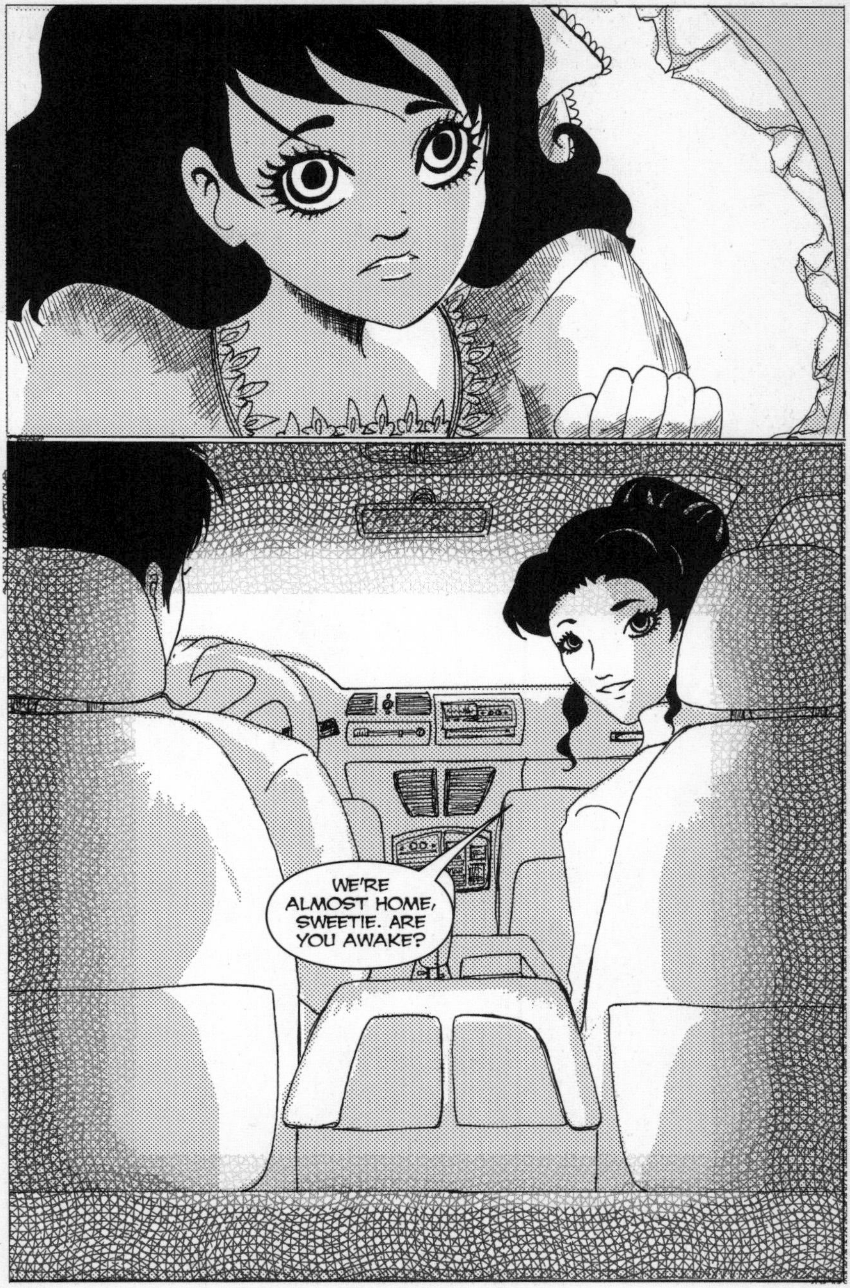
WE'RE ALMOST HOME, SWEETIE. ARE YOU AWAKE?

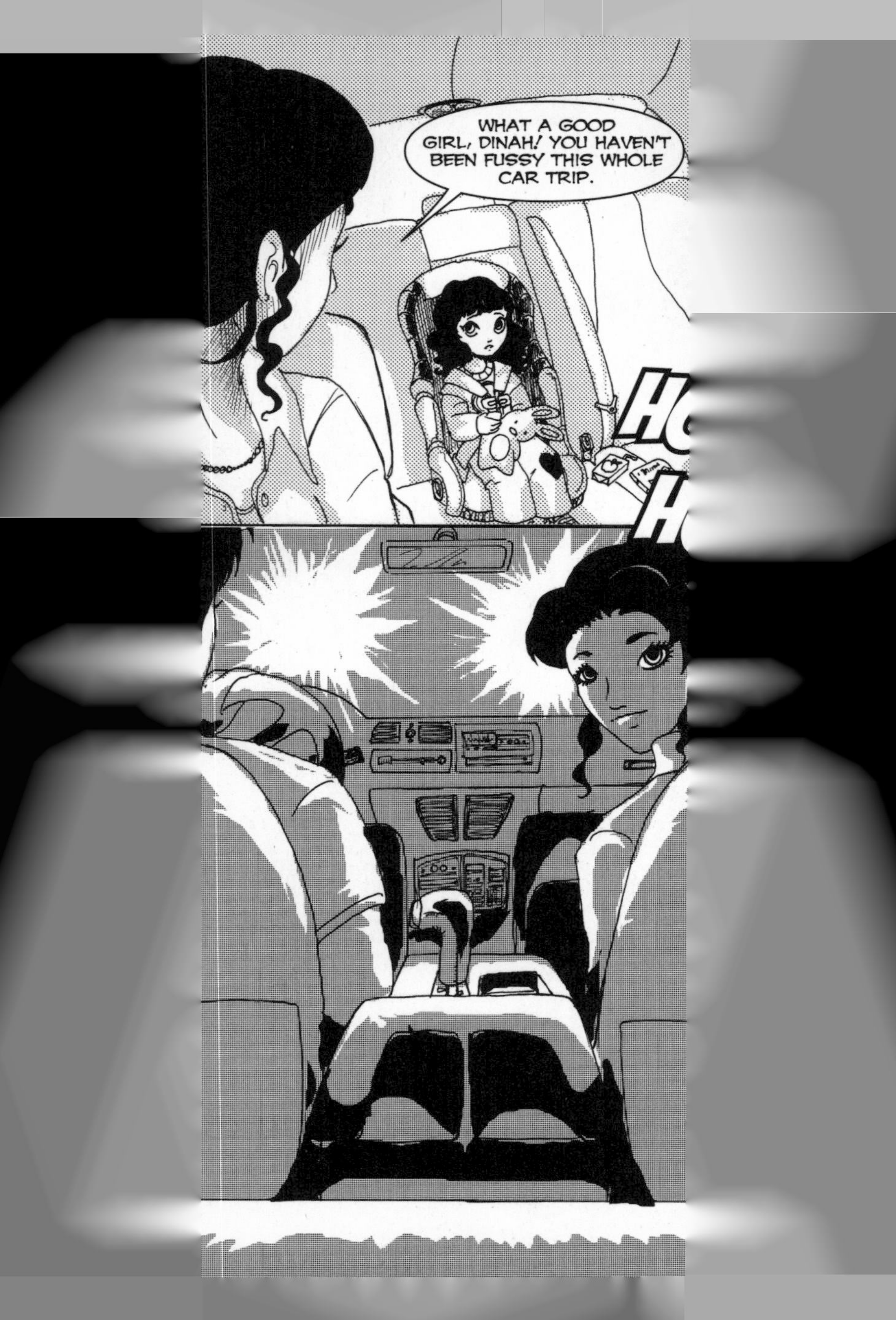
WHAT A GOOD GIRL, DINAH! YOU HAVEN'T BEEN FUSSY THIS WHOLE CAR TRIP.

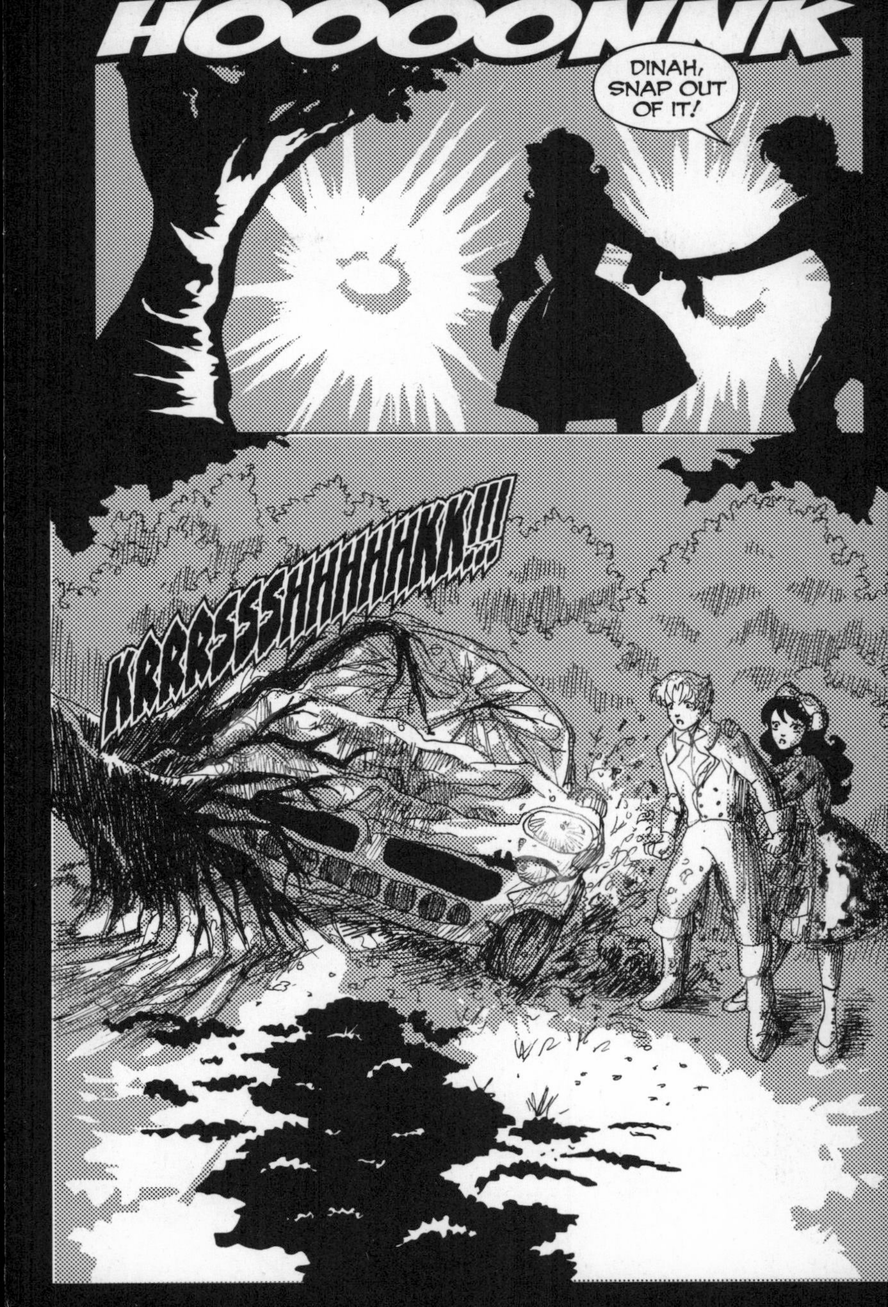
HOOOOONNK
DINAH, SNAP OUT OF IT!
KRRRSSSHHHHHHHKK!!!

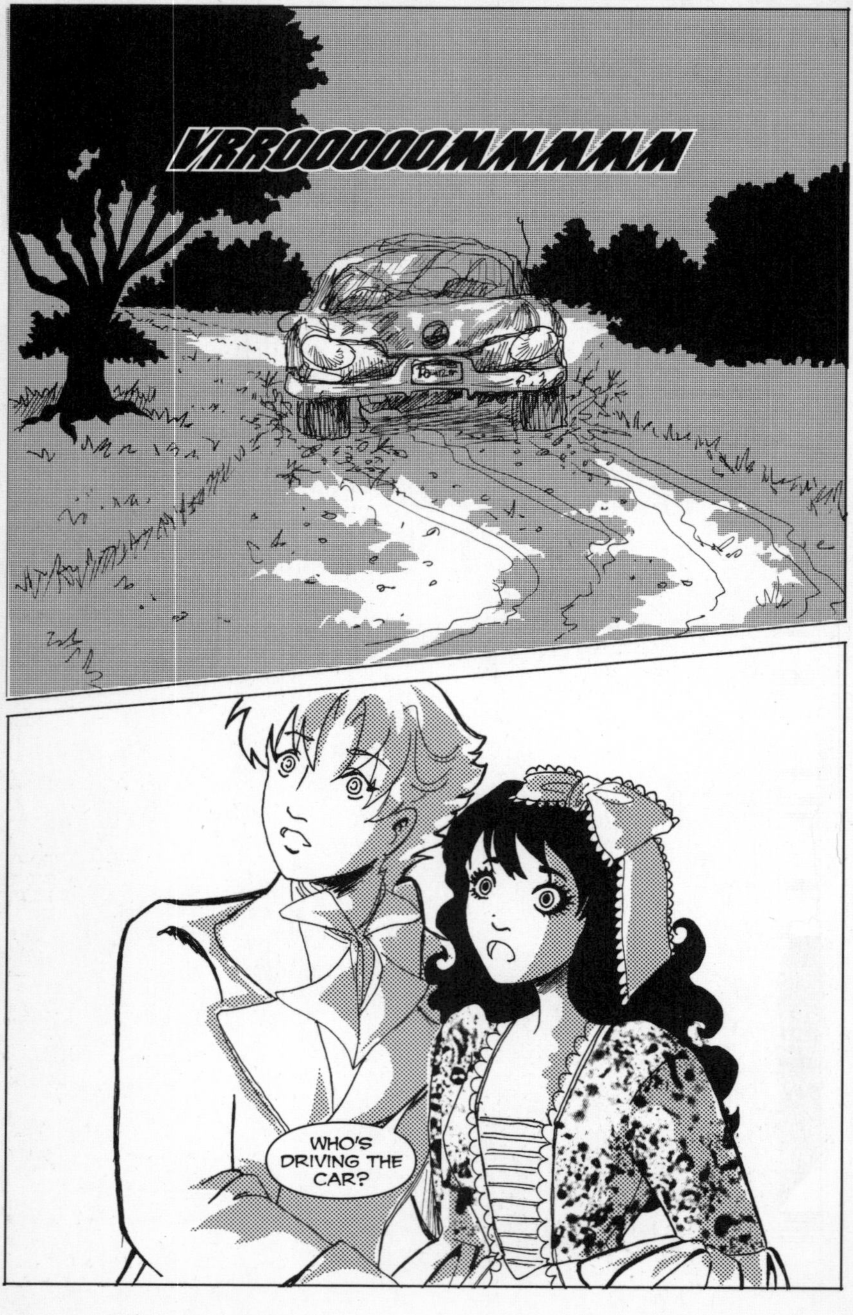
VRROOOOOOMMMMMM
WHO'S DRIVING THE CAR?

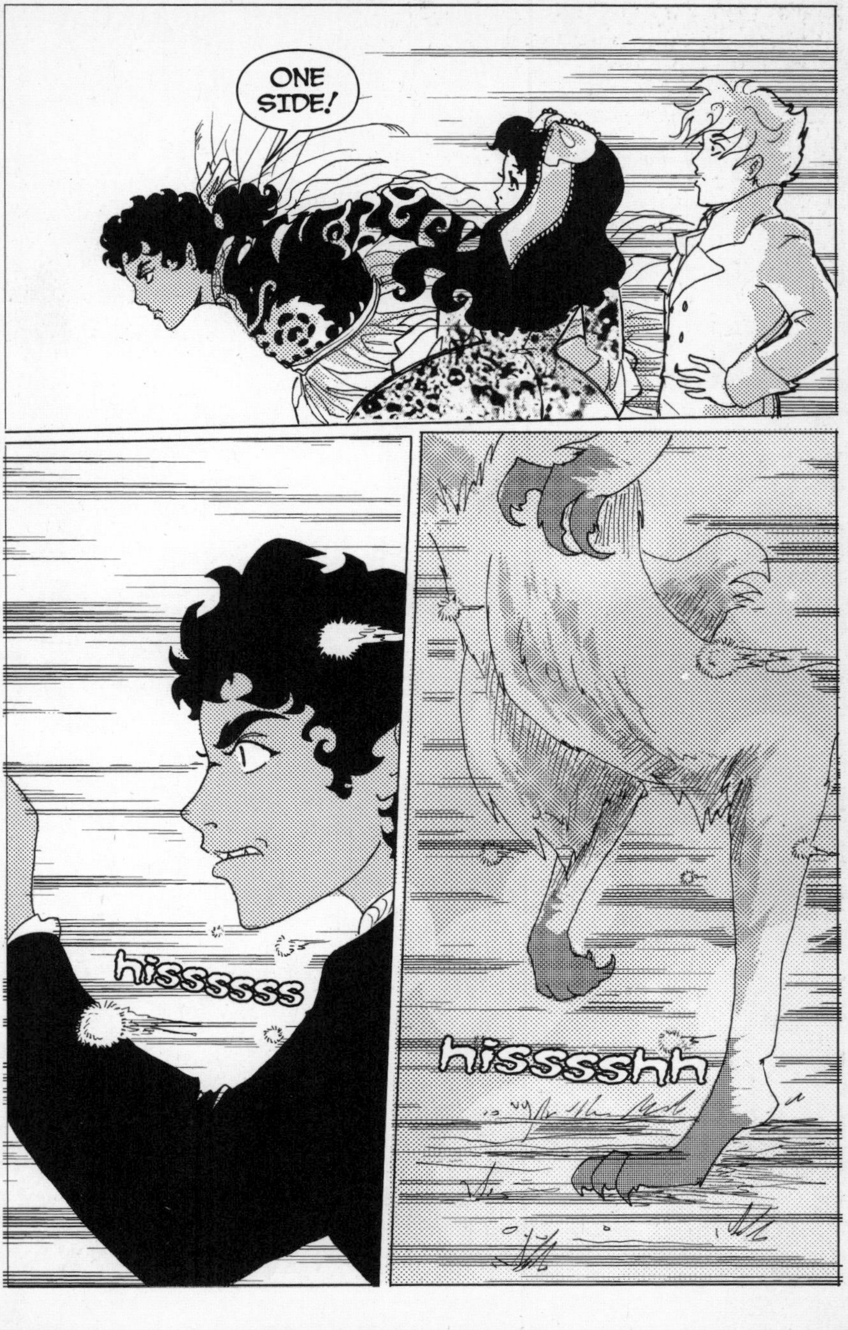
ONE SIDE!
hisssssss
hissssshh

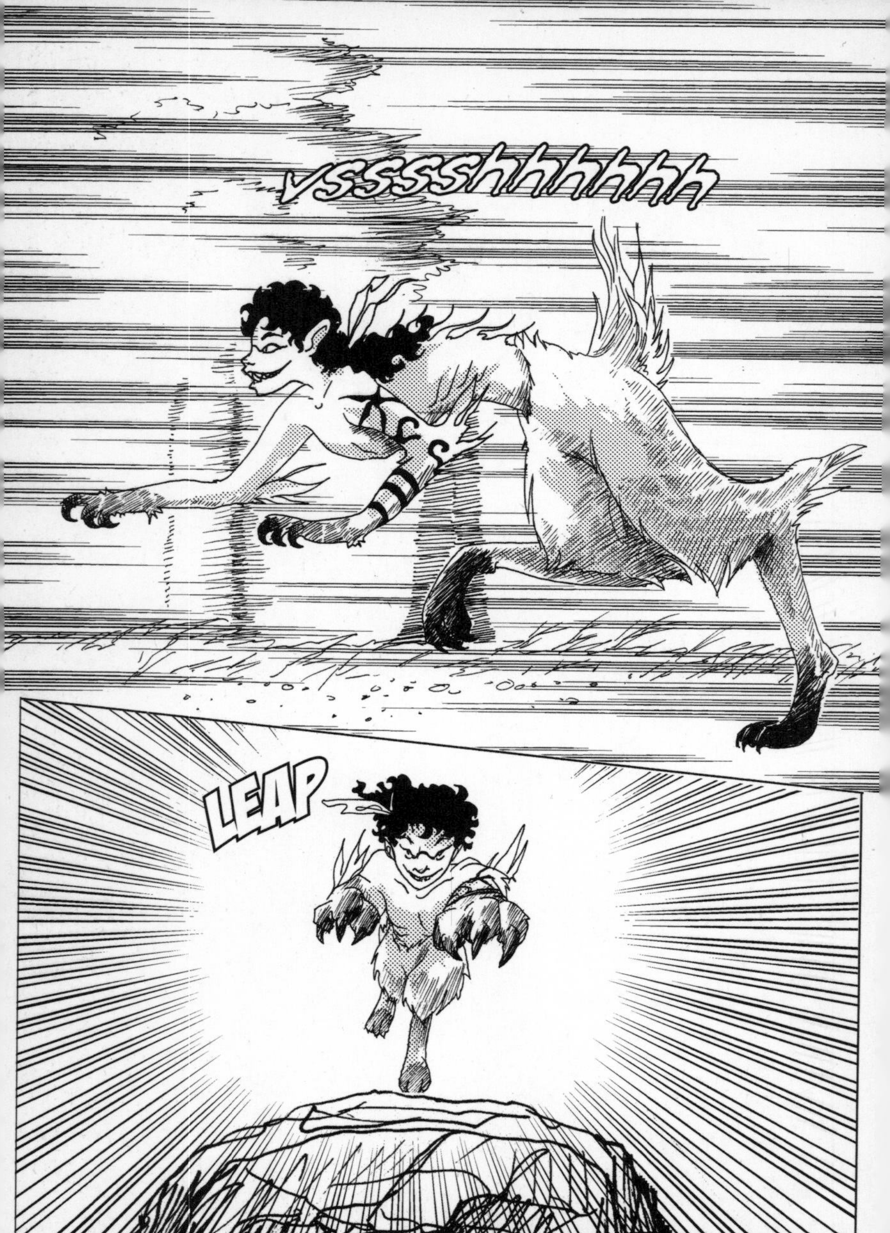
vsssshhhhhh
LEAP

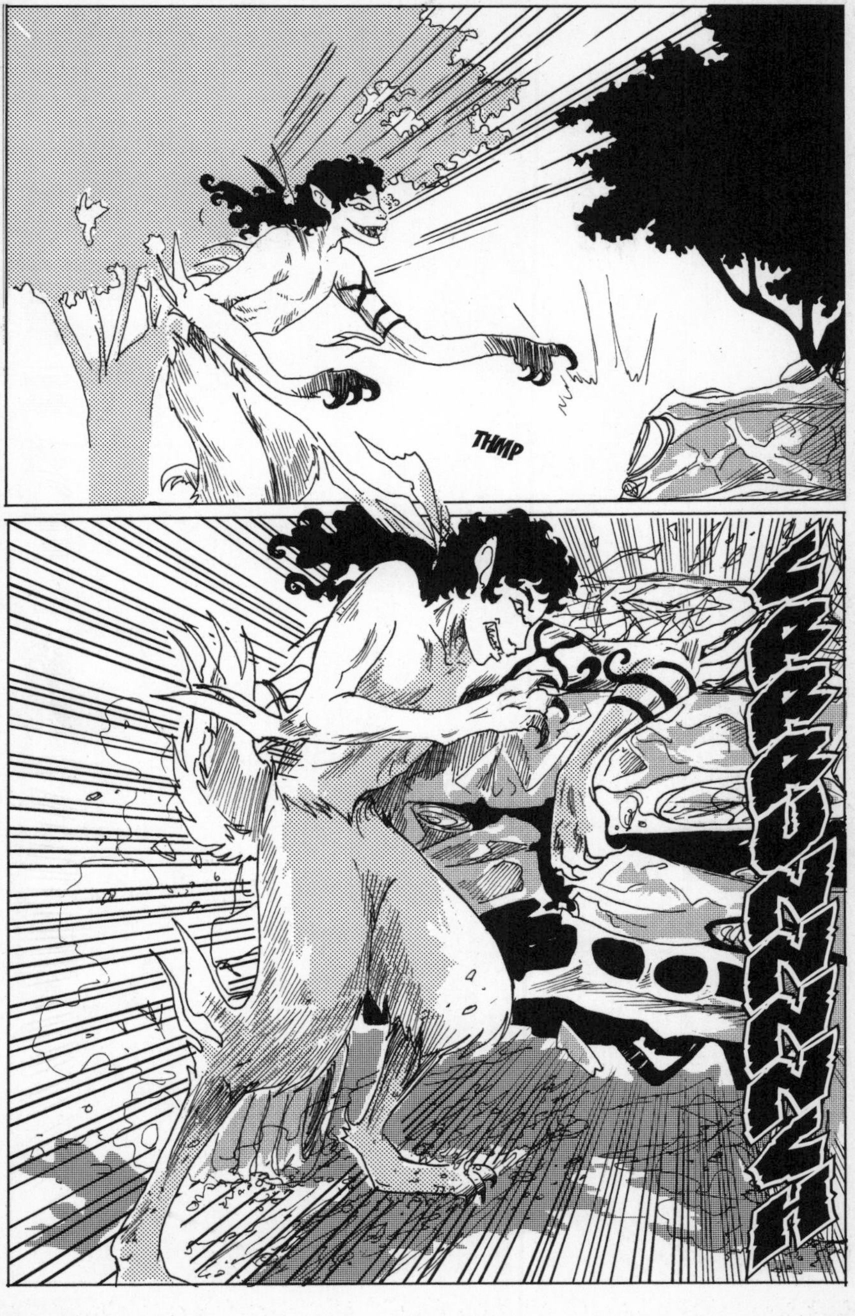
THMP

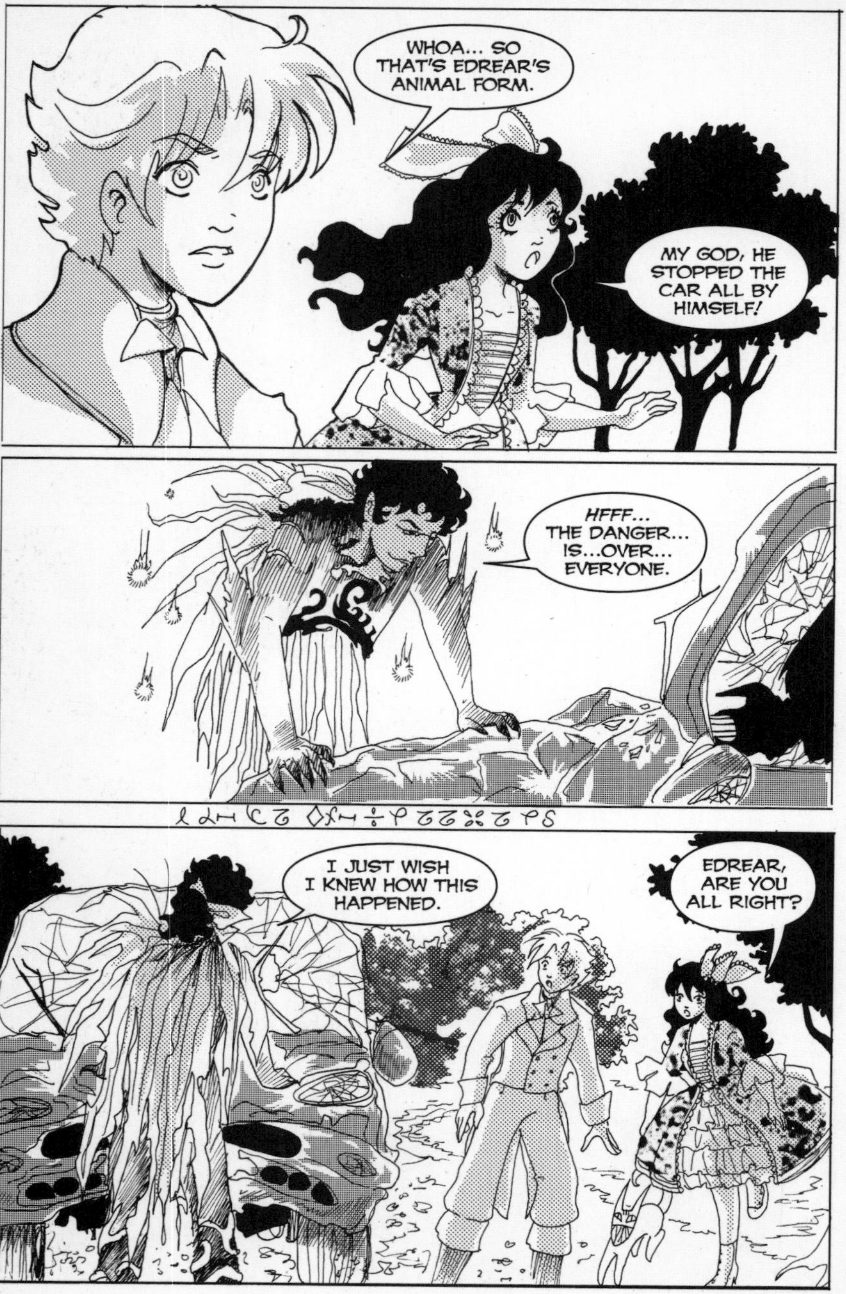
WHOA... SO THAT'S EDREAR'S ANIMAL FORM.
MY GOD, HE STOPPED THE CAR ALL BY HIMSELF!
HFFF... THE DANGER... IS...OVER... EVERYONE.
I JUST WISH I KNEW HOW THIS HAPPENED.
EDREAR, ARE YOU ALL RIGHT?

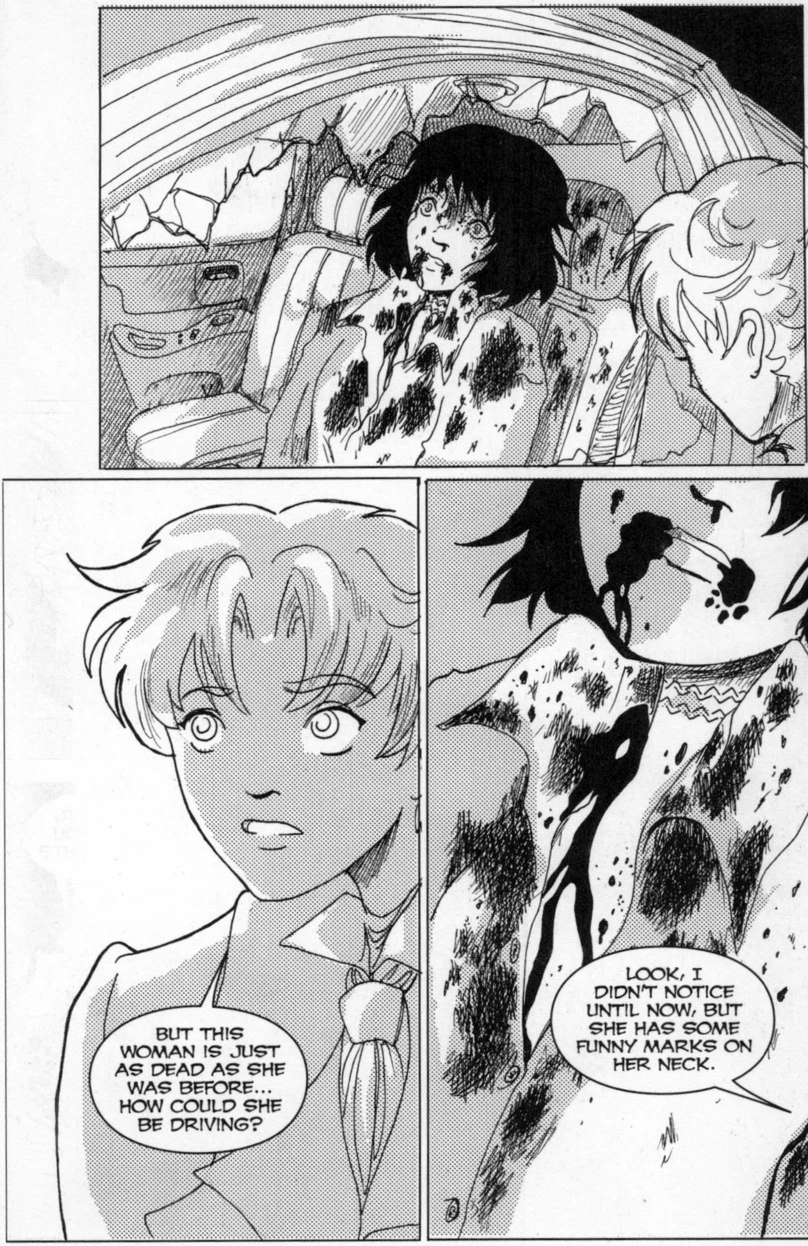
BUT THIS WOMAN IS JUST AS DEAD AS SHE WAS BEFORE... HOW COULD SHE BE DRIVING?
LOOK, I DIDN'T NOTICE UNTIL NOW, BUT SHE HAS SOME FUNNY MARKS ON HER NECK.

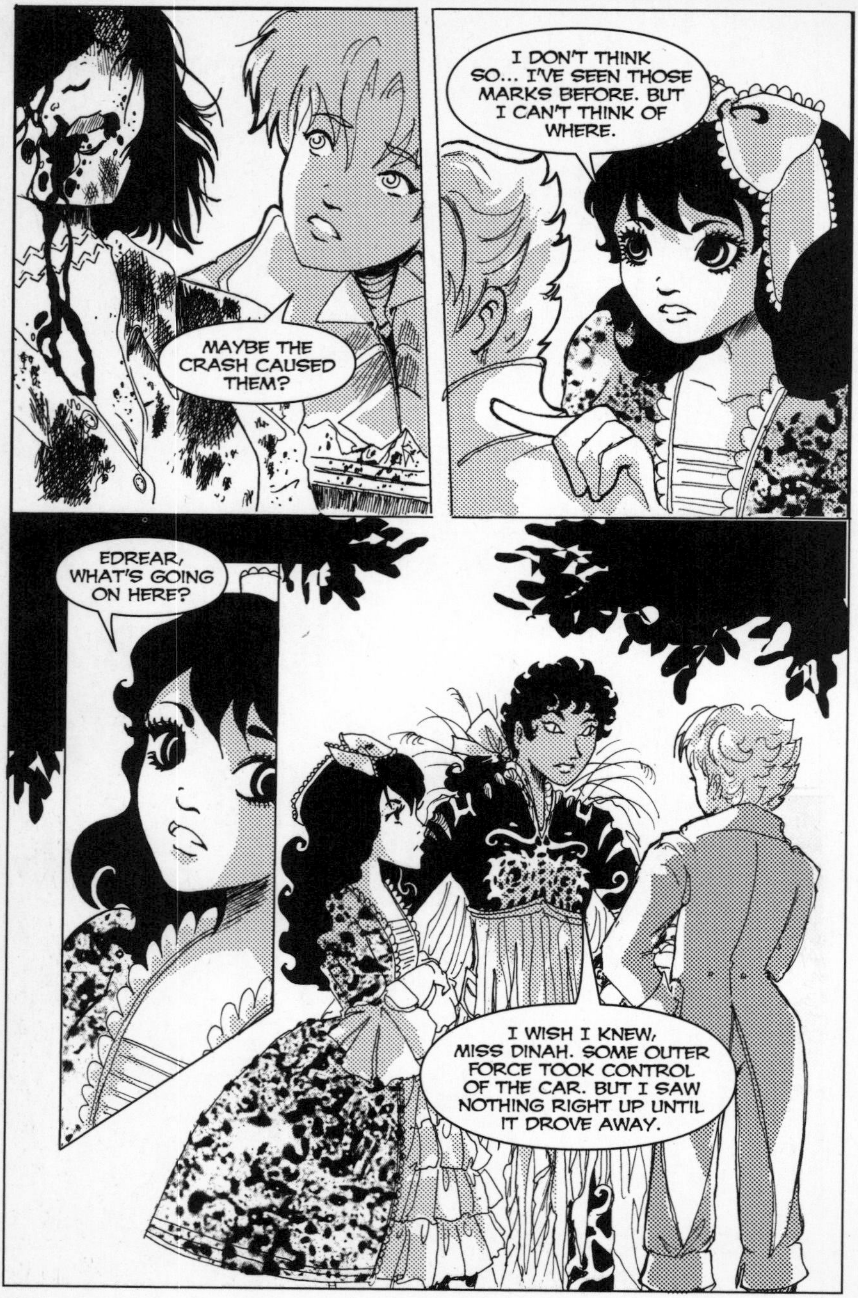
MAYBE THE CRASH CAUSED THEM?
I DON'T THINK SO... I'VE SEEN THOSE MARKS BEFORE. BUT I CAN'T THINK OF WHERE.
EDREAR, WHAT'S GOING ON HERE?
I WISH I KNEW, MISS DINAH. SOME OUTER FORCE TOOK CONTROL OF THE CAR. BUT I SAW NOTHING RIGHT UP UNTIL IT DROVE AWAY.

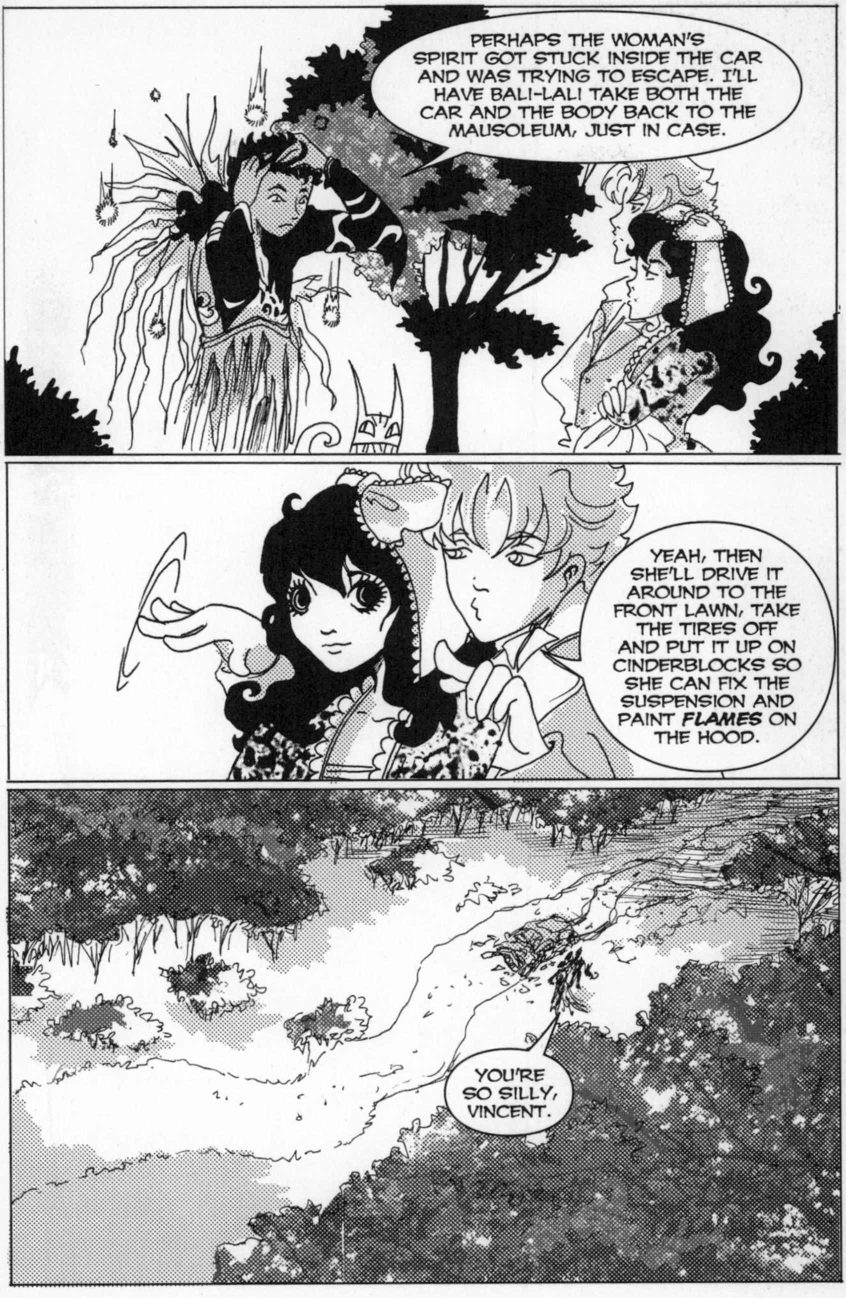
PERHAPS THE WOMAN'S SPIRIT GOT STUCK INSIDE THE CAR AND WAS TRYING TO ESCAPE. I'LL HAVE BALI-LALI TAKE BOTH THE CAR AND THE BODY BACK TO THE MAUSOLEUM, JUST IN CASE.
YEAH, THEN SHE'LL DRIVE IT AROUND TO THE FRONT LAWN, TAKE THE TIRES OFF AND PUT IT UP ON CINDERBLOCKS SO SHE CAN FIX THE SUSPENSION AND PAINT *FLAMES* ON THE HOOD.
YOU'RE SO SILLY, VINCENT.

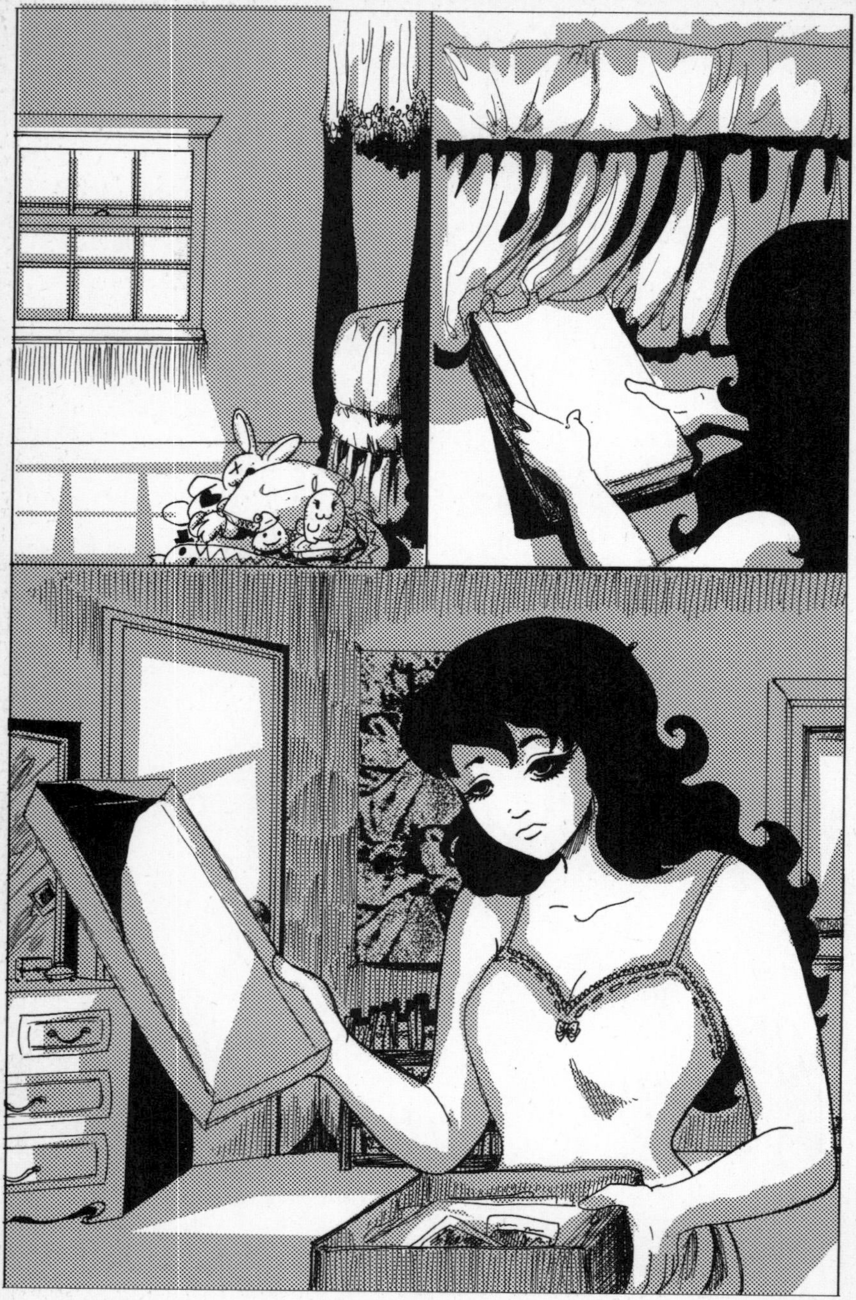

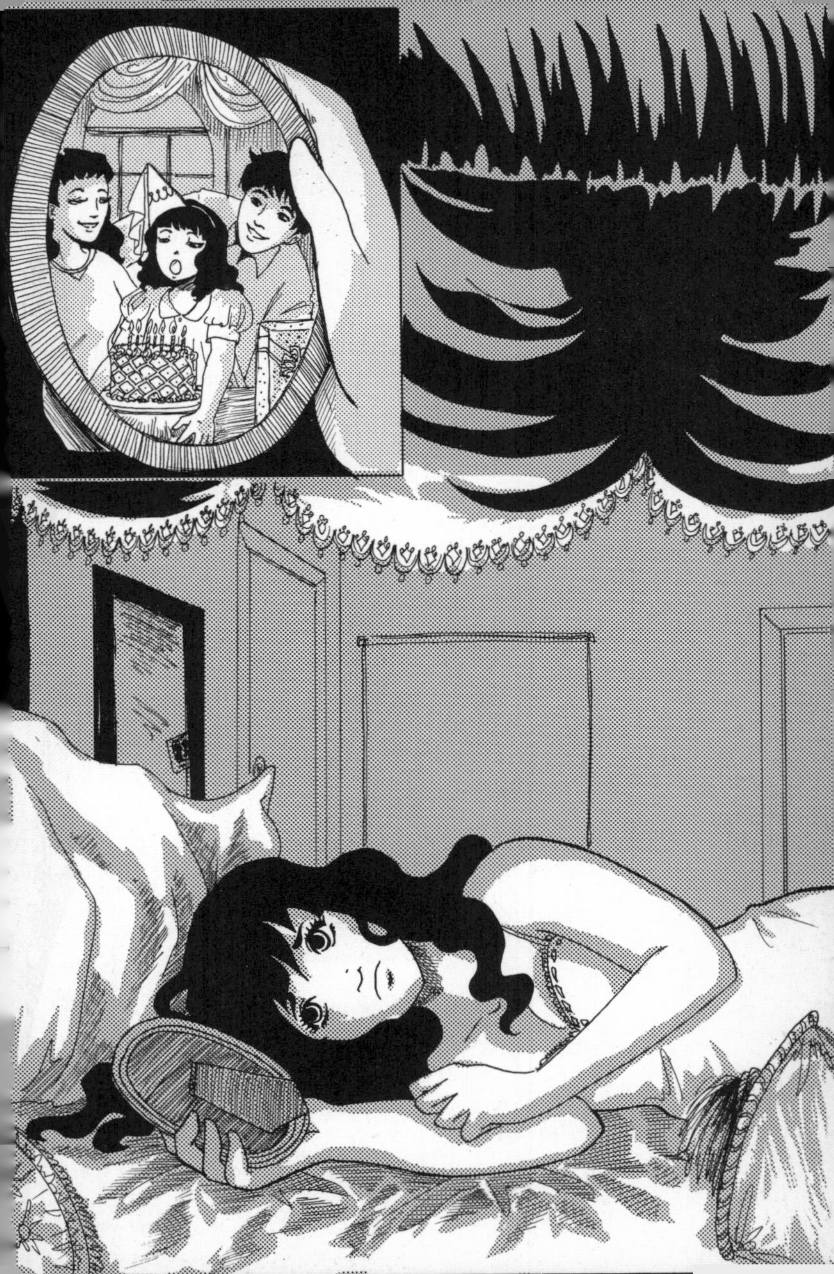

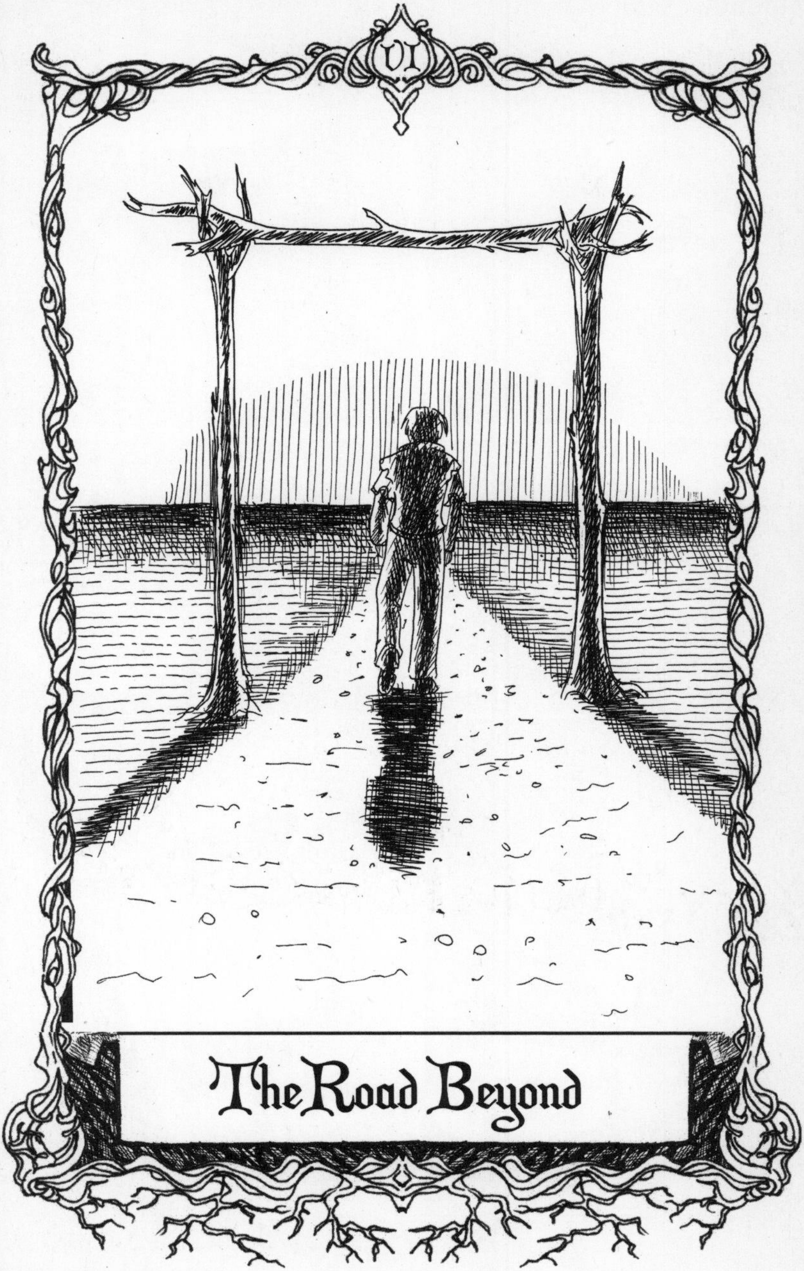
VI
The Road Beyond

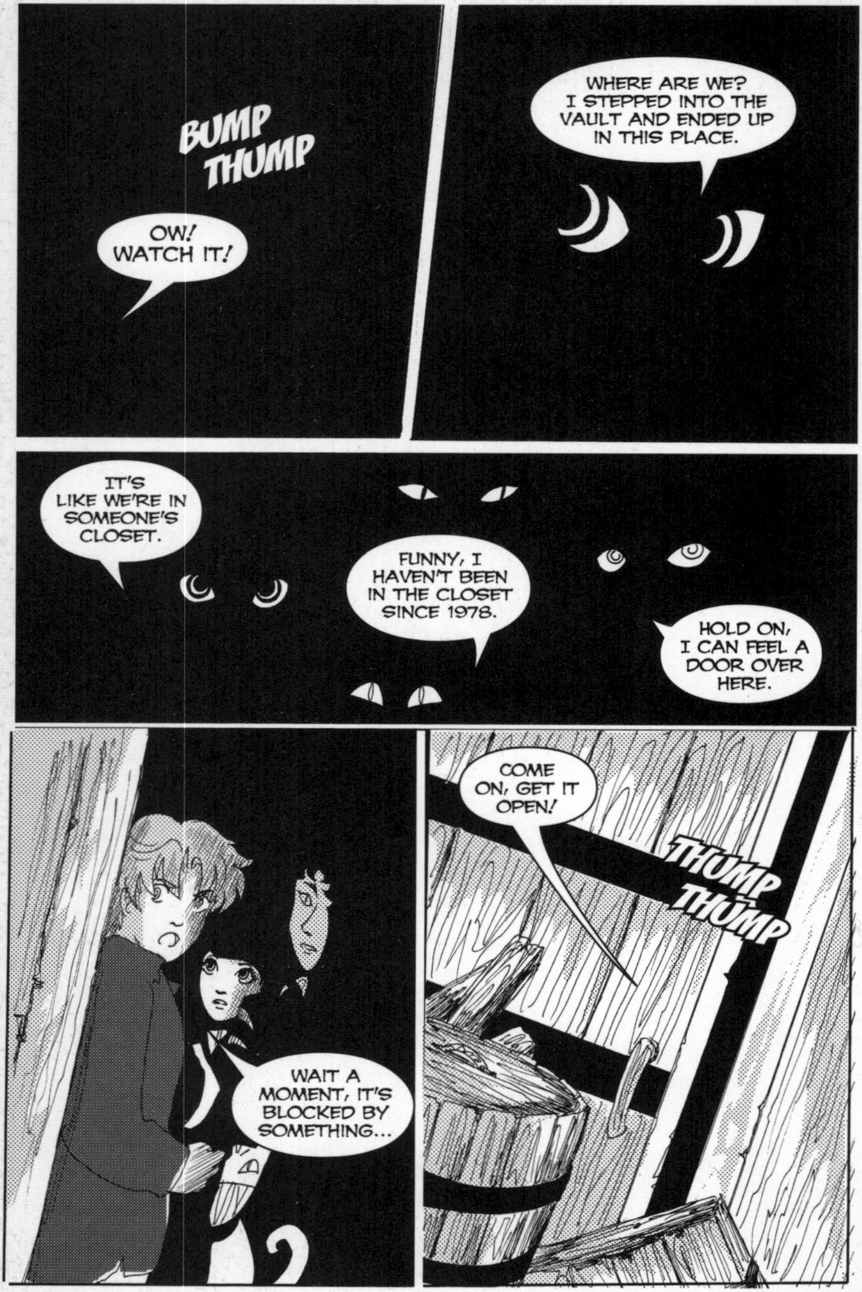
BUMP THUMP
OW! WATCH IT!
WHERE ARE WE? I STEPPED INTO THE VAULT AND ENDED UP IN THIS PLACE.
IT'S LIKE WE'RE IN SOMEONE'S CLOSET.
FUNNY, I HAVEN'T BEEN IN THE CLOSET SINCE 1978.
HOLD ON, I CAN FEEL A DOOR OVER HERE.
WAIT A MOMENT, IT'S BLOCKED BY SOMETHING...
COME ON, GET IT OPEN!
THUMP THUMP

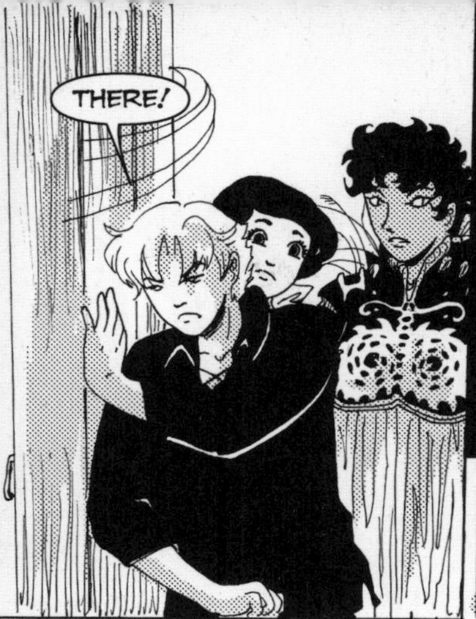
THERE!

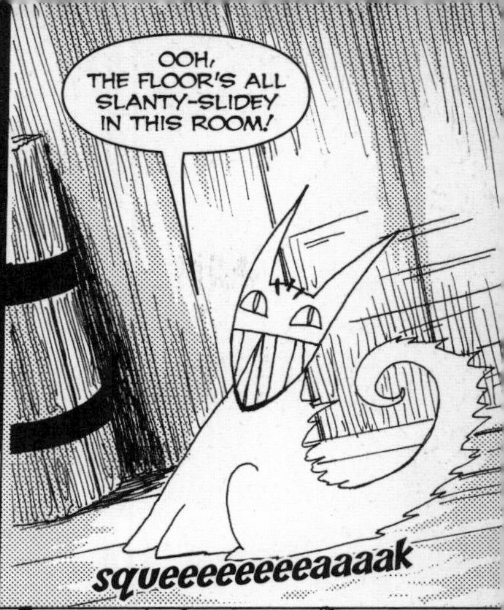
OOH, THE FLOOR'S ALL SLANTY-SLIDEY IN THIS ROOM!
squeeeeeeeeeaaaak

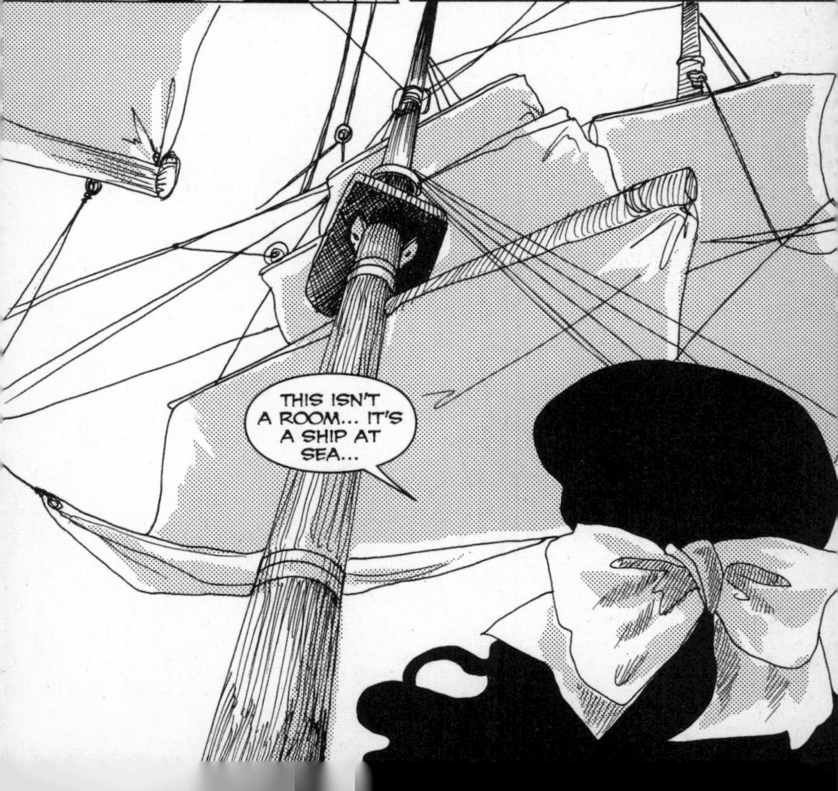
THIS ISN'T A ROOM... IT'S A SHIP AT SEA...

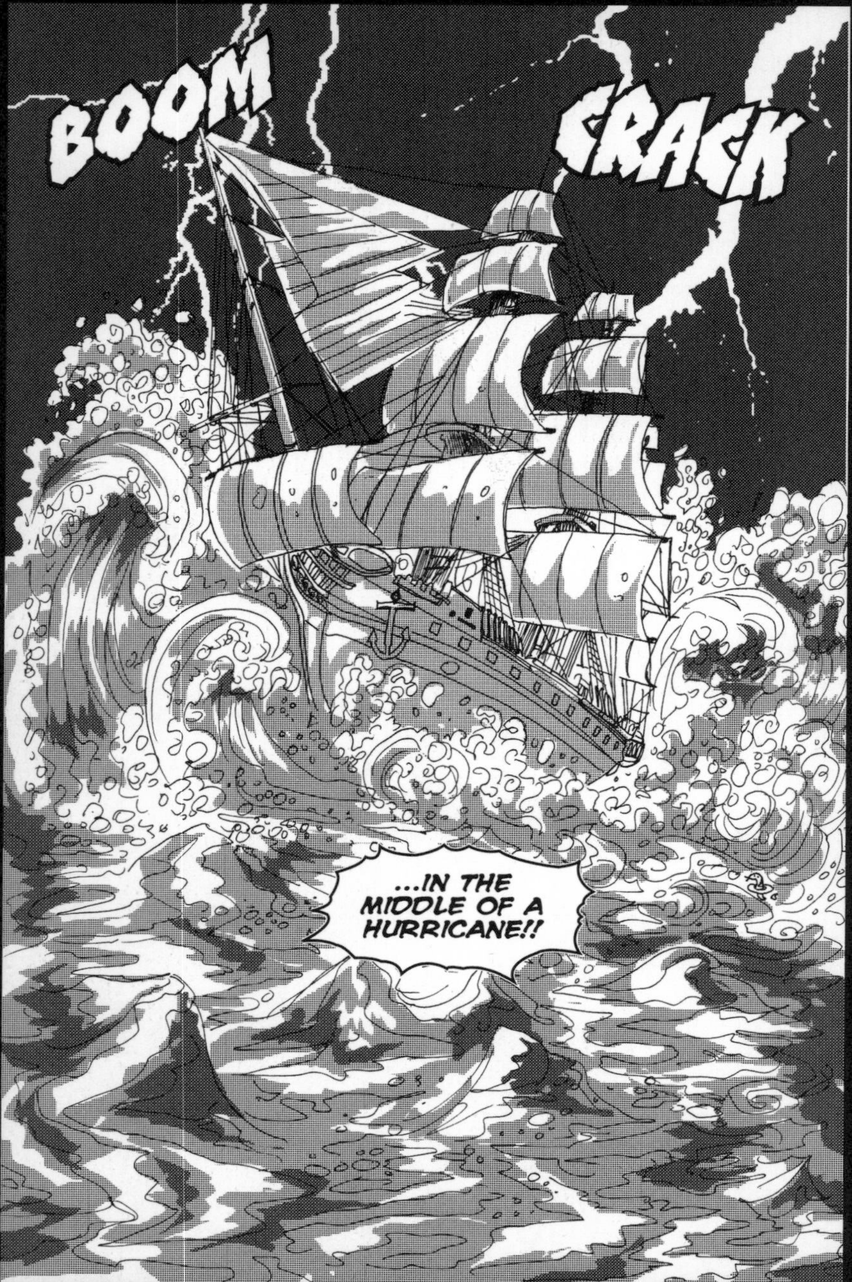
BOOM
CRACK
...IN THE MIDDLE OF A HURRICANE!!

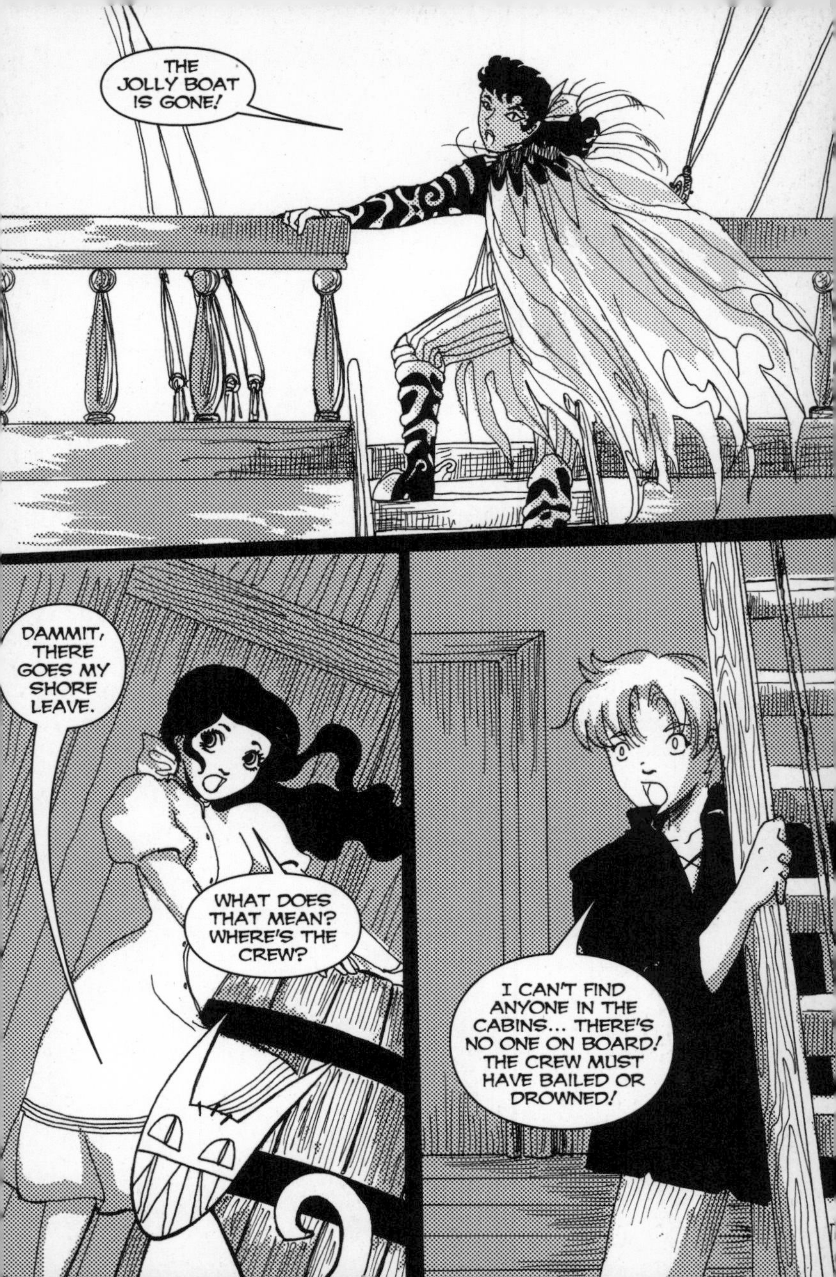
THE JOLLY BOAT IS GONE!
DAMMIT, THERE GOES MY SHORE LEAVE.
WHAT DOES THAT MEAN? WHERE'S THE CREW?
I CAN'T FIND ANYONE IN THE CABINS... THERE'S NO ONE ON BOARD! THE CREW MUST HAVE BAILED OR DROWNED!

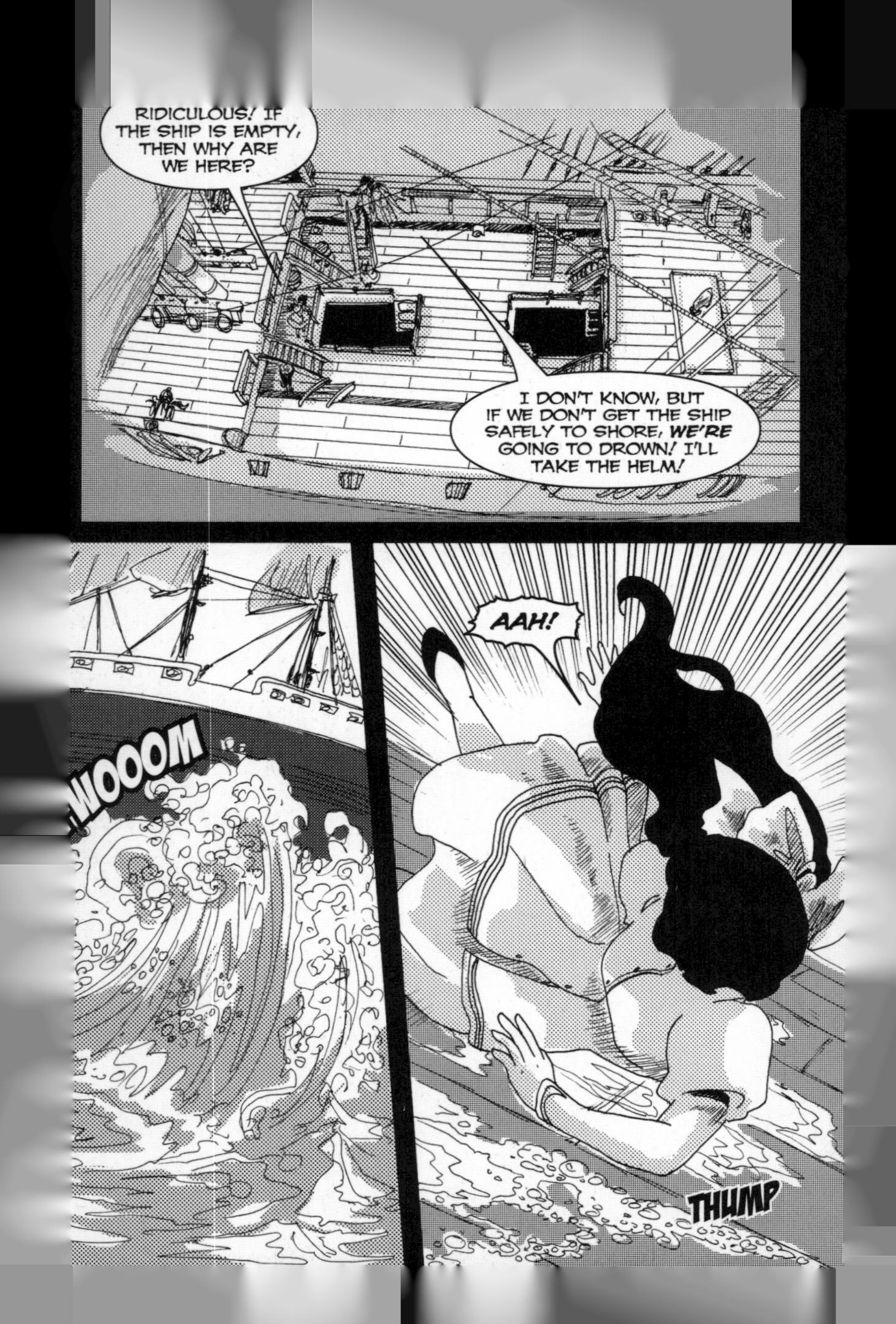
RIDICULOUS! IF THE SHIP IS EMPTY, THEN WHY ARE WE HERE?
I DON'T KNOW, BUT IF WE DON'T GET THE SHIP SAFELY TO SHORE, *WE'RE* GOING TO DROWN! I'LL TAKE THE HELM!
WOOOM
AAH!
THUMP

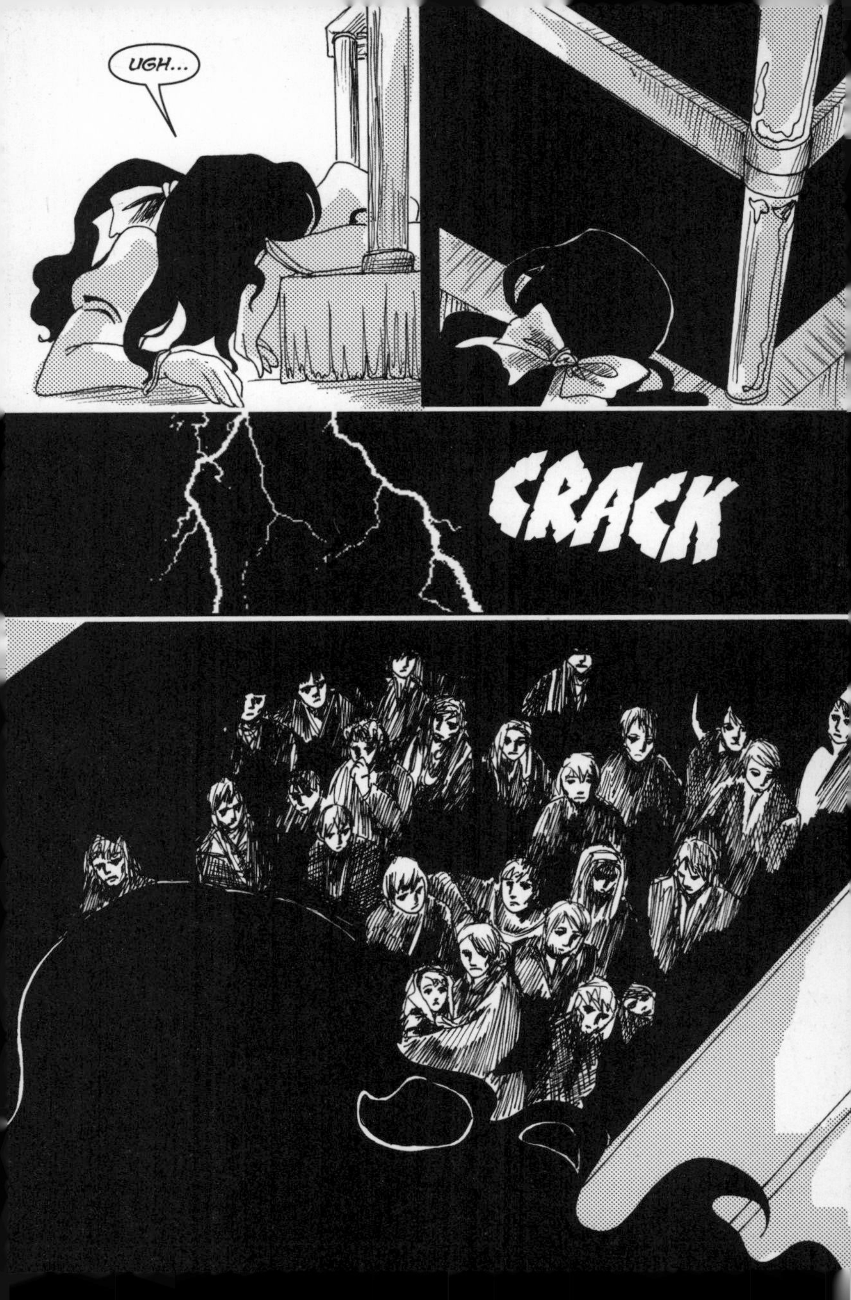
UGH...
CRACK

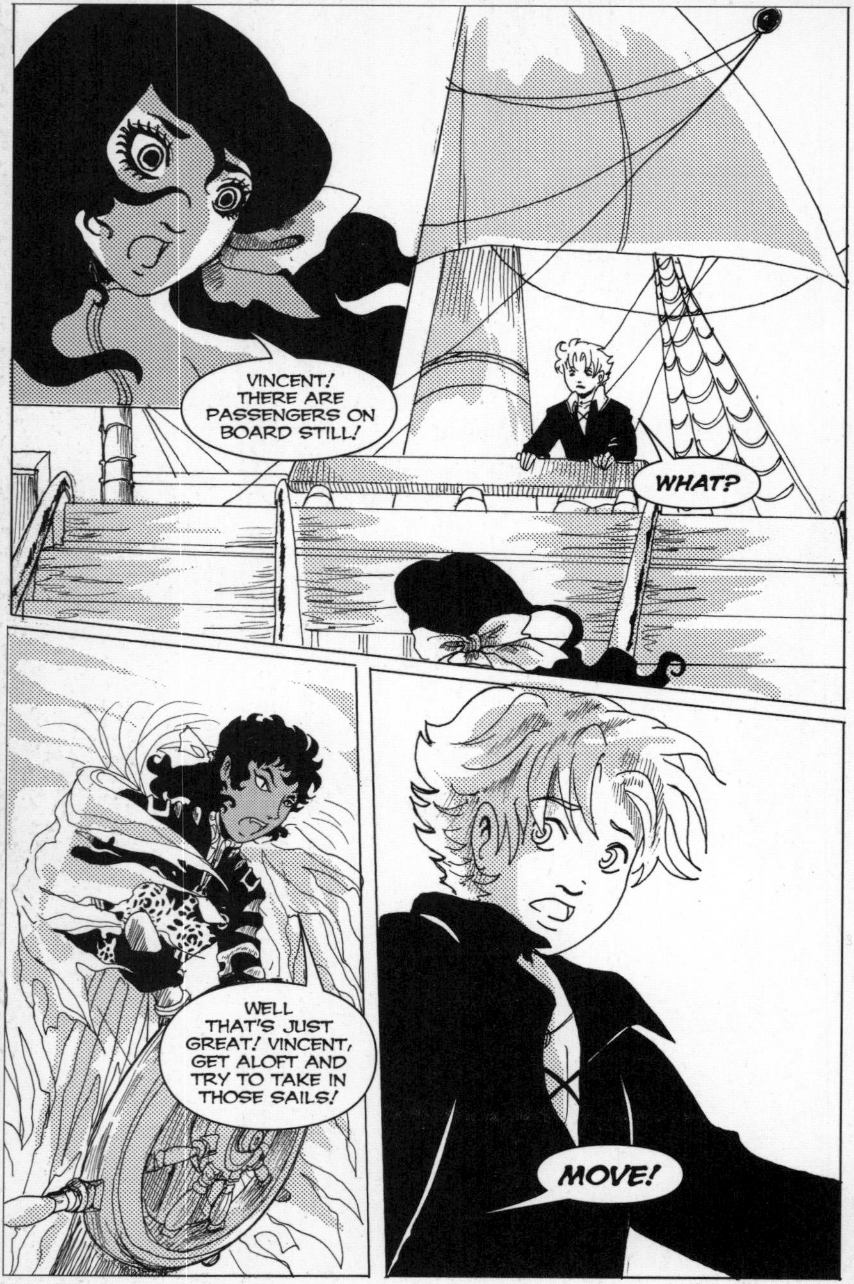
VINCENT! THERE ARE PASSENGERS ON BOARD STILL!
WHAT?
WELL THAT'S JUST GREAT! VINCENT, GET ALOFT AND TRY TO TAKE IN THOSE SAILS!
MOVE!

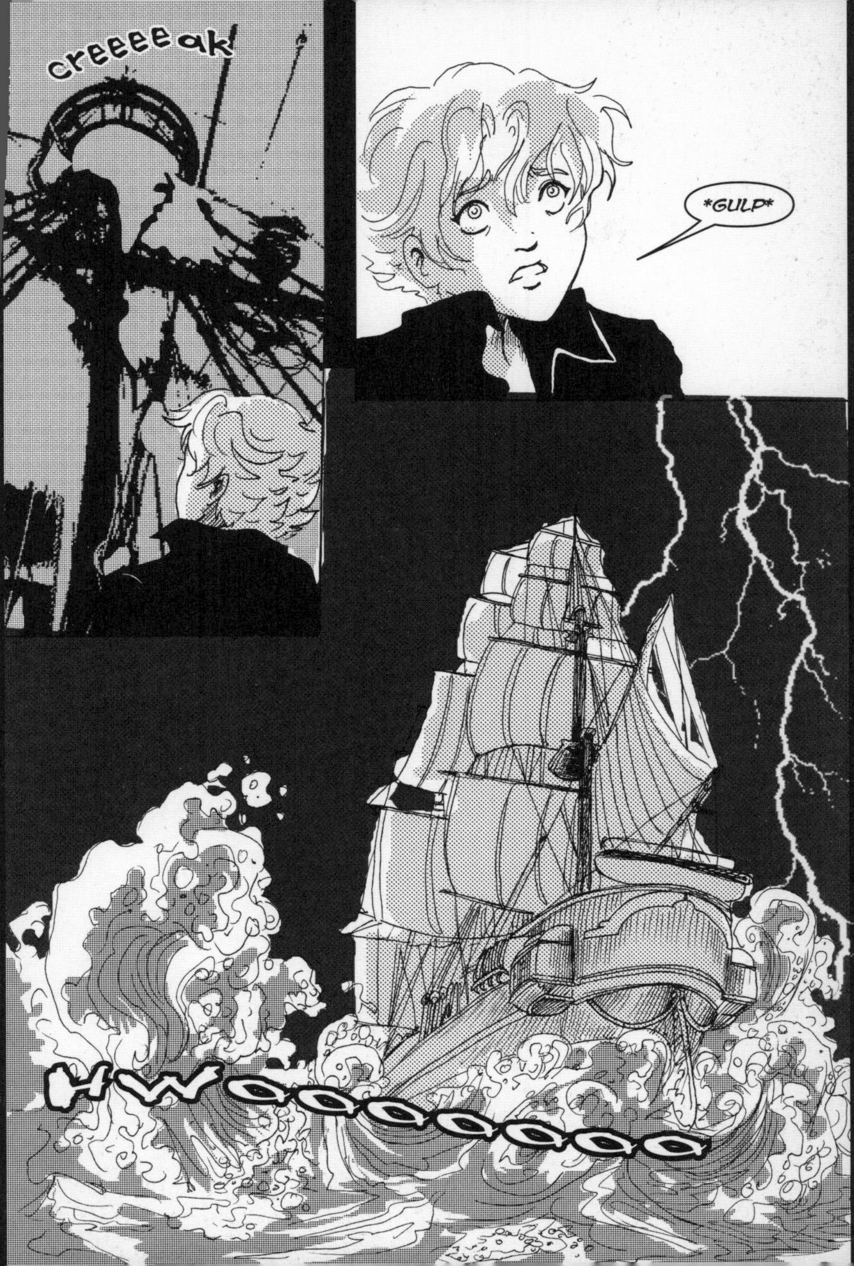
creeeeak
GULP
HWaaaaaaa

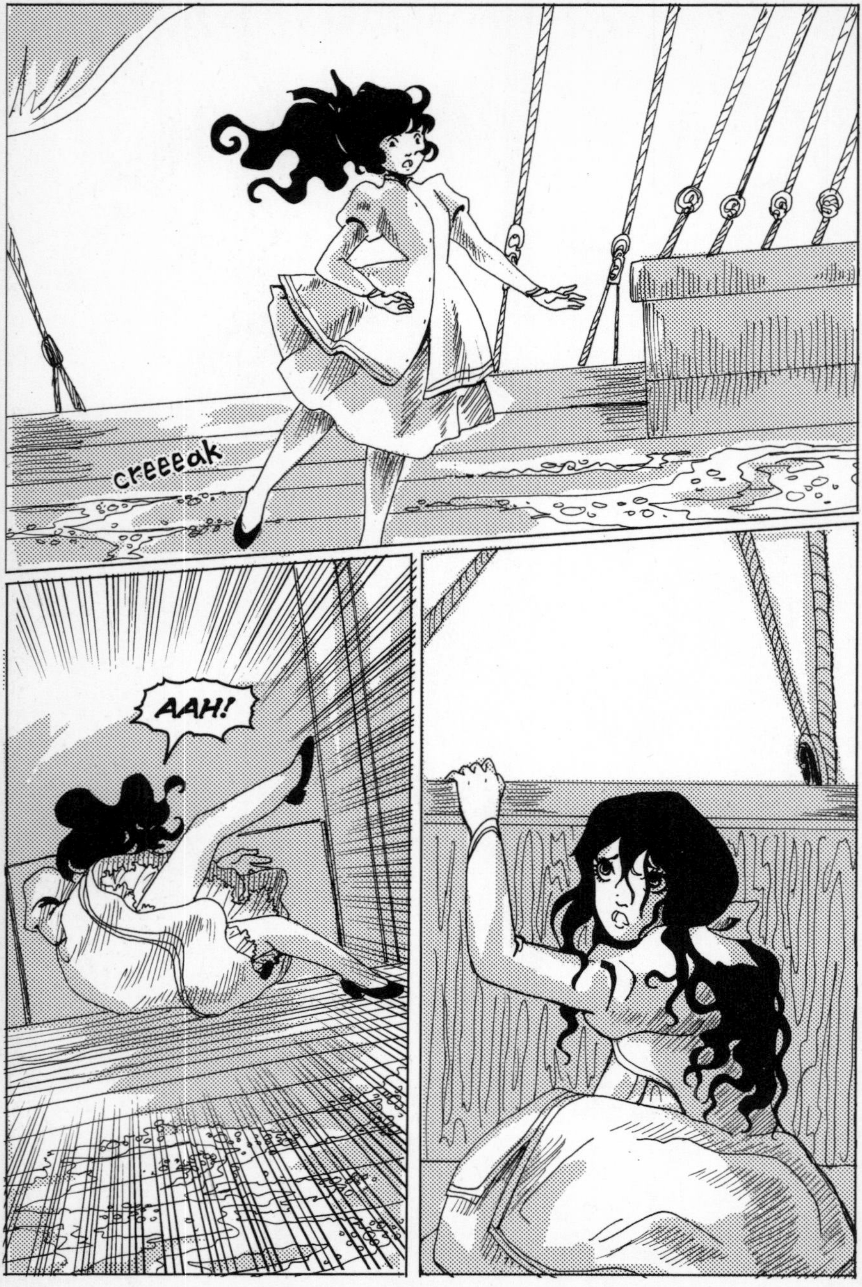
creeeak
AAH!

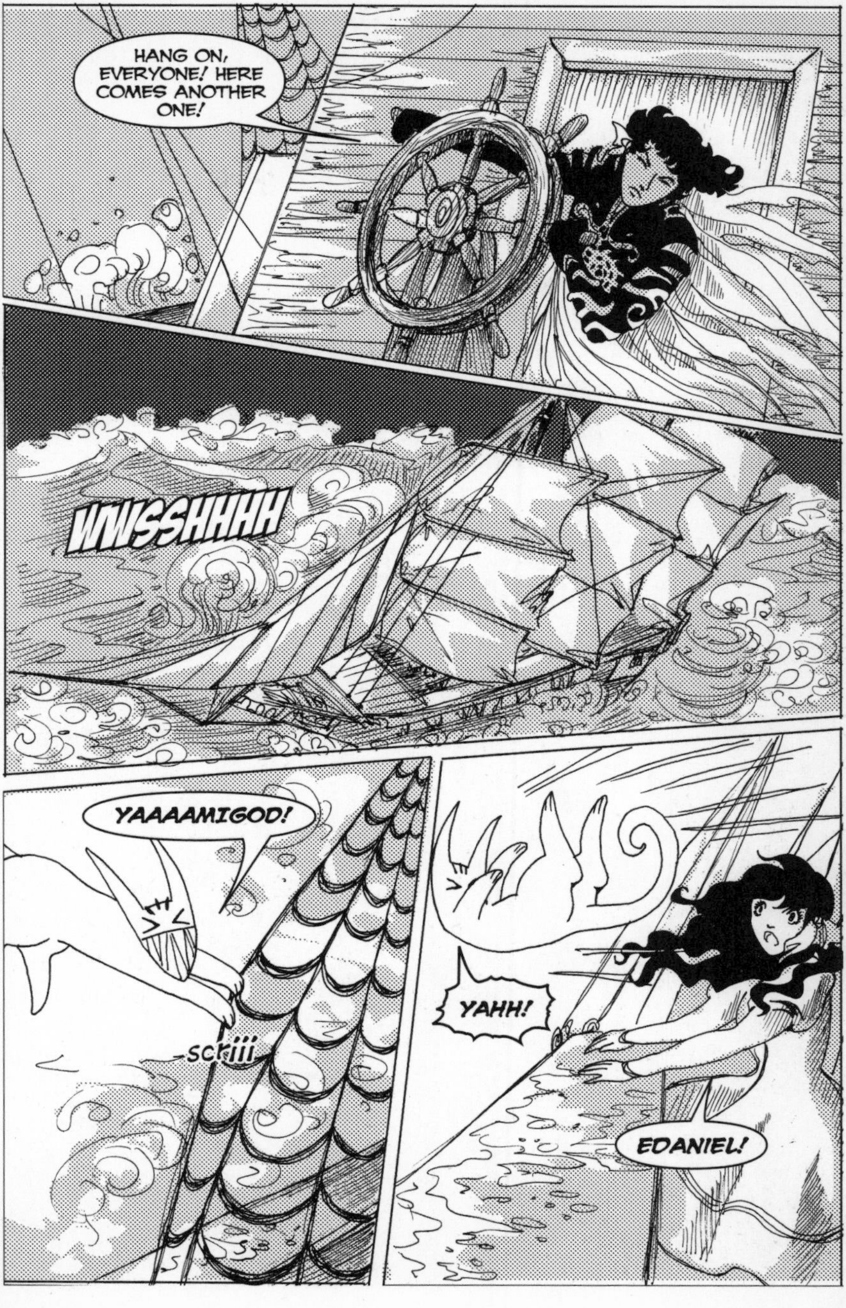
HANG ON, EVERYONE! HERE COMES ANOTHER ONE!
WWSSHHHH
YAAAAMIGOD!
scriii
YAHH!
EDANIEL!

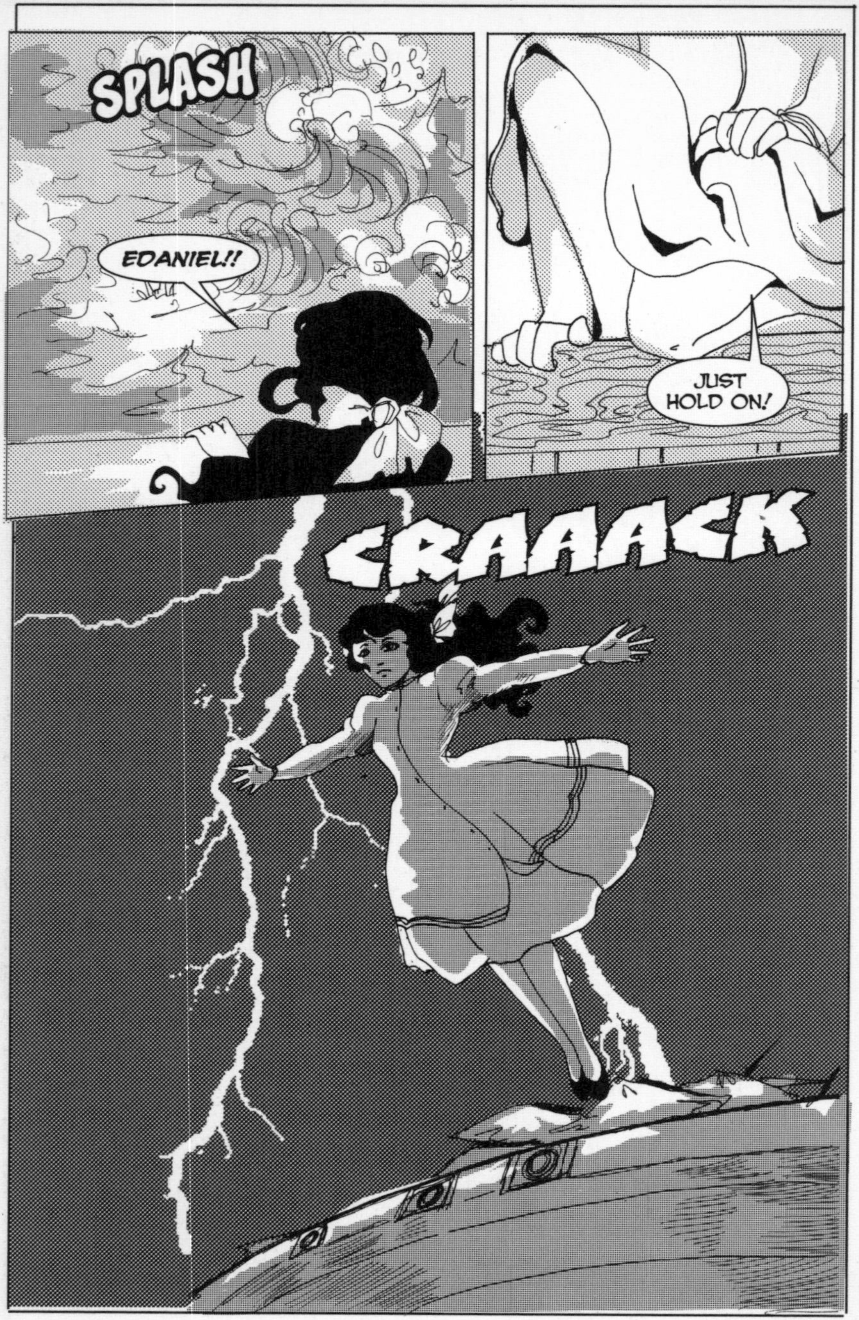
SPLASH
EDANIEL!!
JUST HOLD ON!
CRAAACK

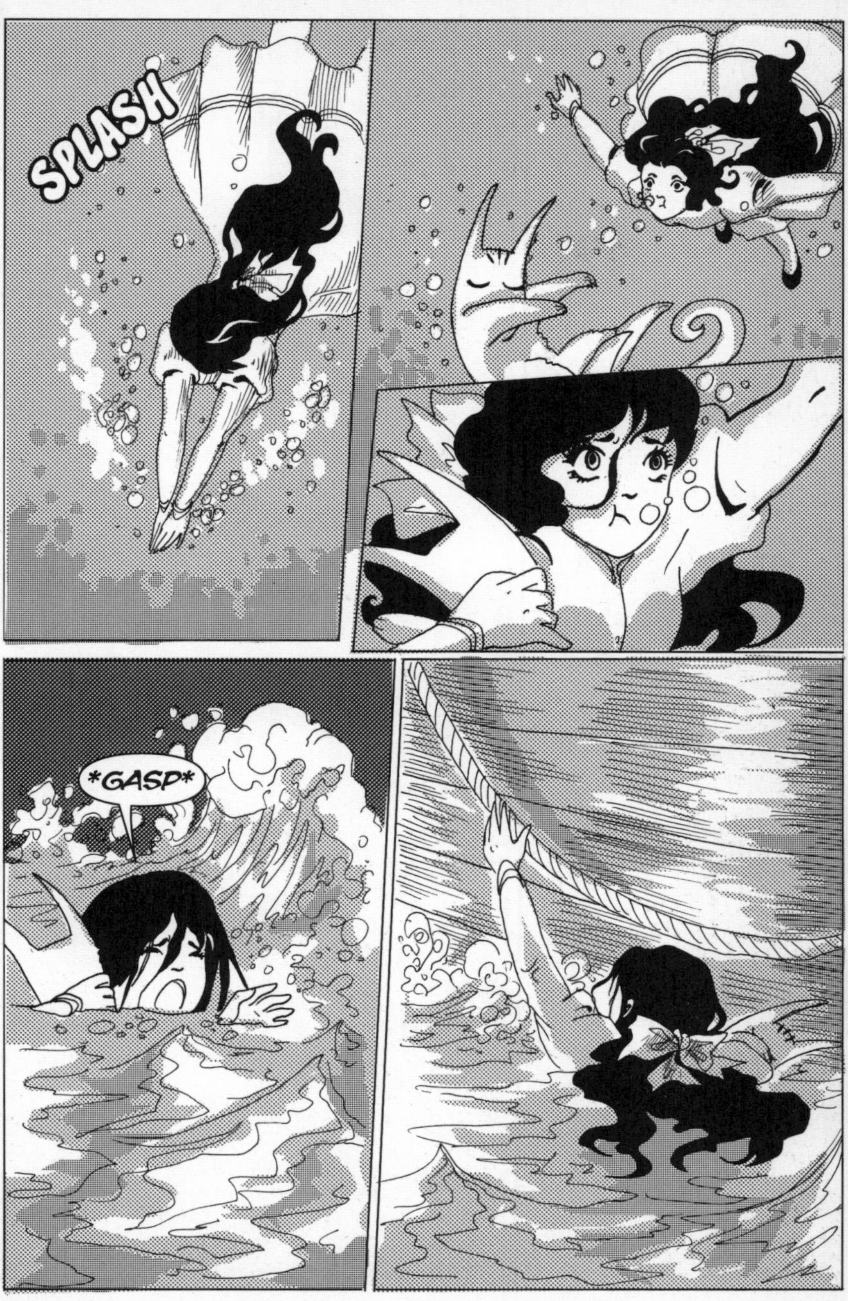
SPLASH
GASP

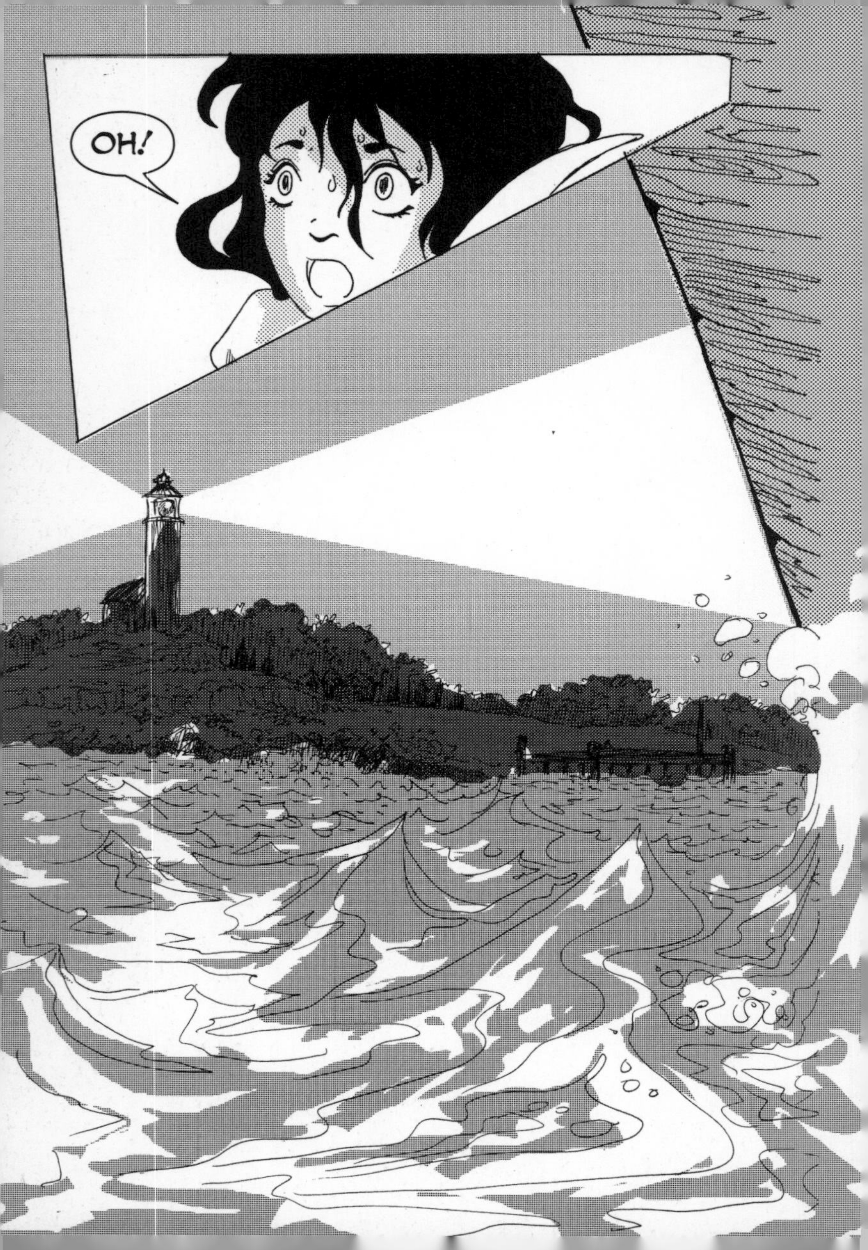
OH!

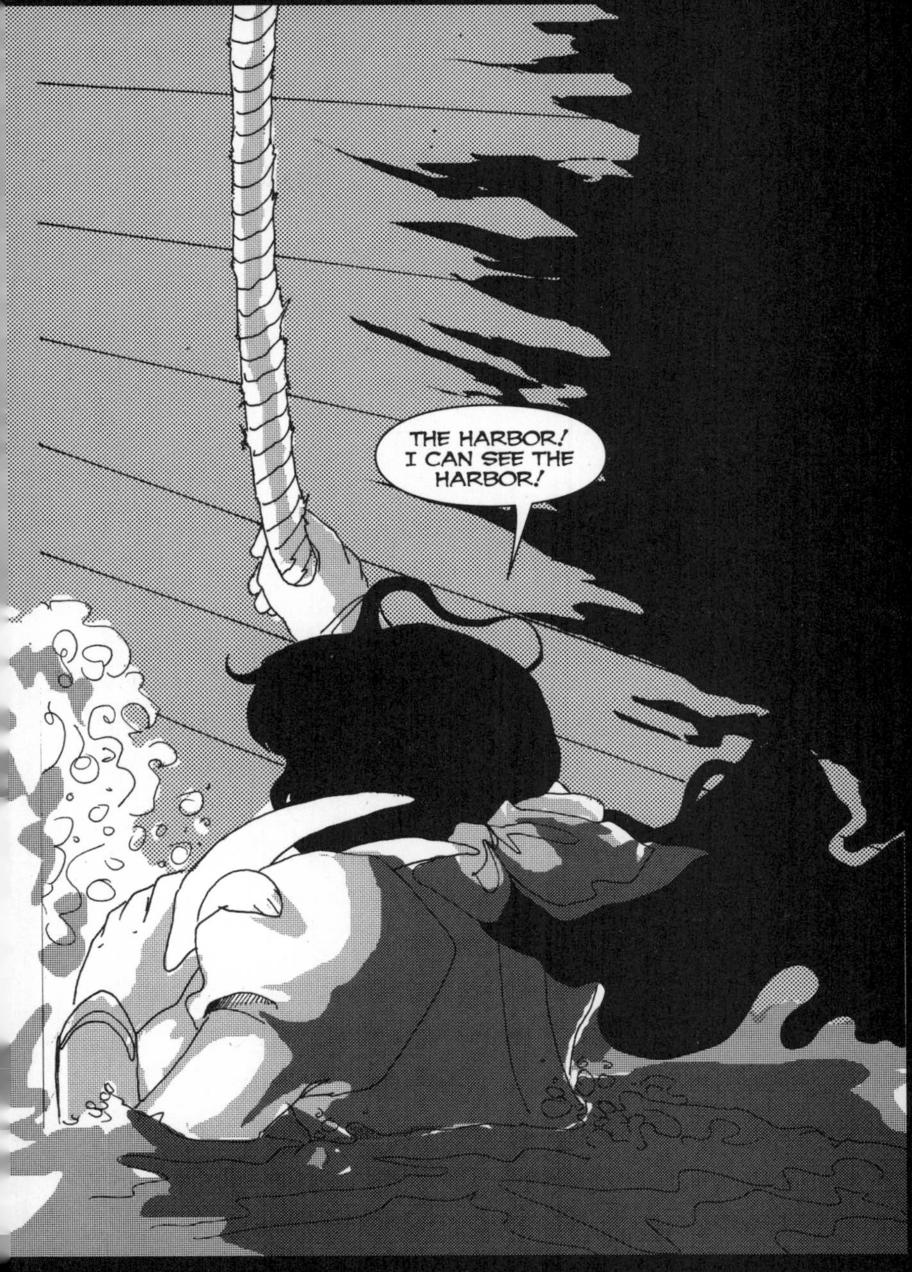
THE HARBOR! I CAN SEE THE HARBOR!

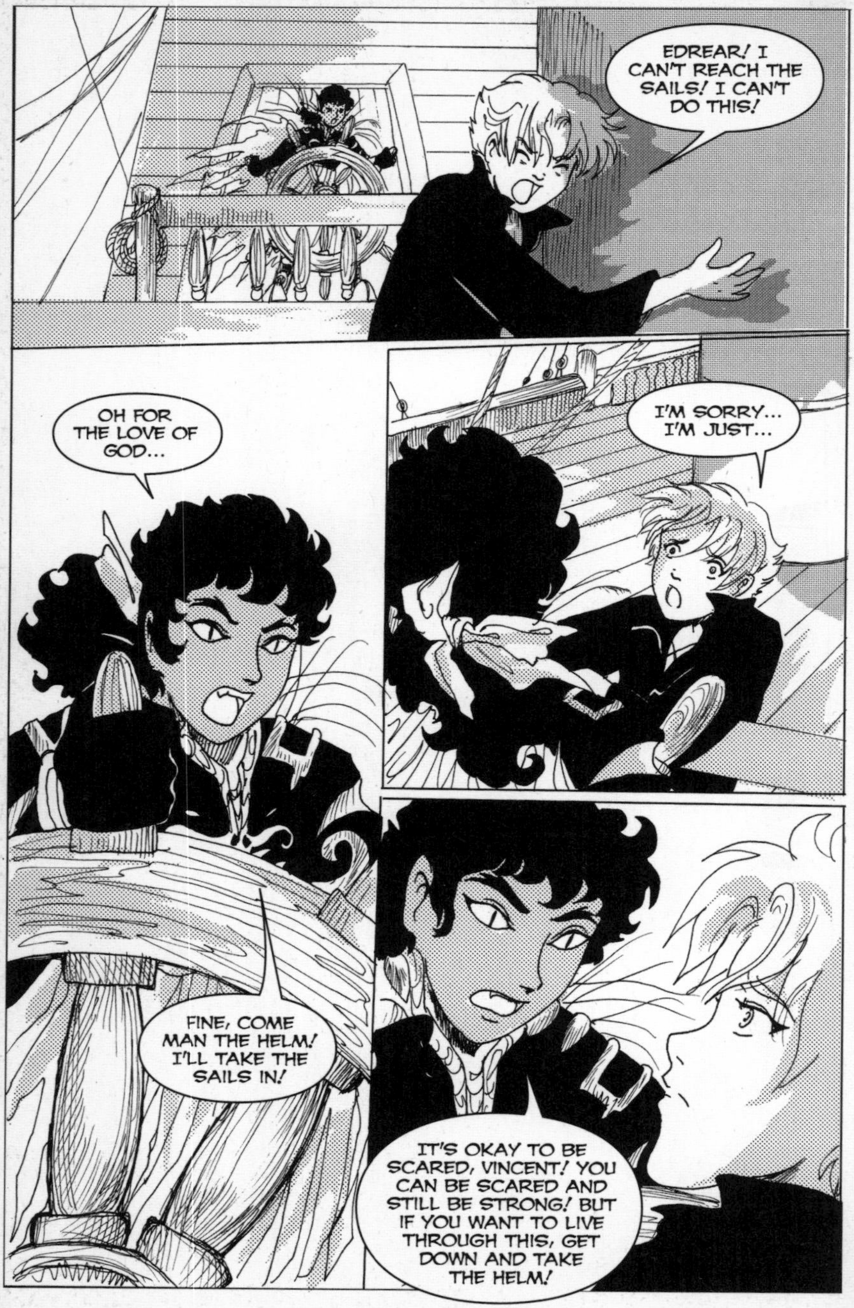
EDREAR! I CAN'T REACH THE SAILS! I CAN'T DO THIS!
OH FOR THE LOVE OF GOD...
I'M SORRY... I'M JUST...
FINE, COME MAN THE HELM! I'LL TAKE THE SAILS IN!
IT'S OKAY TO BE SCARED, VINCENT! YOU CAN BE SCARED AND STILL BE STRONG! BUT IF YOU WANT TO LIVE THROUGH THIS, GET DOWN AND TAKE THE HELM!

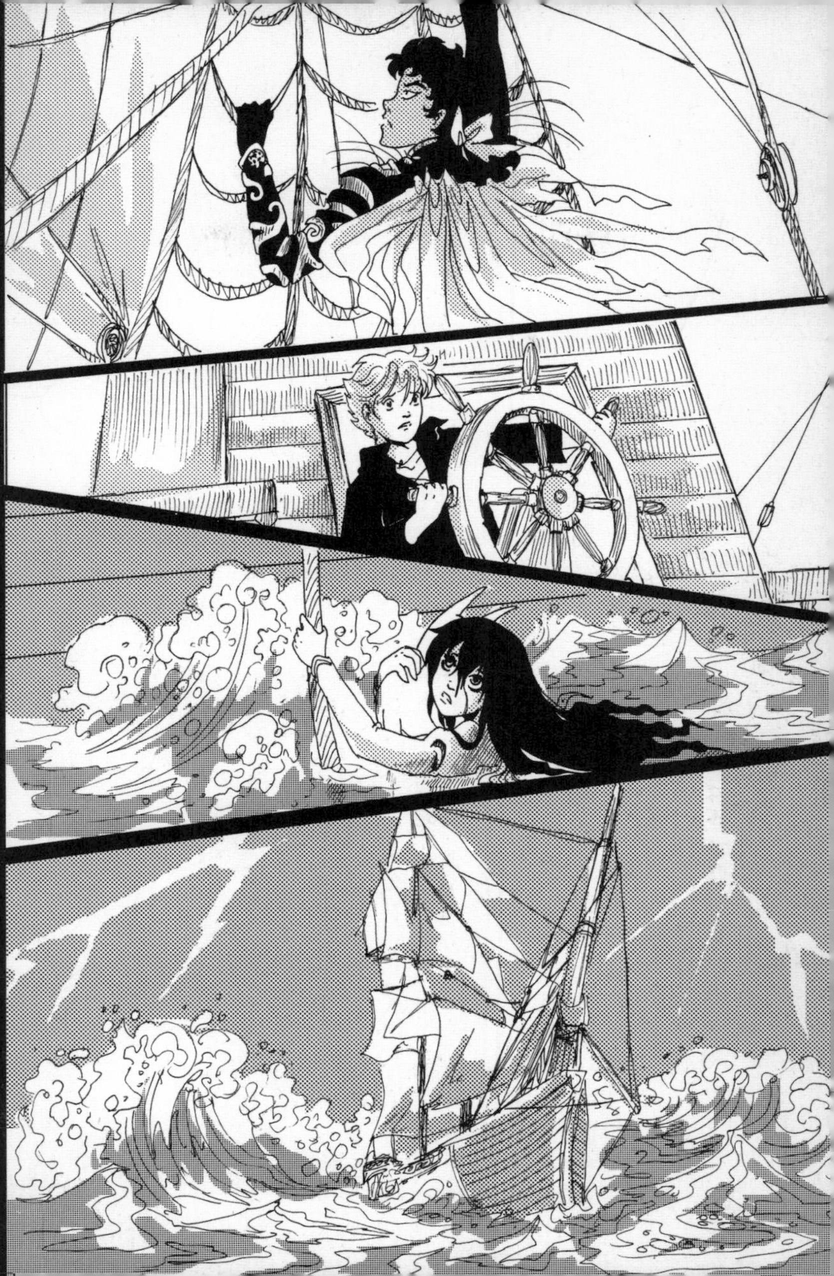

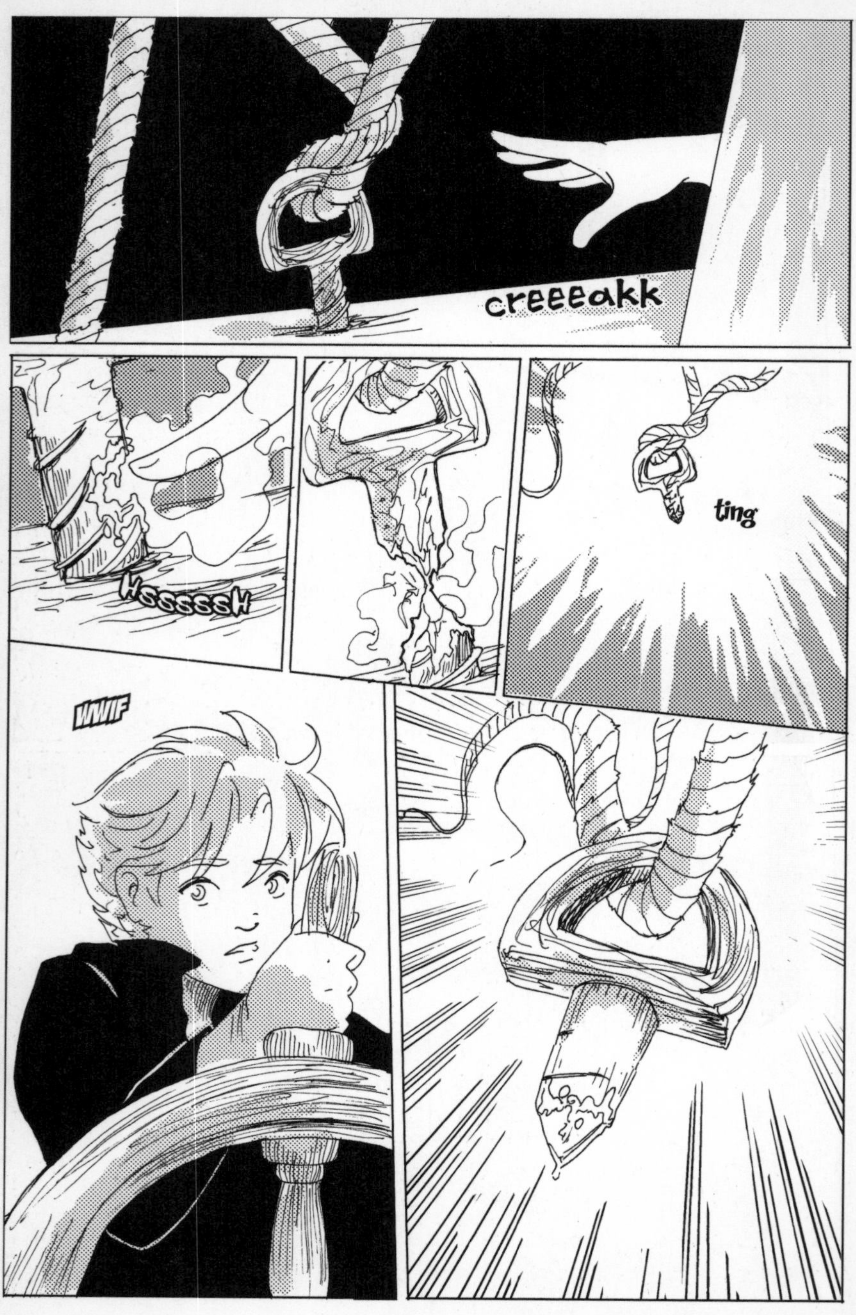
creeeakk
HSSSSSH
ting
WWIF

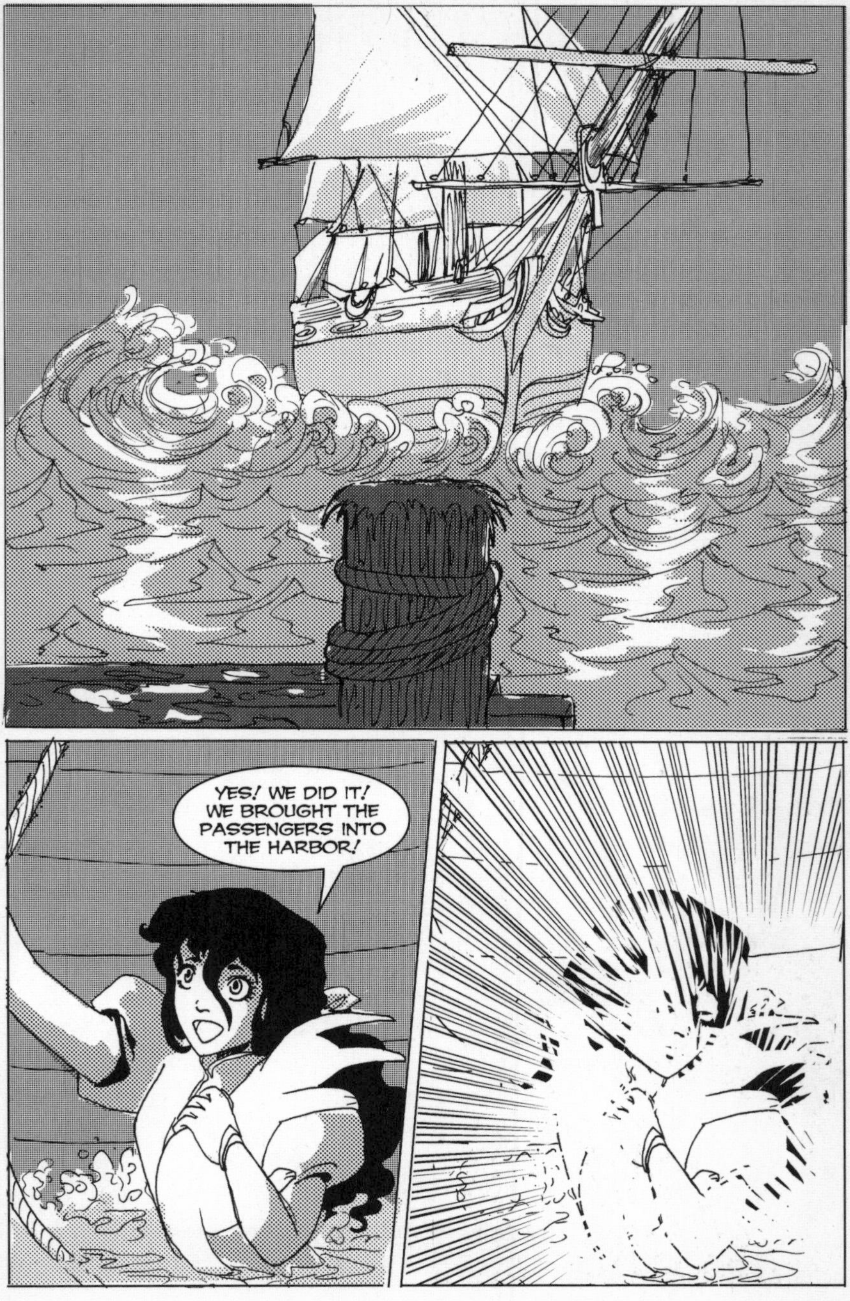
YES! WE DID IT! WE BROUGHT THE PASSENGERS INTO THE HARBOR!

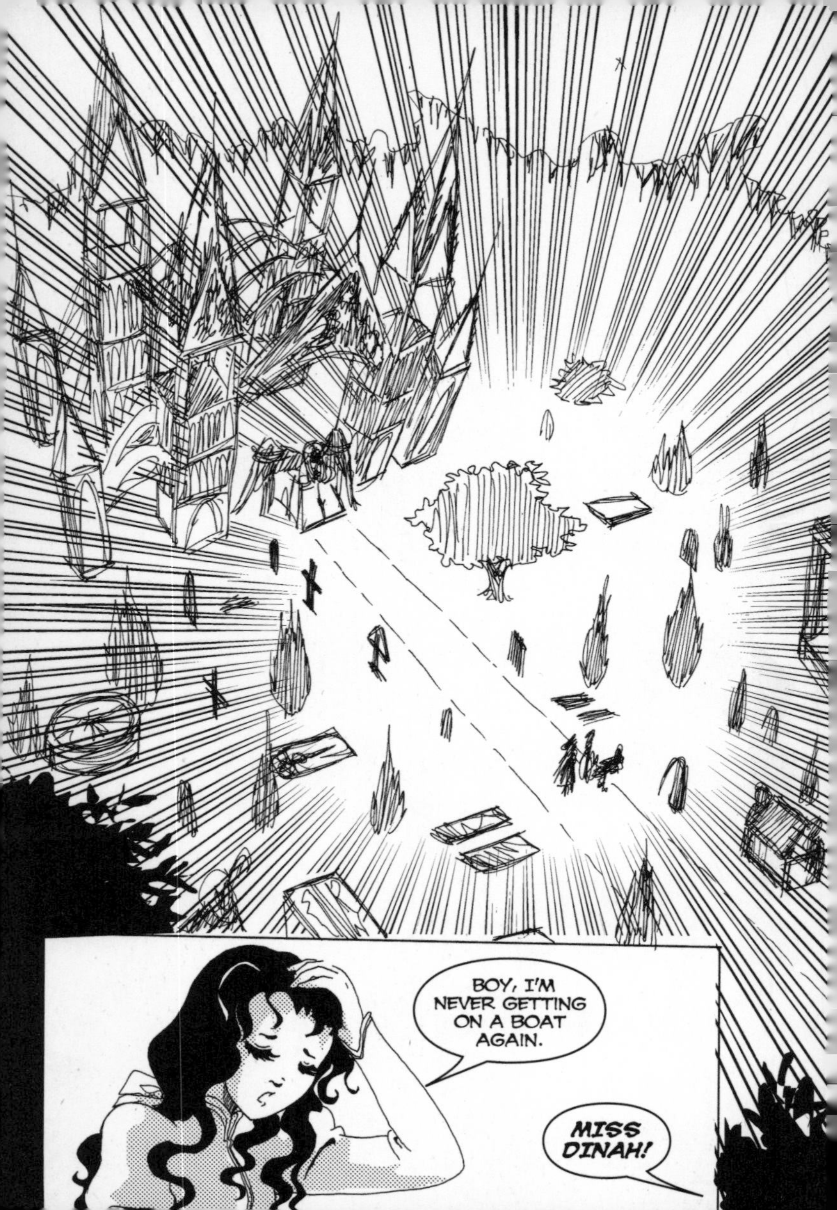
BOY, I'M NEVER GETTING ON A BOAT AGAIN.
MISS DINAH!

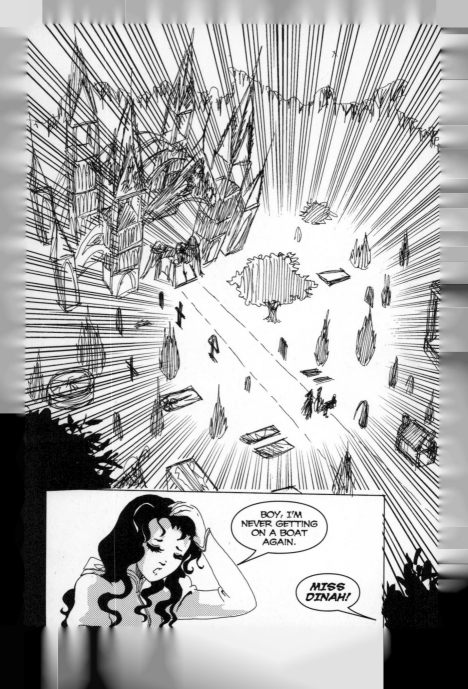

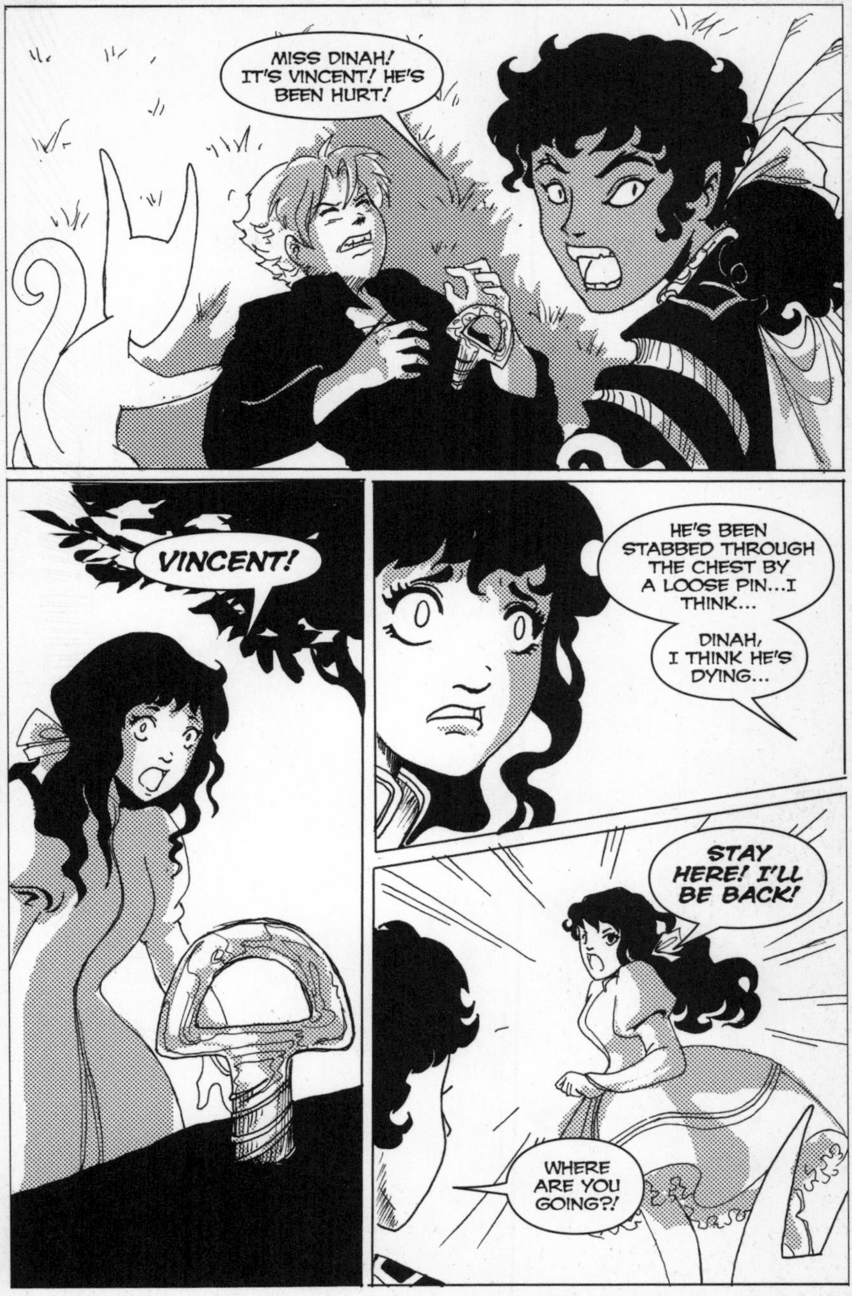
MISS DINAH! IT'S VINCENT! HE'S BEEN HURT!
VINCENT!
HE'S BEEN STABBED THROUGH THE CHEST BY A LOOSE PIN...I THINK...
DINAH, I THINK HE'S DYING...
STAY HERE! I'LL BE BACK!
WHERE ARE YOU GOING?!

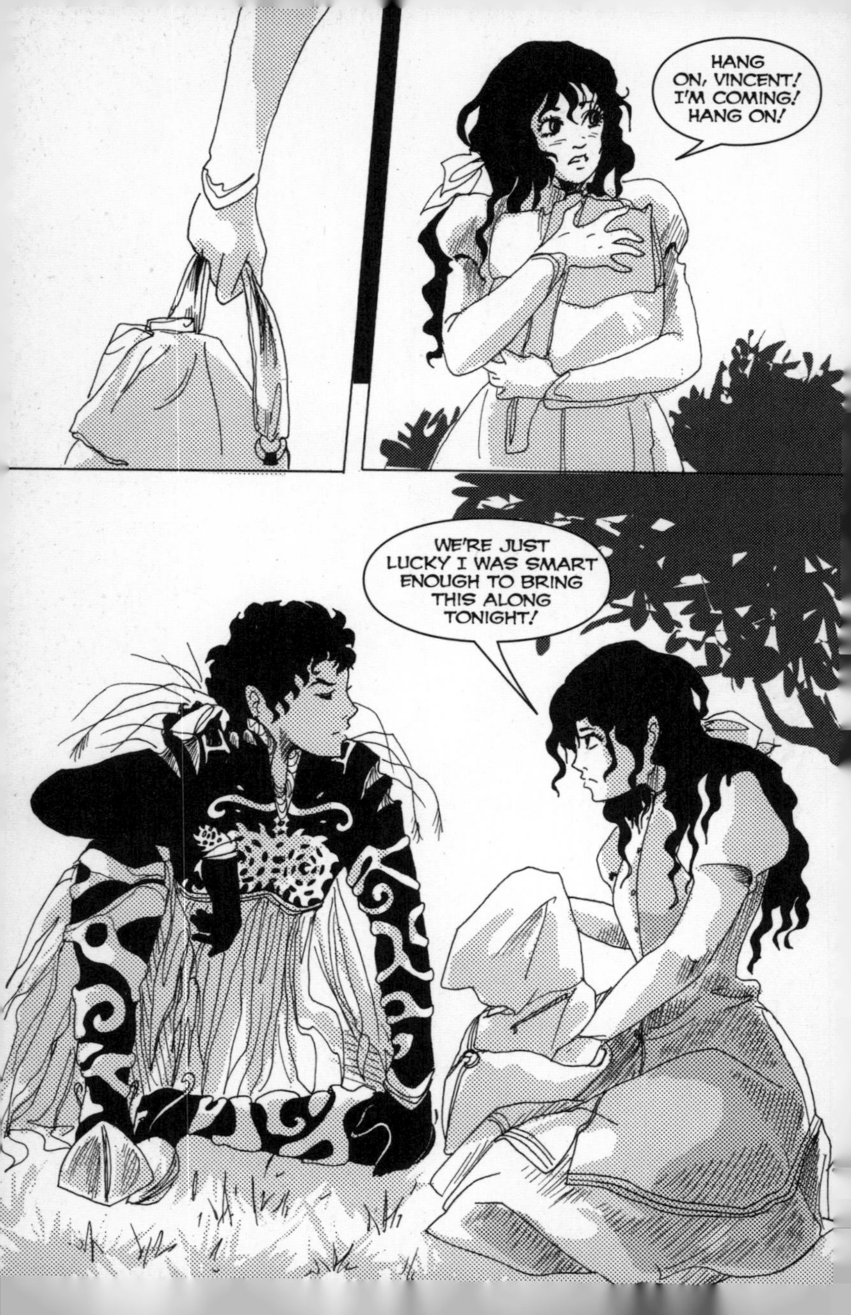
HANG ON, VINCENT! I'M COMING! HANG ON!
WE'RE JUST LUCKY I WAS SMART ENOUGH TO BRING THIS ALONG TONIGHT!

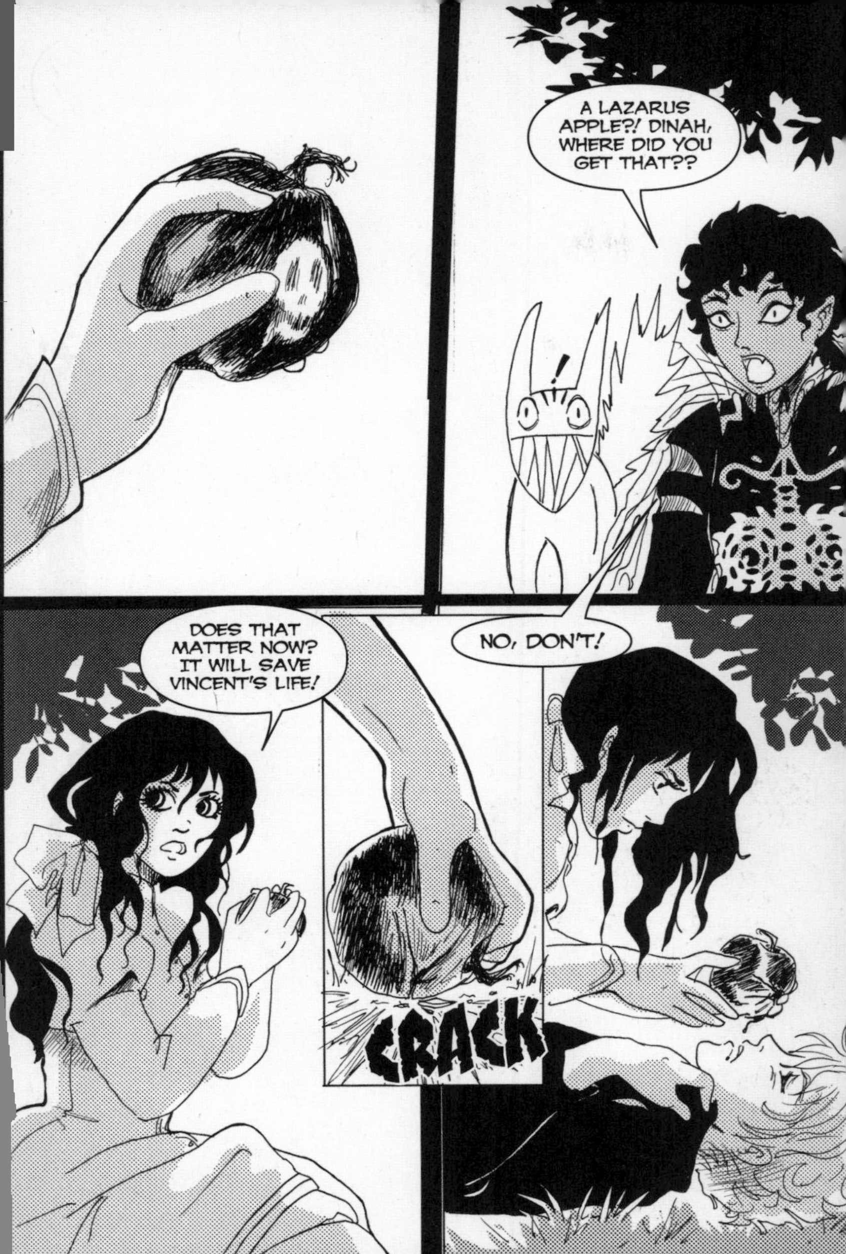
A LAZARUS APPLE?! DINAH, WHERE DID YOU GET THAT??
!
DOES THAT MATTER NOW? IT WILL SAVE VINCENT'S LIFE!
NO, DON'T!
CRACK

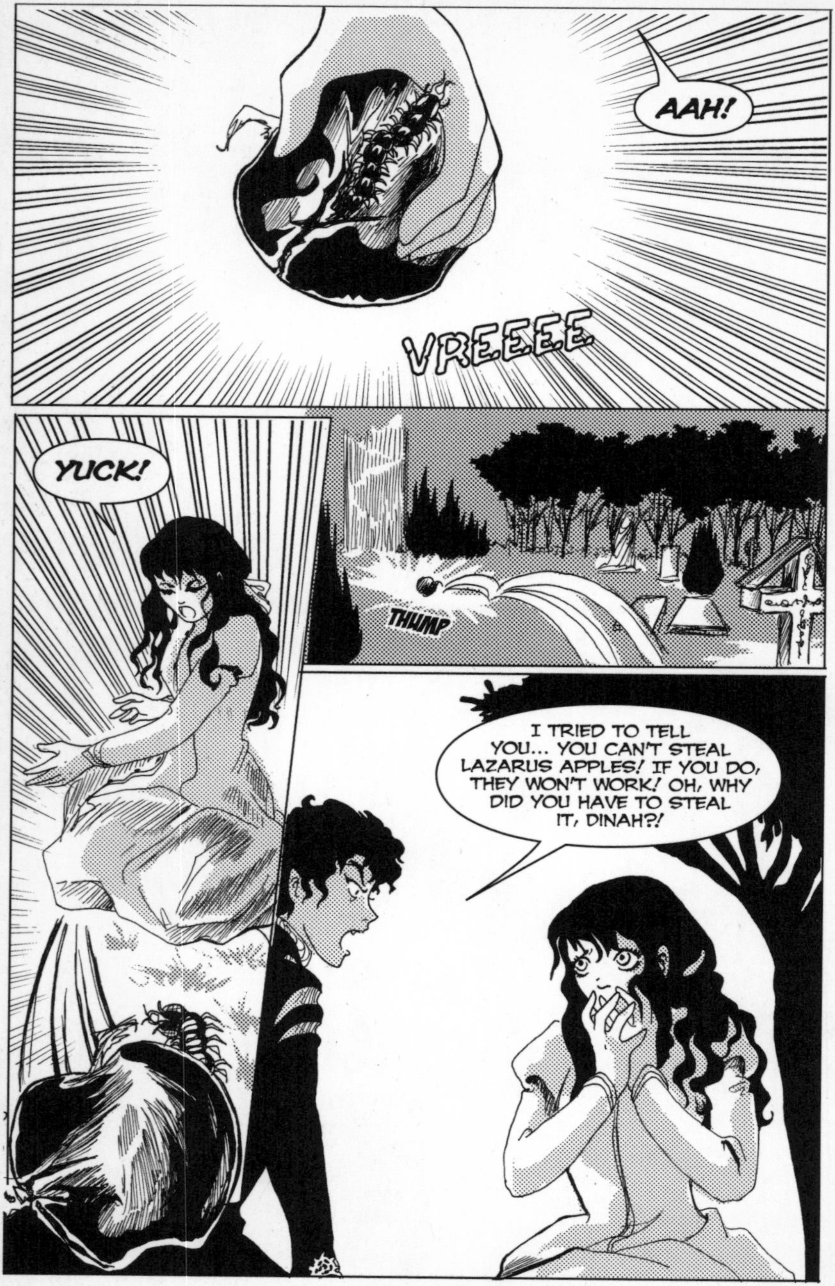
AAH!
VREEEE
YUCK!
THUMP
I TRIED TO TELL YOU... YOU CAN'T STEAL LAZARUS APPLES! IF YOU DO, THEY WON'T WORK! OH, WHY DID YOU HAVE TO STEAL IT, DINAH?!

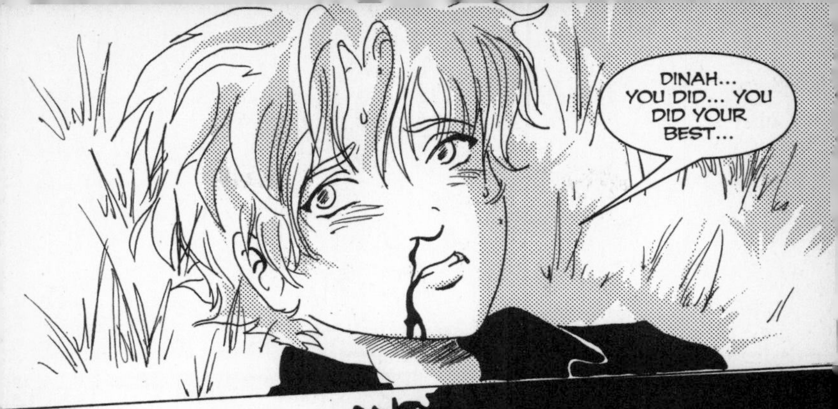
DINAH... YOU DID... YOU DID YOUR BEST...
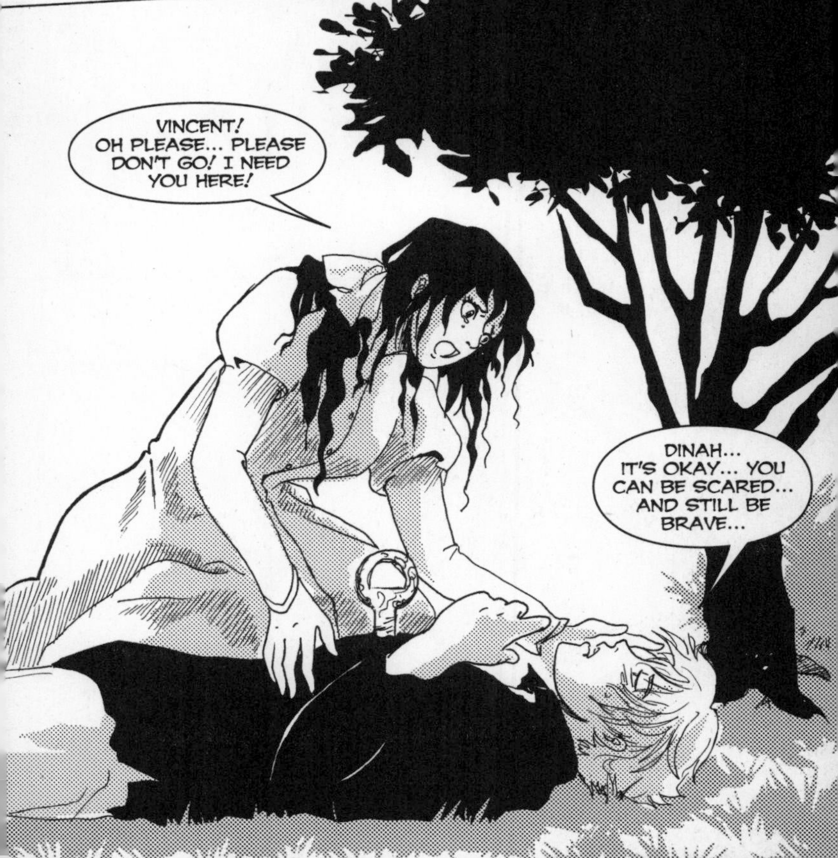
VINCENT! OH PLEASE... PLEASE DON'T GO! I NEED YOU HERE!
DINAH... IT'S OKAY... YOU CAN BE SCARED... AND STILL BE BRAVE...

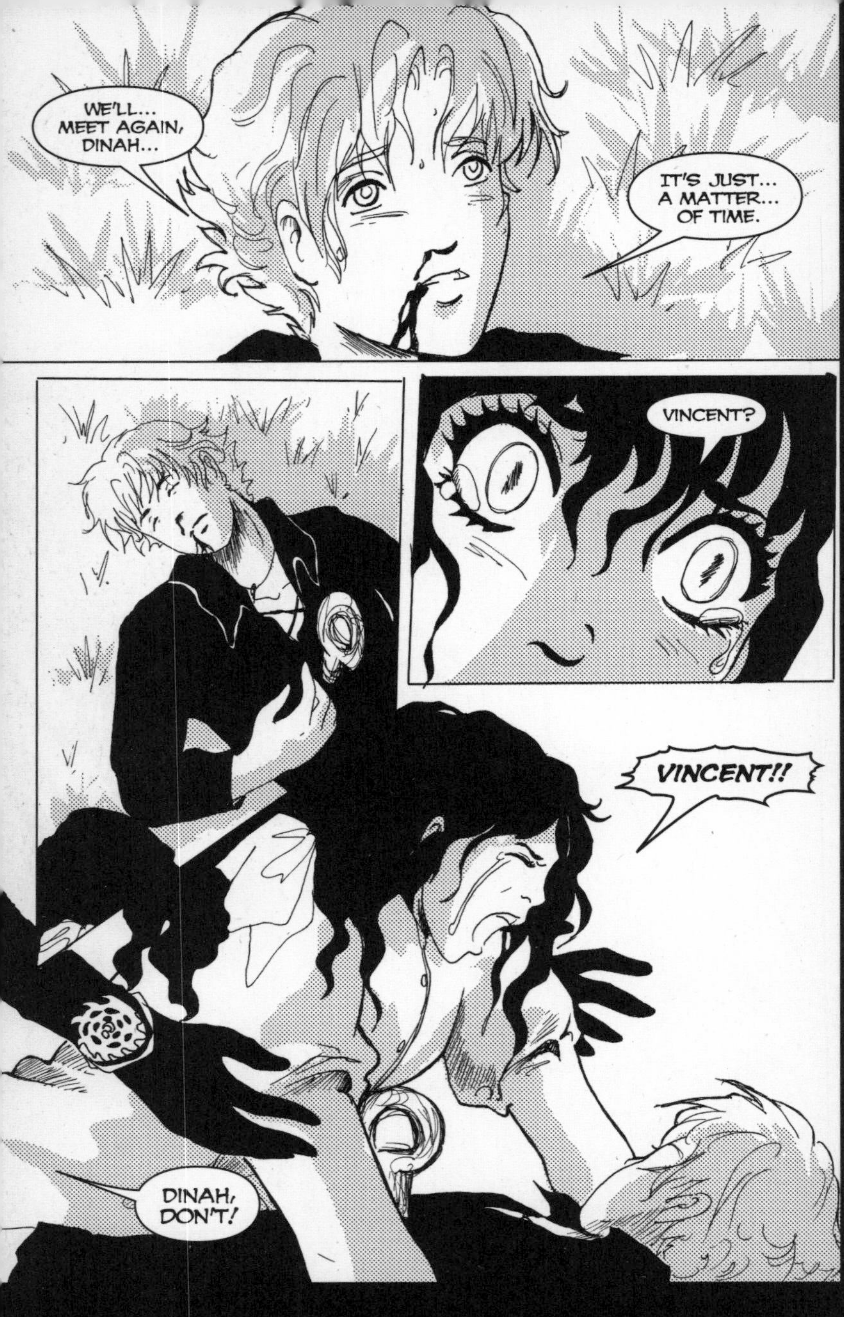
WE'LL... MEET AGAIN, DINAH...
IT'S JUST... A MATTER... OF TIME.
VINCENT?
VINCENT!!
DINAH, DON'T!

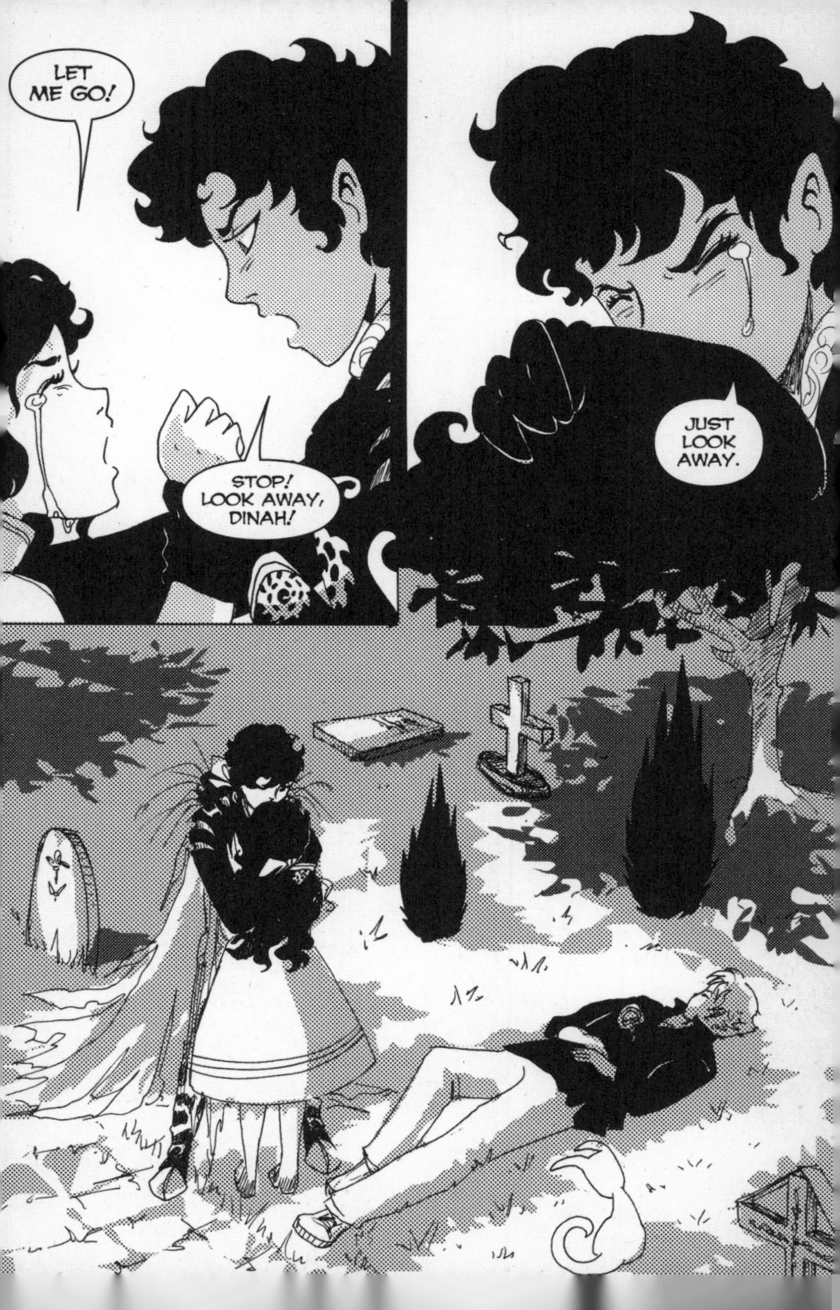
LET ME GO!
STOP! LOOK AWAY, DINAH!
JUST LOOK AWAY.

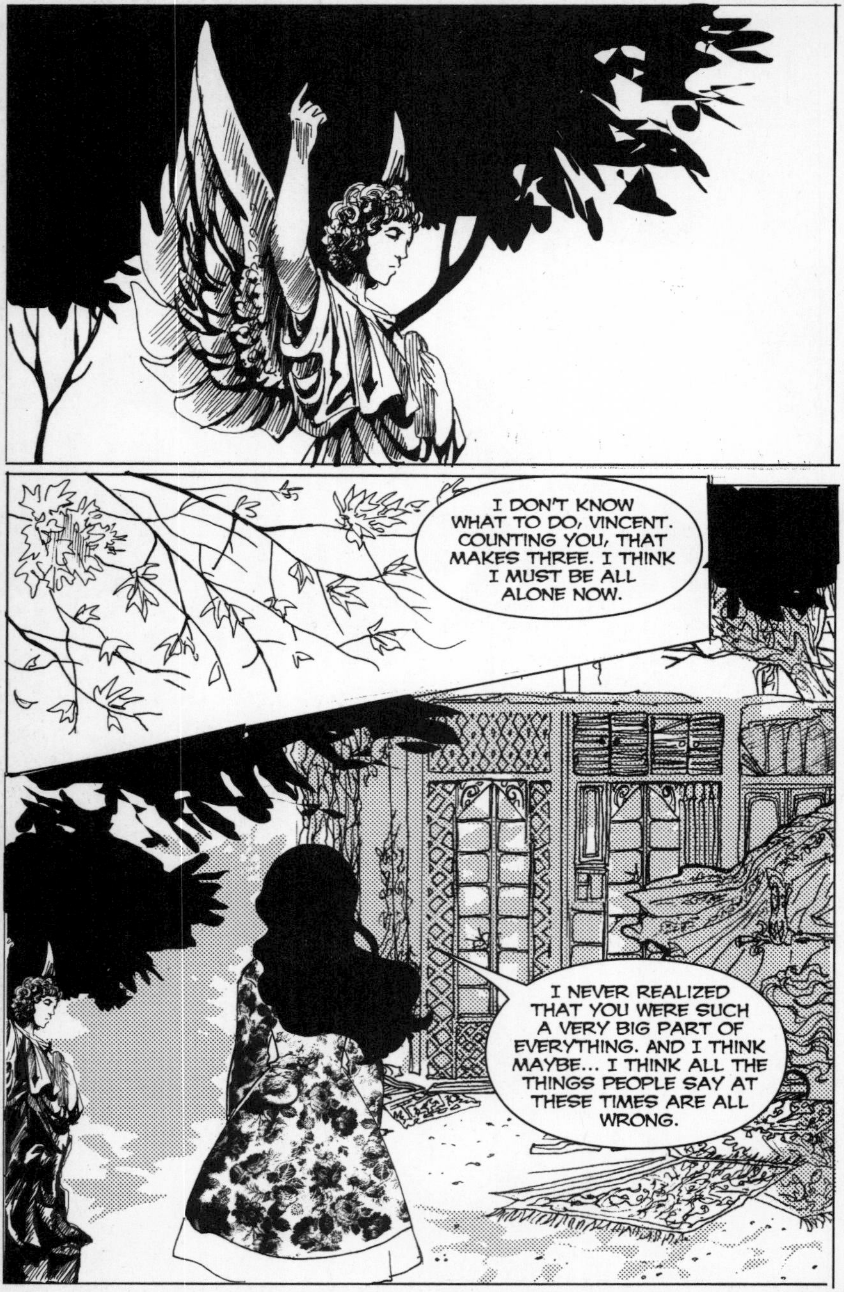
I DON'T KNOW WHAT TO DO, VINCENT. COUNTING YOU, THAT MAKES THREE. I THINK I MUST BE ALL ALONE NOW.
I NEVER REALIZED THAT YOU WERE SUCH A VERY BIG PART OF EVERYTHING. AND I THINK MAYBE... I THINK ALL THE THINGS PEOPLE SAY AT THESE TIMES ARE ALL WRONG.

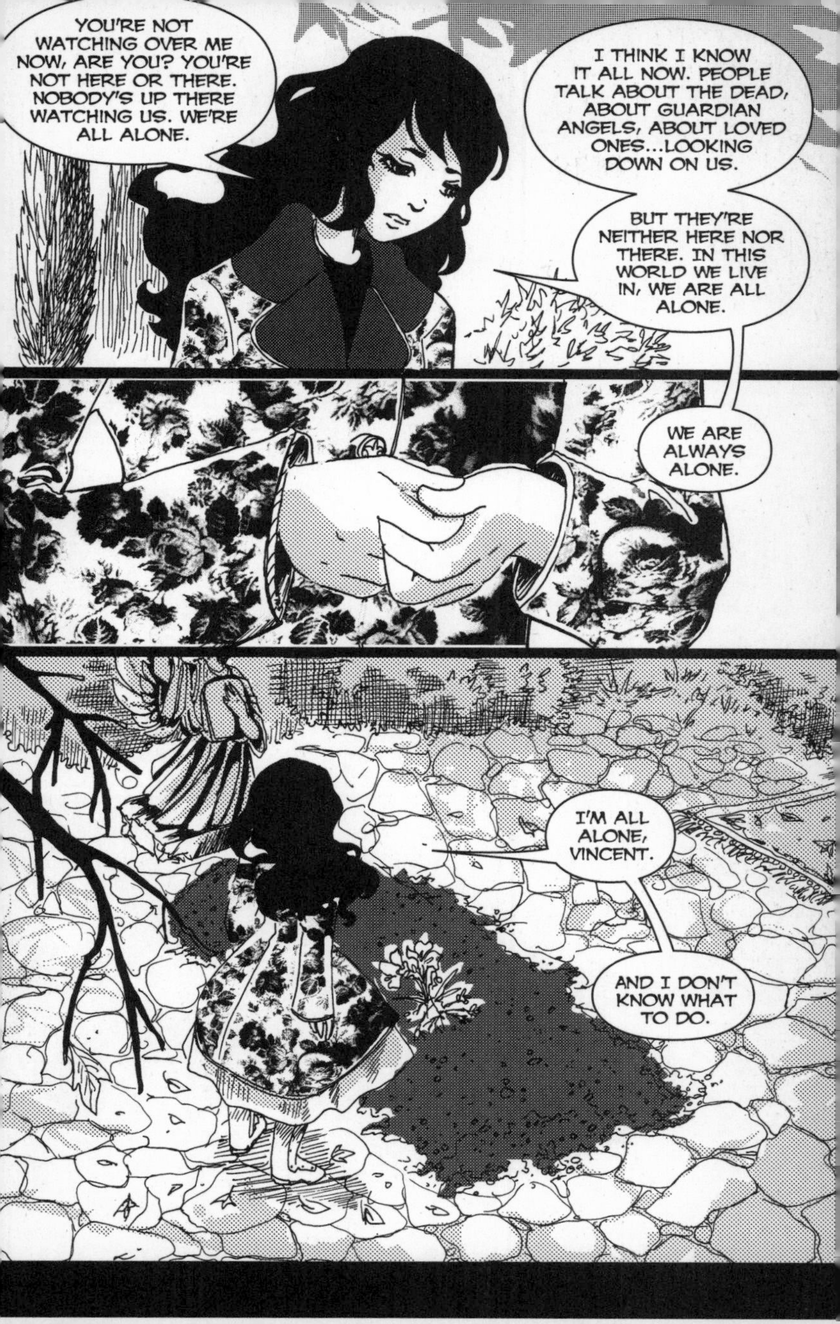
YOU'RE NOT WATCHING OVER ME NOW, ARE YOU? YOU'RE NOT HERE OR THERE. NOBODY'S UP THERE WATCHING US. WE'RE ALL ALONE.
I THINK I KNOW IT ALL NOW. PEOPLE TALK ABOUT THE DEAD, ABOUT GUARDIAN ANGELS, ABOUT LOVED ONES...LOOKING DOWN ON US.
BUT THEY'RE NEITHER HERE NOR THERE. IN THIS WORLD WE LIVE IN, WE ARE ALL ALONE.
WE ARE ALWAYS ALONE.
I'M ALL ALONE, VINCENT.
AND I DON'T KNOW WHAT TO DO.

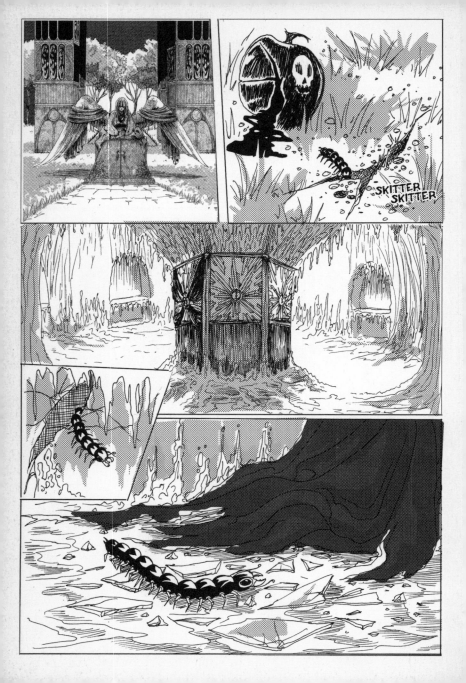

SKITTER
SKITTER

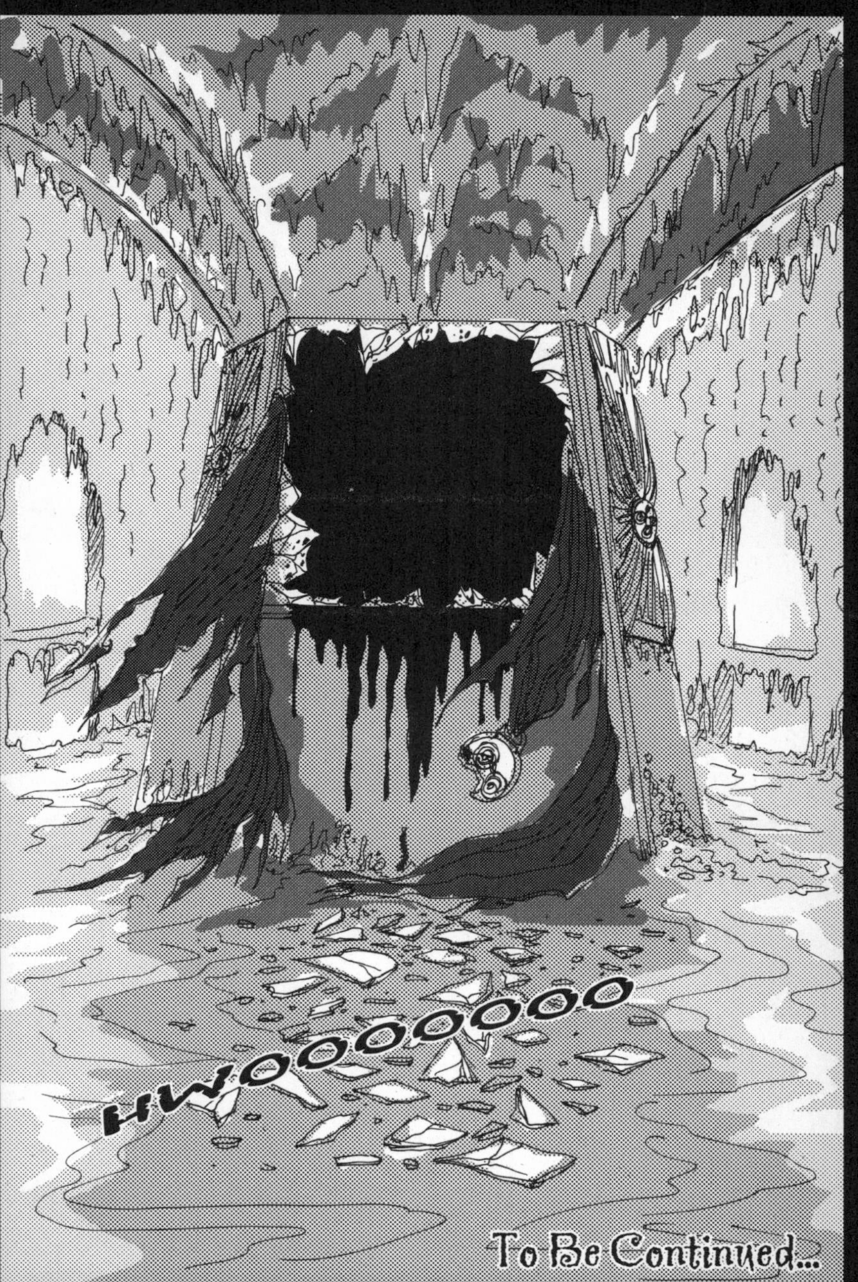
HWOOOOOOO
To Be Continued...

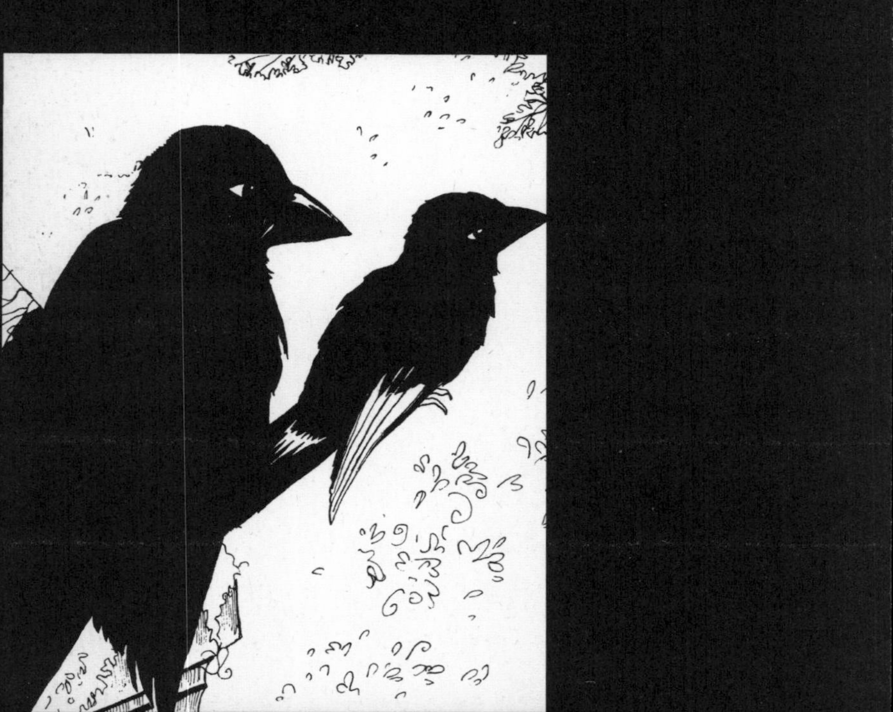

In Volume Five of Bizenghast:

Adrift and in despair, Dinah will have to fight to keep her sanity, keep her life together and keep all hell from breaking loose in the Mausoleum! The town of Bizenghast holds many secrets, and Dinah must grow up and grow strong if she intends to seek out the truth behind the mystery. Hatred and murder underlie the very foundations of the town and Dinah's struggle is only just beginning...

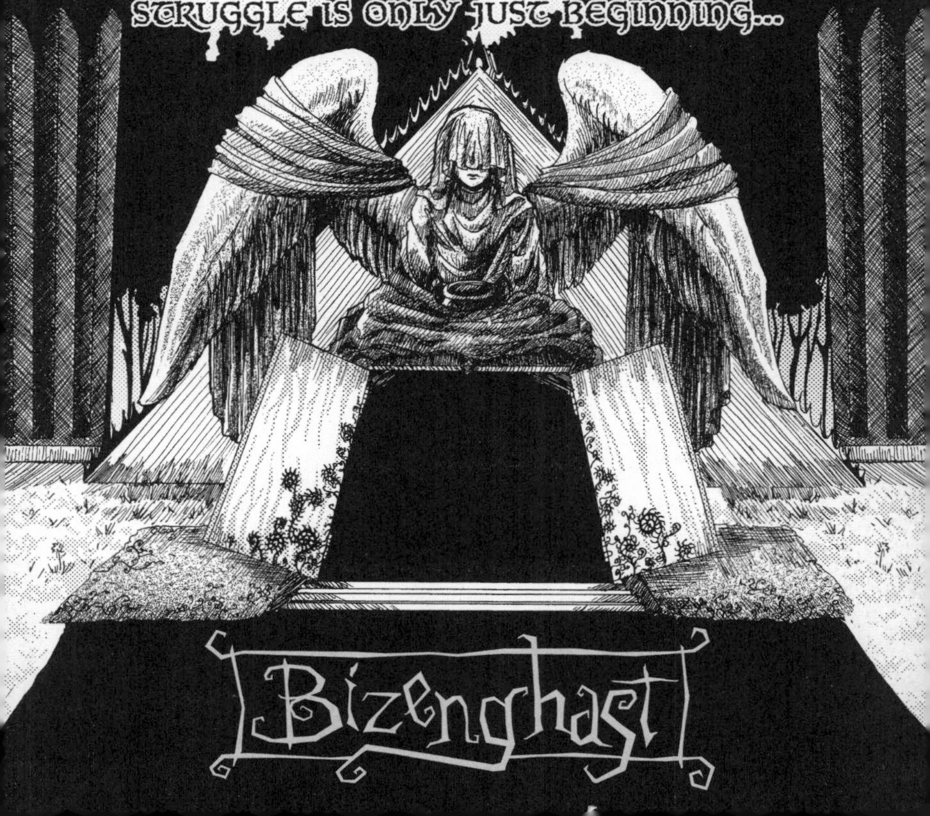
Bizenghast

THE FOLLOWING PAGES CONTAIN THE EARLIEST SKETCHES OF THE CAST OF BIZENGHAST, DUG UP FROM MY SKETCHBOOKS FROM A FEW YEARS BACK.

THEY'RE KINDA PRETTY AWFUL.
ENJOY.

WHEN I FIRST DESIGNED DINAH, SHE HAD SHORT BLACK STRAIGHT HAIR, AND HER FEATURES WERE VERY SIMPLIFIED...I'M PRETTY SURE BECAUSE MY DRAWING SKILLS WERE JUST AWFUL. NOT FOR ANY FANTASTIC ARTISTIC REASON.

BIZENGHAST WAS EXTREMELY DIFFERENT IN THE BEGINNING. I CAN'T EVEN WRITE OUT ALL THE CHANGES IT WENT THROUGH BEFORE I FINALLY PITCHED IT. IT WAS SORT OF LIKE A LITTLE BALLOON THAT JUST KEPT EXPANDING AND EXPANDING. I THINK ACCORDING TO THAT ANALOGY, IT'LL POP WHEN THE SERIES IS FINISHED. OR SOMETHING.

VINCENT WAS NOT DINAH'S ONLY FRIEND ORIGINALLY...JUST HER BEST FRIEND. IN THE BEGINNING, THEY BOTH HAD THE SAME CIRCLE OF FRIENDS WHO WERE TOTAL IDIOTS. I GOT RID OF THEM BECAUSE I JUST COULDN'T FIGURE OUT WHY DI AND VI WERE FRIENDS WITH THEM IN THE FIRST PLACE.

MAN, LOOK AT THAT SHIRT. THAT'S HILARIOUS.

DINAH DIDN'T START TO HAVE
LONG HAIR AND LOLITA-ISH
FASHIONS UNTIL AROUND MY
GRADUATION FROM COLLEGE.
I WAS HEAVILY INTO LOLITA
STUFF AT THAT TIME, HENCE
ALL THE OUTFITS.

DURING THIS TIME I
WAS TRYING TO COME
UP WITH A GOOD NAME
FOR DINAH, AND HAD A
FEW CHOICES:

*CHARLOTTE
*DIANA
*MOIRA
*SARAH
*MOLLY

AROUND THIS TIME, I STARTED THINKING ABOUT WHAT EDANIEL AND EDREAR WOULD LOOK LIKE.

EDREAR'S ORIGINAL NAME WAS MORDRED, AND IT EVOLVED FROM THERE. EDANIEL IS NAMED AFTER A GUY NAMED DANIEL THAT I PICKED RANDOMLY FROM MY MIDDLE SCHOOL YEARBOOK :)

AS YOU CAN SEE, THEY CHANGED DESIGNS A LOT!

Dinah

Edaniel

Edrear

Vincent

HERE'S THE WHOLE GANG TOGETHER AT LAST! THIS
WAS BASICALLY THE FINAL DESIGN FOR EVERYONE
BEFORE I STARTED WORKING ON CHARACTER
TRAITS AND THE ENVIRONMENT OF BIZENGHAST.
DI'S HAIR BECAME CURLY AND EDREAR GOT
THAT WEIRD ARMOR. FYI: THAT'S NOT ARMOR.
THAT'S AN EXOSKELETON. EDREAR'S LIKE A GIANT
INSECT. HE NEVER TAKES IT OFF, ONLY SHEDS IT
OR DISGUISES IT BY MAGIC.

MAN AM I GLAD VI DITCHED THE FEATHER SHIRT.

THIS WAS THE LAST DESIGN I DID OF DINAH AND
VINCENT BEFORE SUBMITTING THE SERIES TO
TOKYOPOP. THESE ARE BASICALLY THEIR FIRST
CHAPTER OUTFITS WITH SMALL CHANGES. EVERY
CHAPTER, I DRAW A PIC JUST LIKE THIS FOR
REFERENCE OF THEIR OUTFITS.

HERE'S THE DRAWING THAT BEGAN THE ENTIRE BIZENGHAST SERIES. I HAD AN ASSIGNMENT IN ART SCHOOL TO DRAW AN OPEN DOOR. WHILE IN ANOTHER CLASS, I DOODLED WHAT WOULD LATER BECOME THE HOODED ANGEL.

ALSO I WROTE DOWN A TOP SECRET GROCERY LIST. I DON'T THINK I TOOK DOWN ANY REAL NOTES FOR THIS CLASS. STILL GOT AN A, THOUGH.

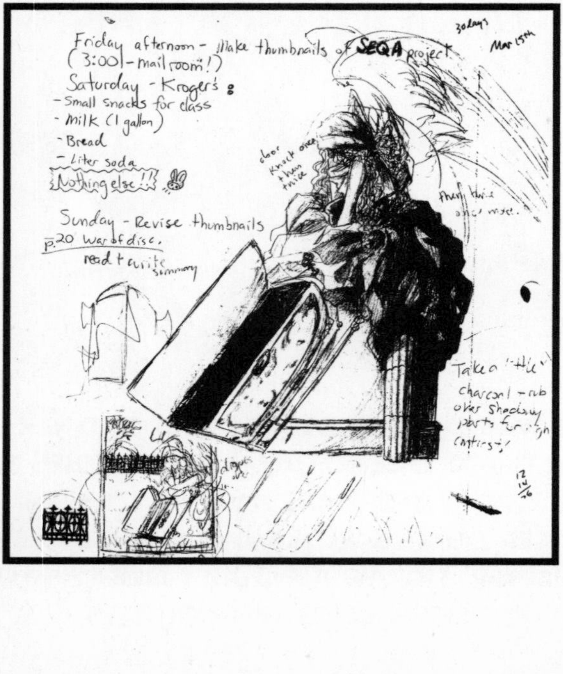
Friday afternoon - Make thumbnails of SEQA project
(3:00 - mailroom!)
Saturday - Kroger's:
- Small snacks for class
- Milk (1 gallon)
- Bread
- Liter soda
Nothing else!!
Sunday - Revise thumbnails
p.20 War of disc.
read + write summary

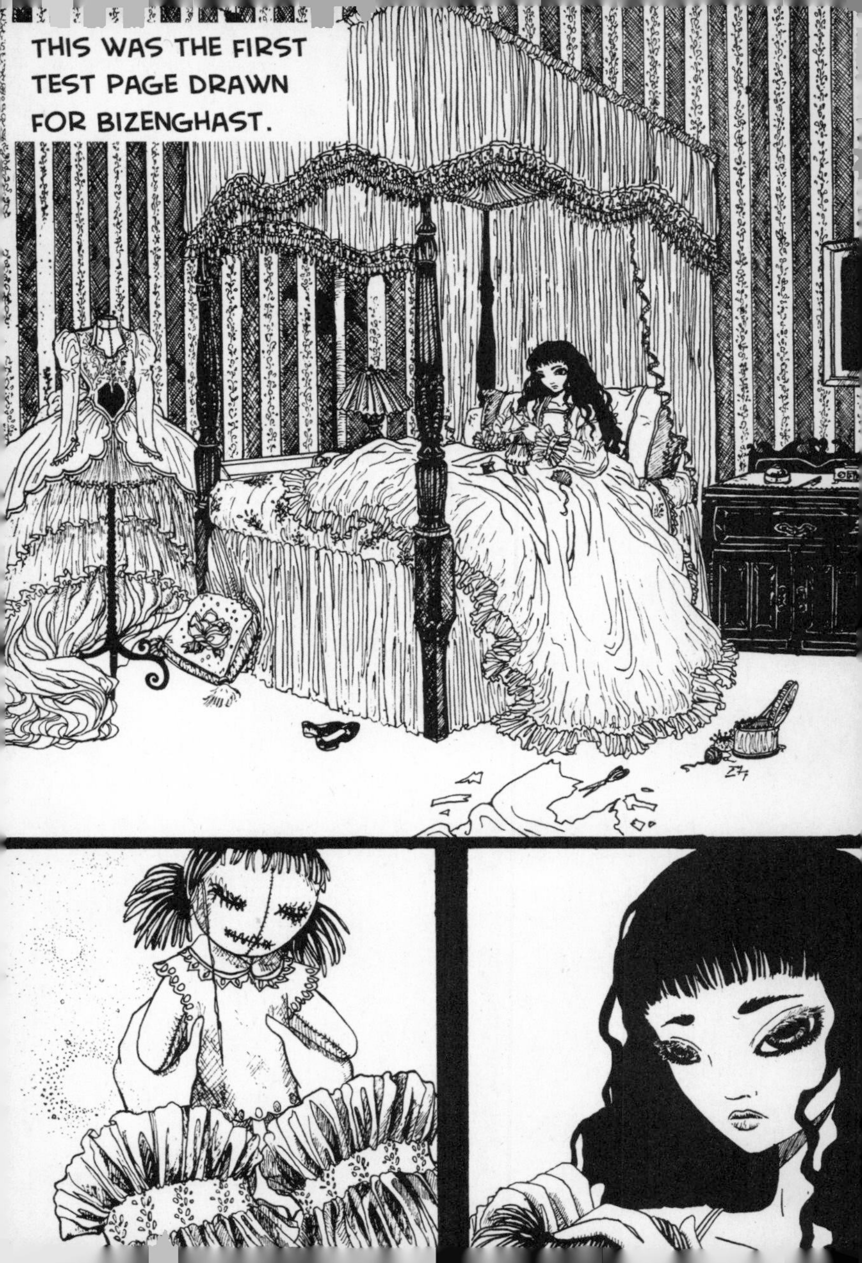
THIS WAS THE FIRST TEST PAGE DRAWN FOR BIZENGHAST.

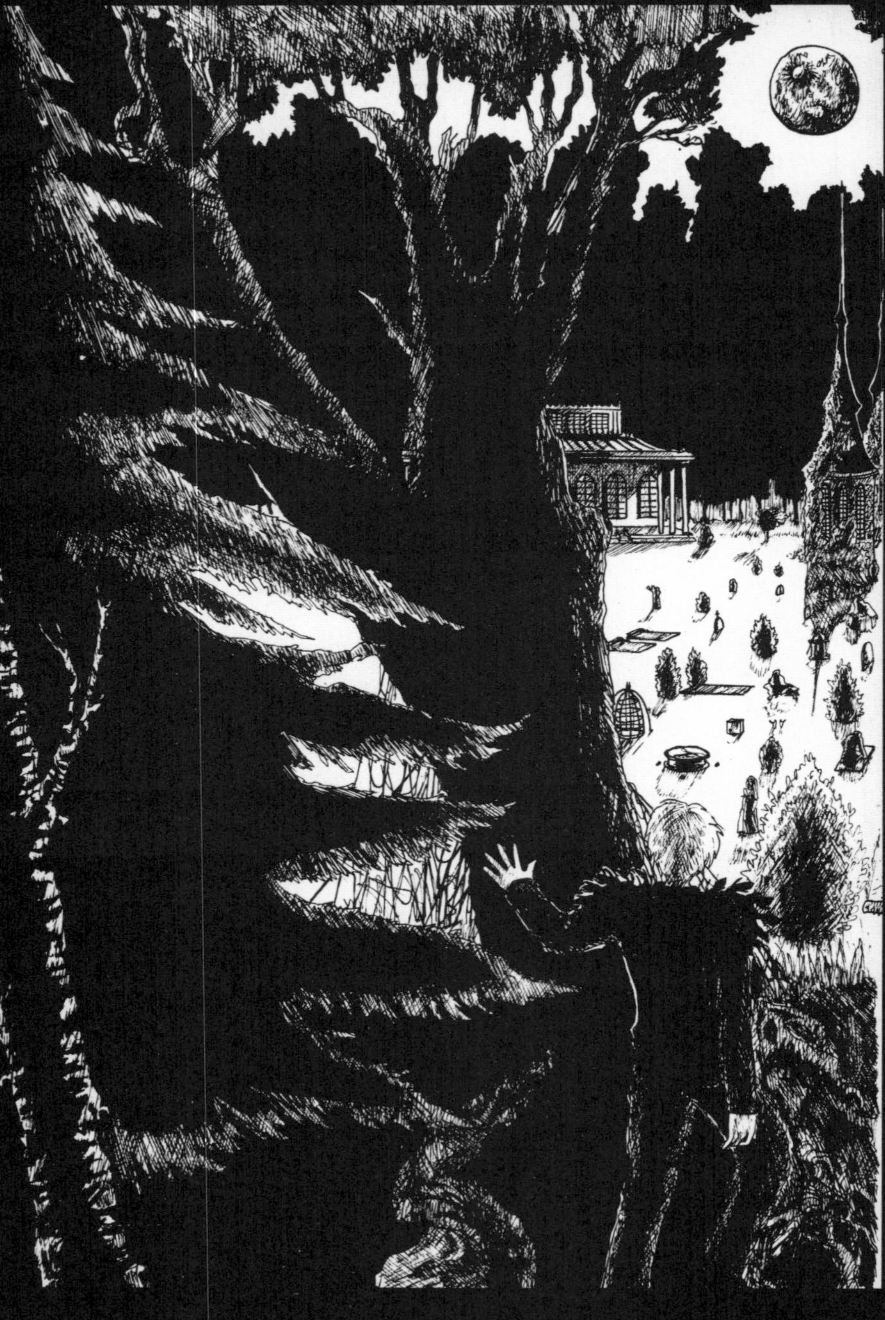

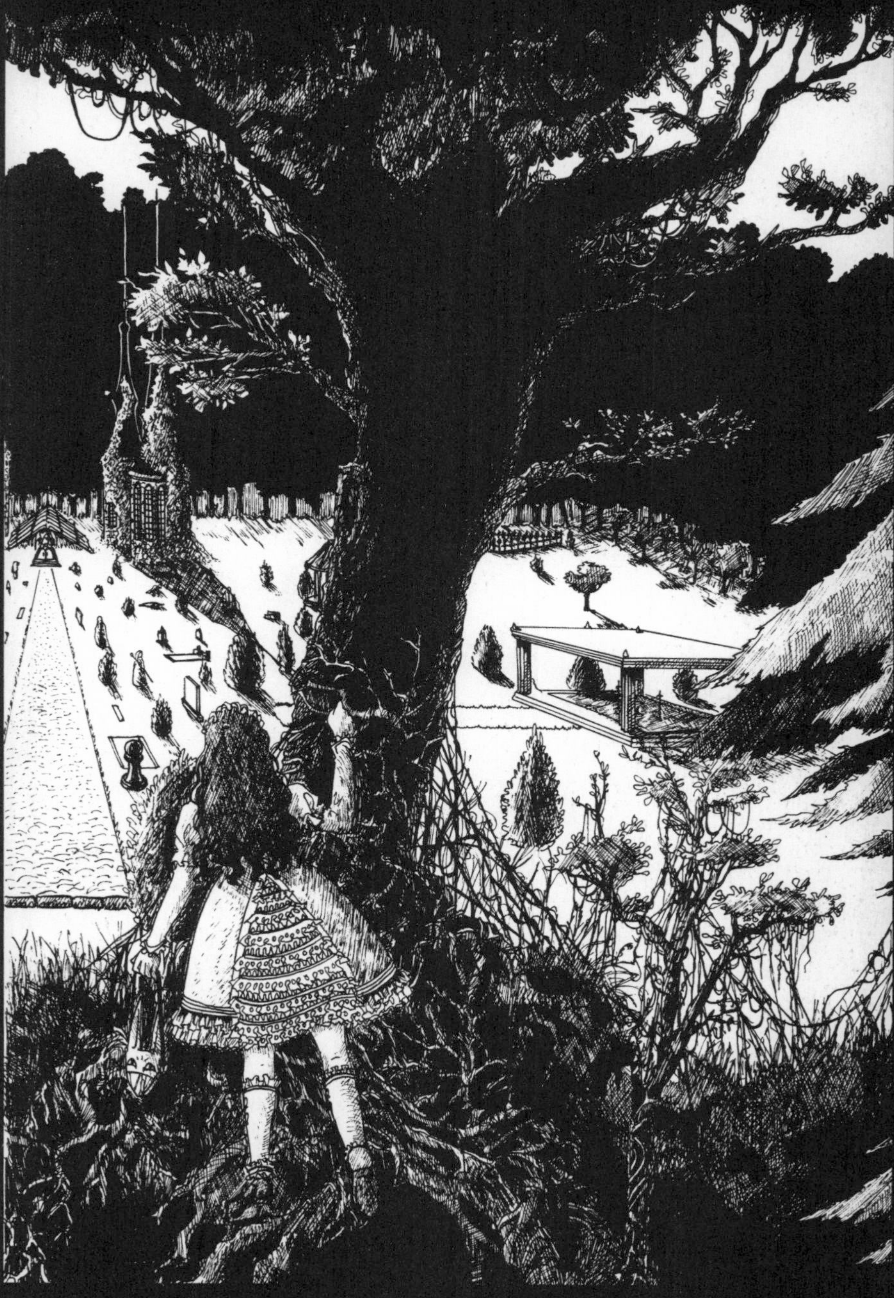

BIZENGHAST COVER ART CONTEST WINNERS!

A WHILE AGO I HAD A CONTEST TO CREATE A COVER FOR THIS VOLUME OF BIZENGHAST. HERE ARE THE AWESOME WINNERS!

FIRST RUNNER UP

"THE FORGET-ME-NOT PRINCE" BY ODDBALLLUCY.

HTTP://ODDBALLLUCY.DEVIANTART.COM

SECOND RUNNER UP

"PUPPET VINCENT" BY RANDOM-CRAZYNESS.

HTTP://RANDOM-CRAZYNESS.DEVIANTART.COM

THIRD RUNNER UP
A TEXT-ONLY ENTRY BY KASPER-LASSIE

VINCENT IS FACING HIS LEFT IN AN OLD, RED TUX WITH SWALLOWTAIL ENDS. THE TUX HAS THAT OLD, GOLDEN, ROPEY LINING. BEHIND HIM IS A ROOM OF GADGETS. BIG ONES, ODD ONES, RED ONES, BLACK ONES. THE GADGETS AREN'T WHAT'S INTERESTING, THOUGH. THE THINGS CREATING THESE MACHINES ARE WIRE-FRAMED FORMS; THE KIND YOU HEM A DRESS TO, WITH THOSE CLOTH FACES.

HTTP://KASPER-LASSIE.DEVIANTART.COM

BIZENGHAST COVER ART CONTEST WINNERS!

WINNER OF THE COVER CONTEST!

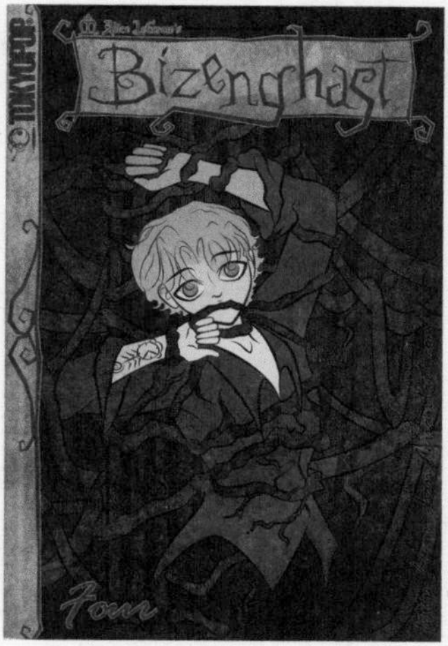
TOKYOPOP
Bizenghast
Four

ART BY COR-CHAN
HTTP://COR-CHAN.DEVIANTART.COM

THIS PIECE REALLY SPOKE TO ME AS A GREAT DESIGN, AND IT ALSO INDIRECTLY INSPIRED THE ACTUAL COVER OF THIS BOOK! FOR THAT, COR-CHAN RECEIVES A BOOK CREDIT AS COVER CONCEPT ARTIST.

THANKS TO EVERYONE WHO ENTERED, AND ALSO TO EVERYONE ON DEVIANTART, FOR ALWAYS GIVING ME HONEST CRITIQUES AND FOR ENJOYING AMAZING COMICS. BIZNIZ SNAKE SEZ: YOU GUYS ARE AWESOME!

COMPLAINT FORM

For faster turnaround on complaints about this
series, please fill out the form below.

Dear Ms. LeGrow,

I am (check all that apply):

☐ A die-hard manga reader.
☐ An angry amateur artist.
☐ Your editor.

☐ An online comic critic.
☐ A TOKYOPOP investor.
☐ A raving madman.

I would just like to register my complete and utter disgust for
your book series, Bizenghast. In my opinion, real manga should be:

☐ Drawn by the Japanese.
☐ Read right-to-left.
☐ Drawn by Americans
with Japanese nicknames.

☐ Read bottom-to-top.
☐ Filled with robots.
☐ Small enough to fit in my mouth.

Your artwork and writing skills are:

☐ Deplorable.
☐ Baffling at the very least.
☐ Not very useful as a hat.

How do you sleep at night, Ms. LeGrow, knowing that:

☐ You're a terrible person?
☐ You're not Japanese?

☐ Your books are devoid of cat-girls?
☐ You left the iron on?

In short, Ms. LeGrow, you are a bad person and I will be
sending a copy of this complaint to:

☐ My mother.
☐ My congressman.

☐ Your mother.
☐ My mailbox.

Sincerely,

_____

(your name here)

FOOL'S GOLD

Everyone knows that-- with rare exception-- girls are fatally drawn to jerks! Upon discovering this sobering truth, Penny takes it upon herself to form her own underground club to identify these boneheads and cure her girlfriends of their addiction to them! Suddenly Penny discovers that she has unintentionally changed the social structure of the school and that she's at the top of the pyramid! But can this revolution last...?

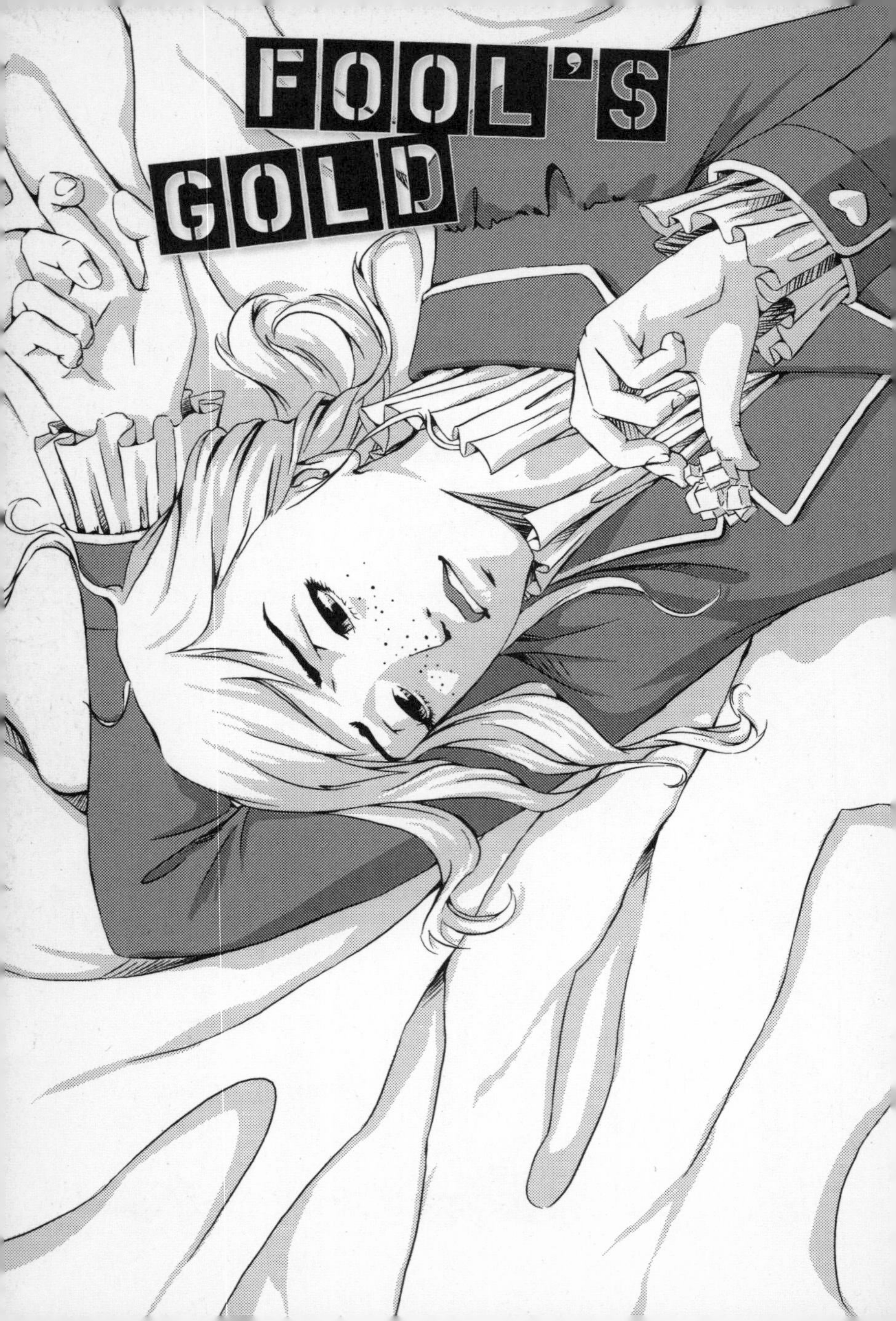
FOOL'S GOLD

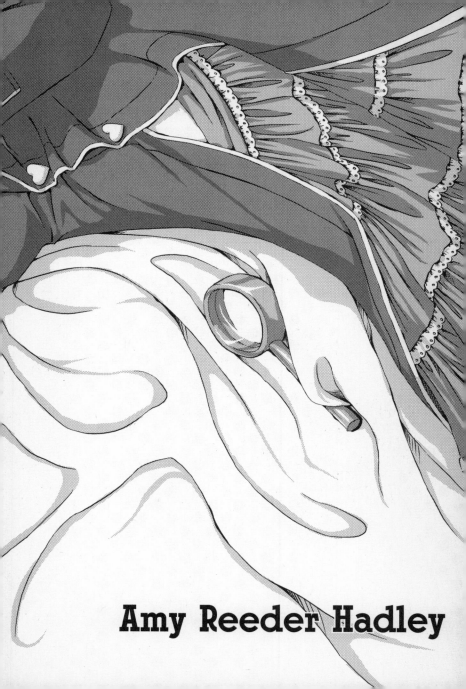

Amy Reeder Hadley

Chapter 1: Sophomore Year

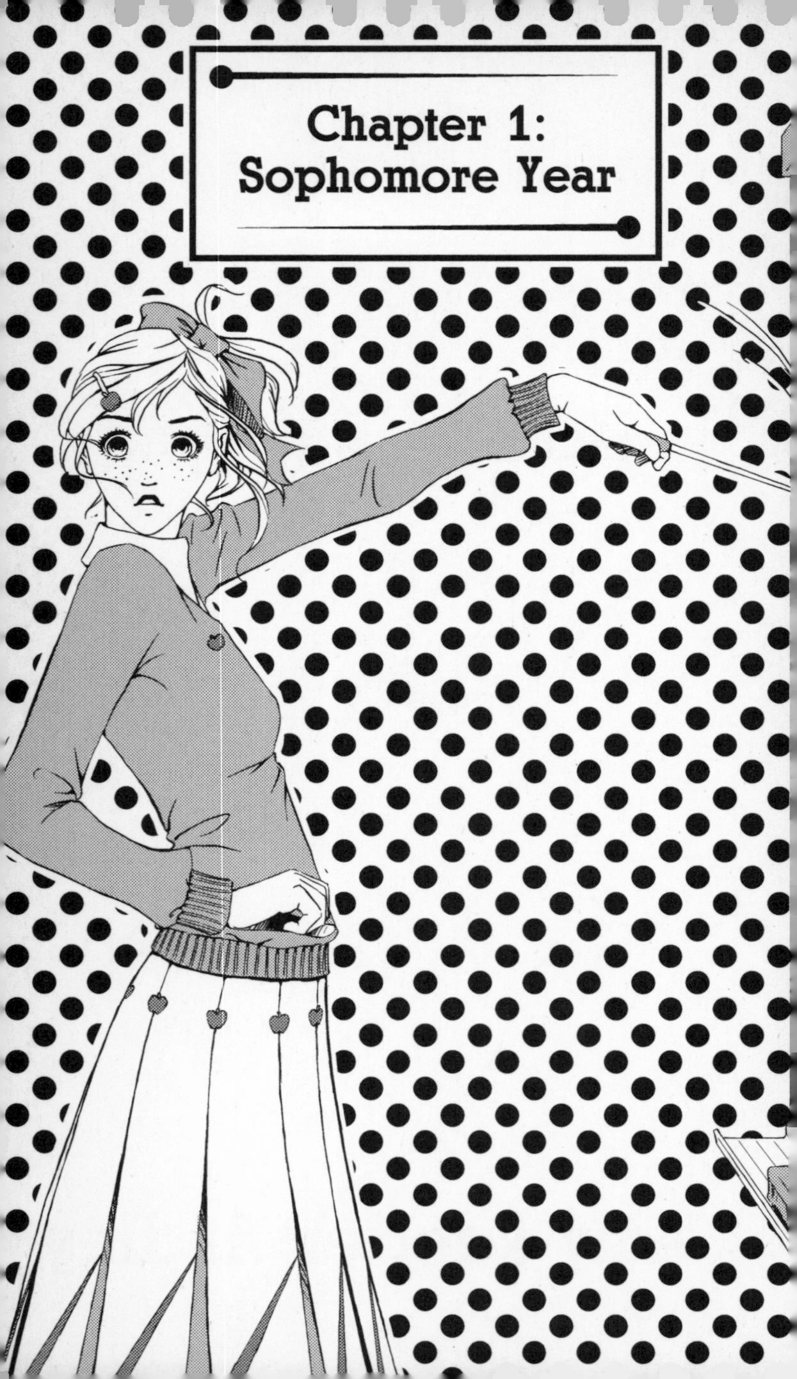

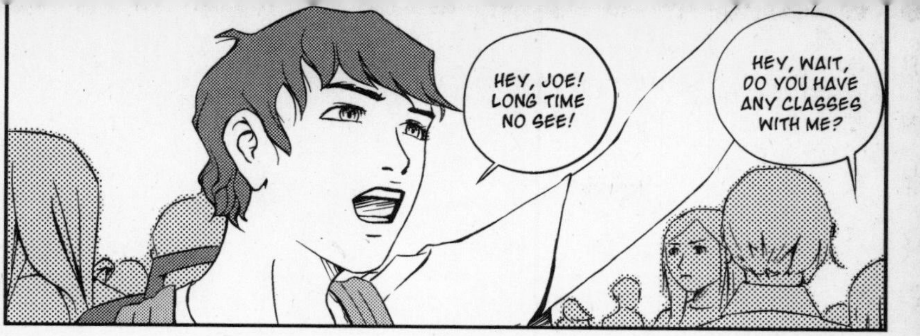
HEY, JOE! LONG TIME NO SEE!
HEY, WAIT, DO YOU HAVE ANY CLASSES WITH ME?

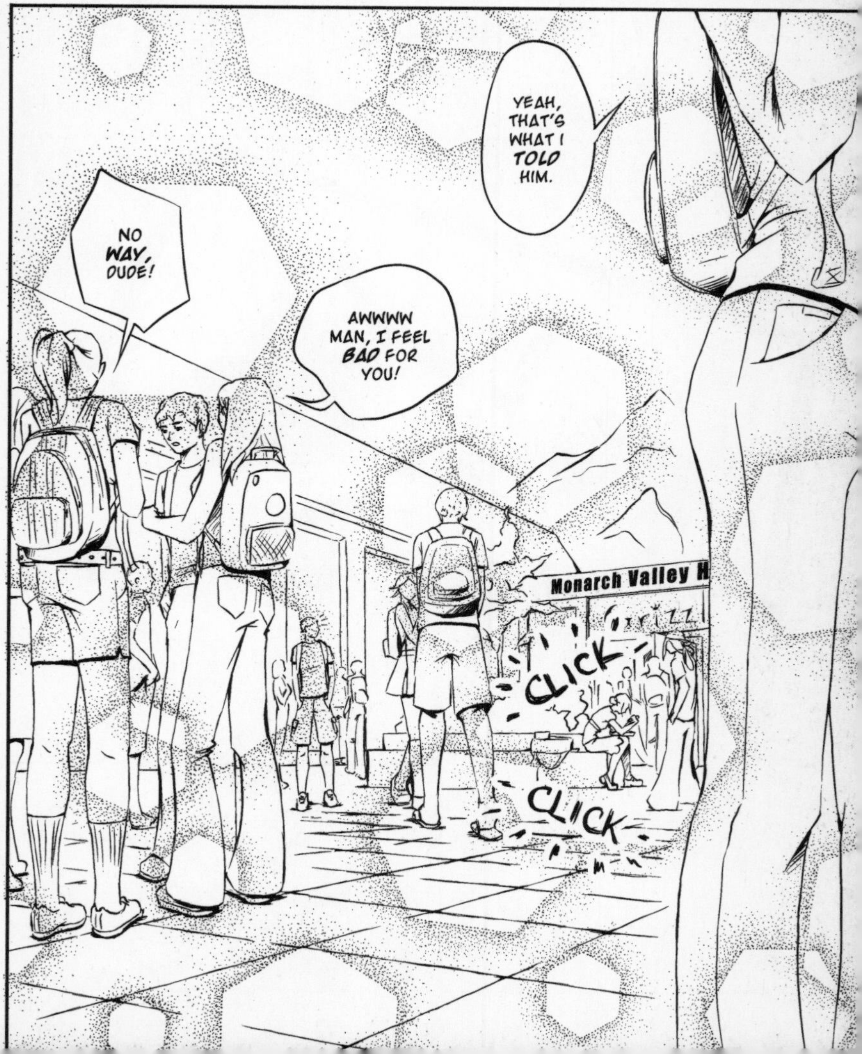
NO WAY, DUDE!
AWWWW MAN, I FEEL BAD FOR YOU!
YEAH, THAT'S WHAT I TOLD HIM.
Monarch Valley H
CLICK
CLICK

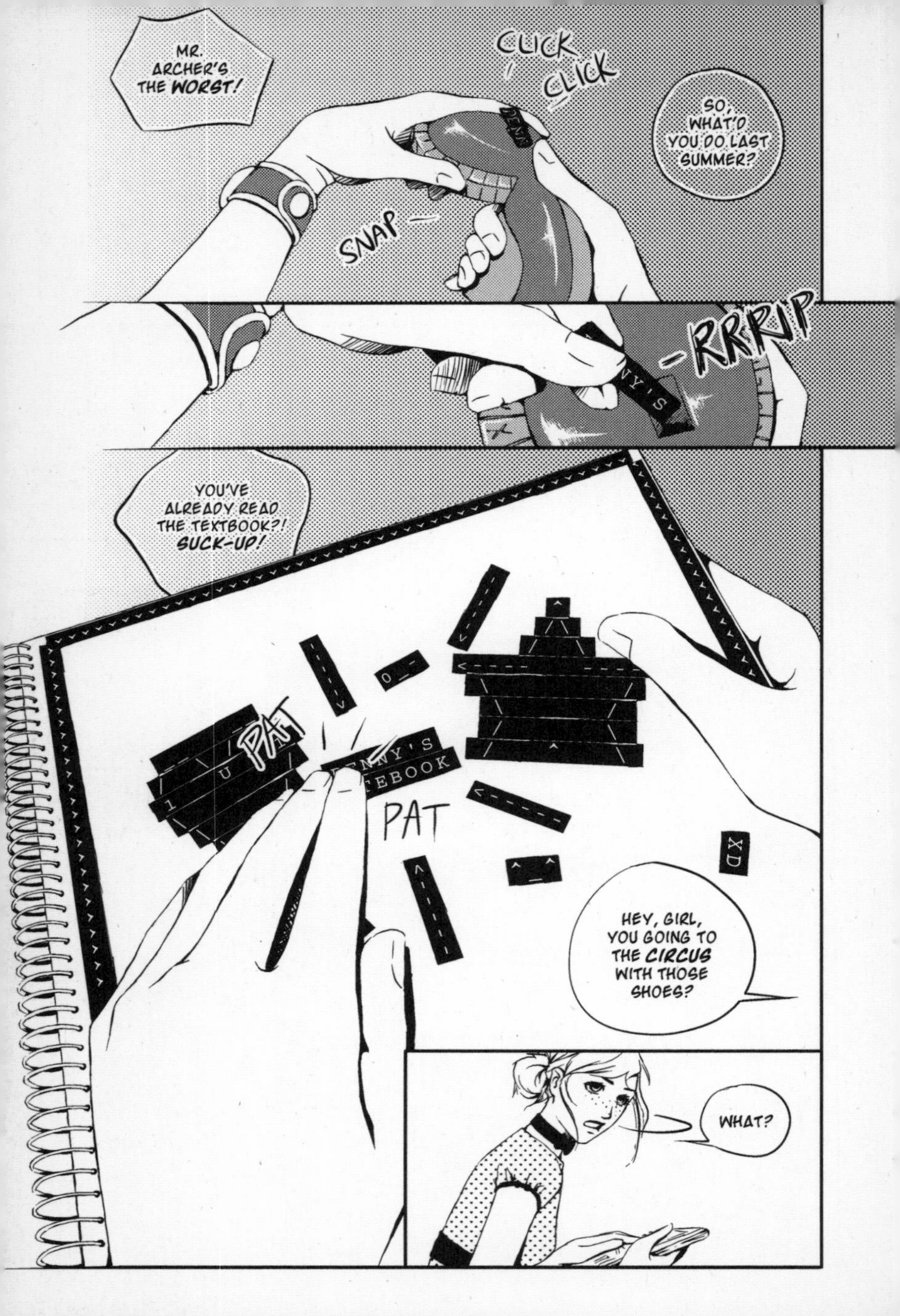
MR. ARCHER'S THE **WORST**!
CLICK
CLICK
SO, WHAT'D YOU DO LAST SUMMER?
SNAP—
-RRRIP
YOU'VE ALREADY READ THE TEXTBOOK?! **SUCK-UP**!
PAT
PAT
XD
HEY, GIRL, YOU GOING TO THE **CIRCUS** WITH THOSE SHOES?
WHAT?

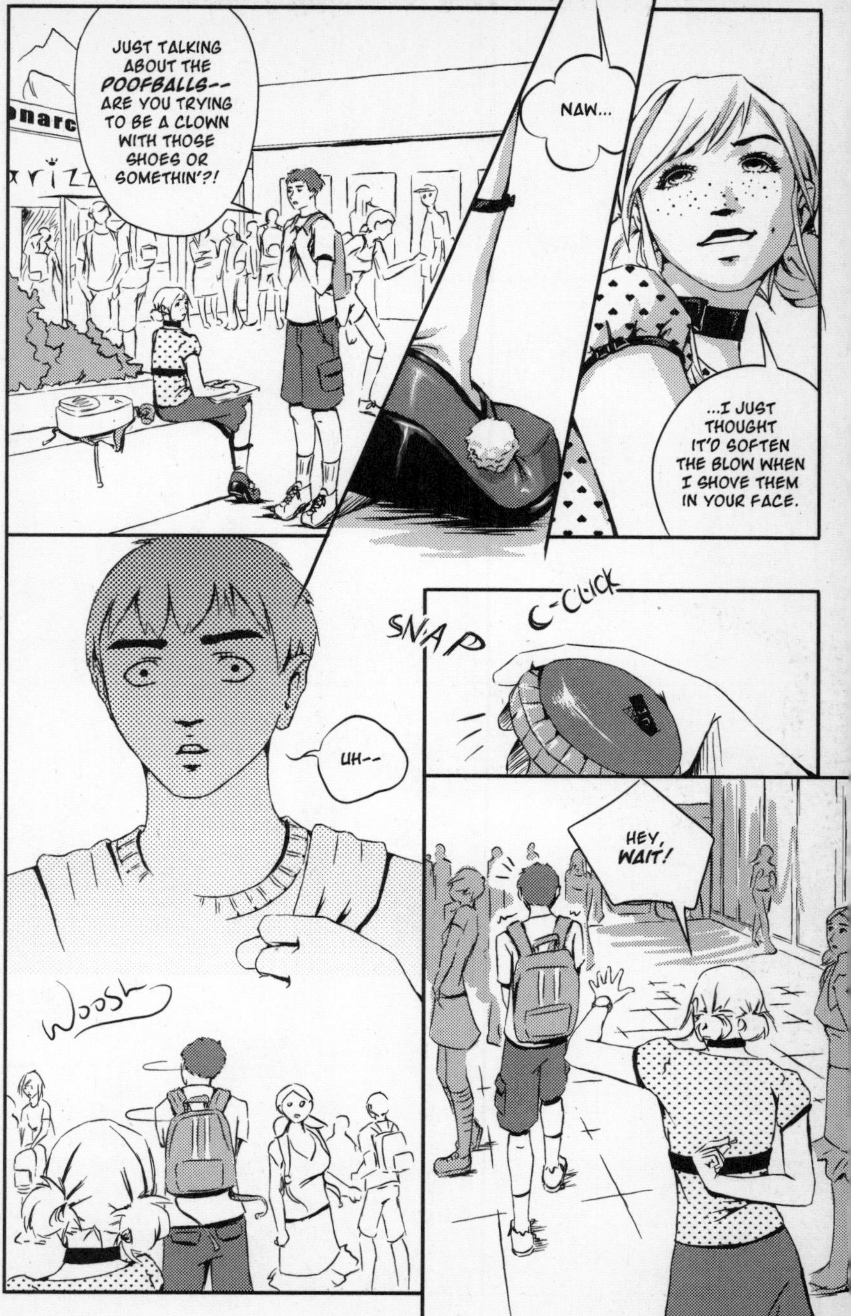
JUST TALKING ABOUT THE POOFBALLS-- ARE YOU TRYING TO BE A CLOWN WITH THOSE SHOES OR SOMETHIN'?!
NAW...
...I JUST THOUGHT IT'D SOFTEN THE BLOW WHEN I SHOVE THEM IN YOUR FACE.
UH--
WOOSH
SNAP
C-CLICK
HEY, WAIT!

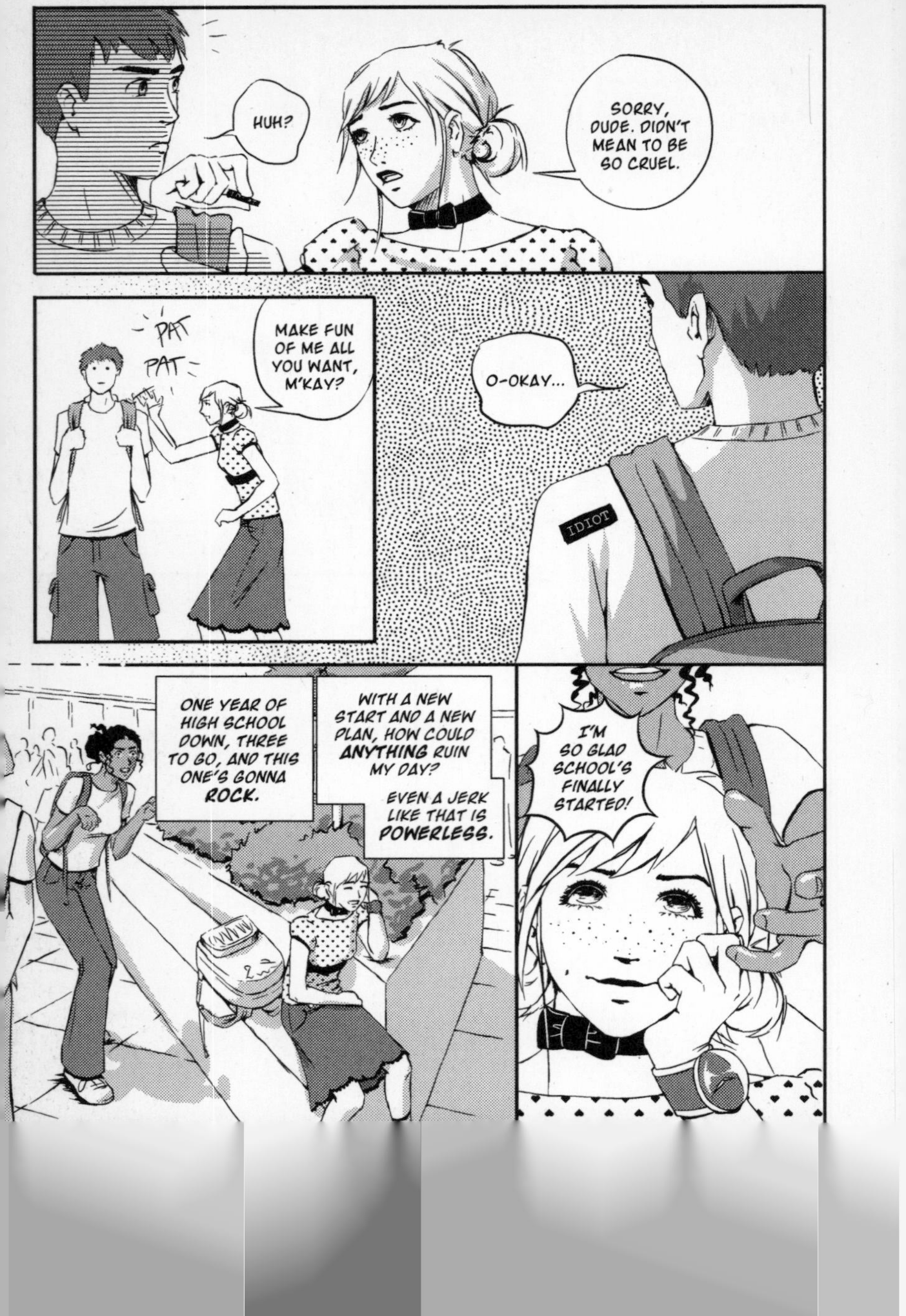
HUH?
SORRY, DUDE. DIDN'T MEAN TO BE SO CRUEL.
PAT PAT
MAKE FUN OF ME ALL YOU WANT, M'KAY?
O-OKAY...
IDIOT
ONE YEAR OF HIGH SCHOOL DOWN, THREE TO GO, AND THIS ONE'S GONNA **ROCK**.
WITH A NEW START AND A NEW PLAN, HOW COULD **ANYTHING** RUIN MY DAY?
EVEN A JERK LIKE THAT IS **POWERLESS**.
I'M SO GLAD SCHOOL'S FINALLY STARTED!

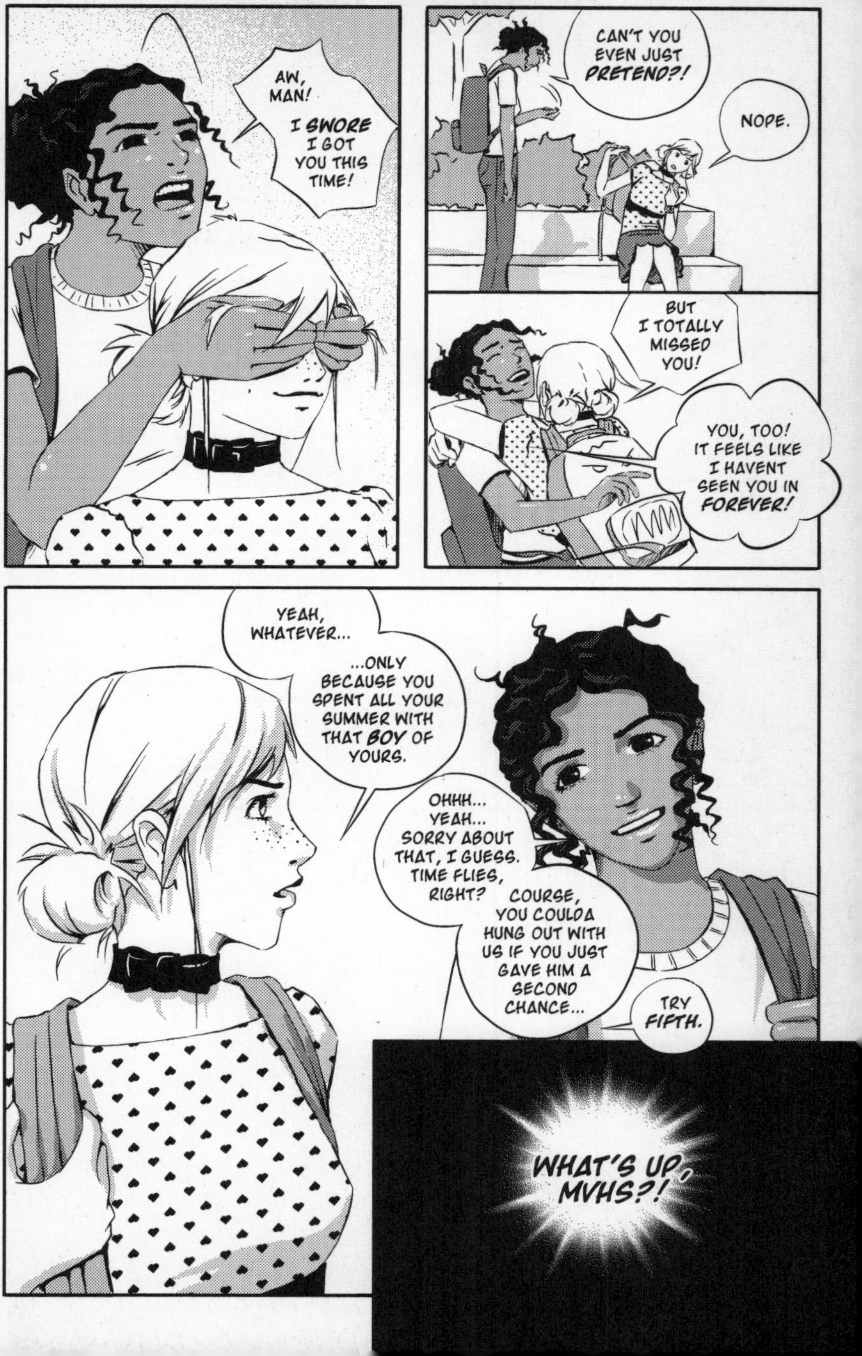
AW, MAN!
I SWORE I GOT YOU THIS TIME!
CAN'T YOU EVEN JUST PRETEND?!
NOPE.
BUT I TOTALLY MISSED YOU!
YOU, TOO! IT FEELS LIKE I HAVENT SEEN YOU IN FOREVER!
YEAH, WHATEVER...
...ONLY BECAUSE YOU SPENT ALL YOUR SUMMER WITH THAT BOY OF YOURS.
OHHH... YEAH... SORRY ABOUT THAT, I GUESS. TIME FLIES, RIGHT?
COURSE, YOU COULDA HUNG OUT WITH US IF YOU JUST GAVE HIM A SECOND CHANCE...
TRY FIFTH.
WHAT'S UP, MVHS?!

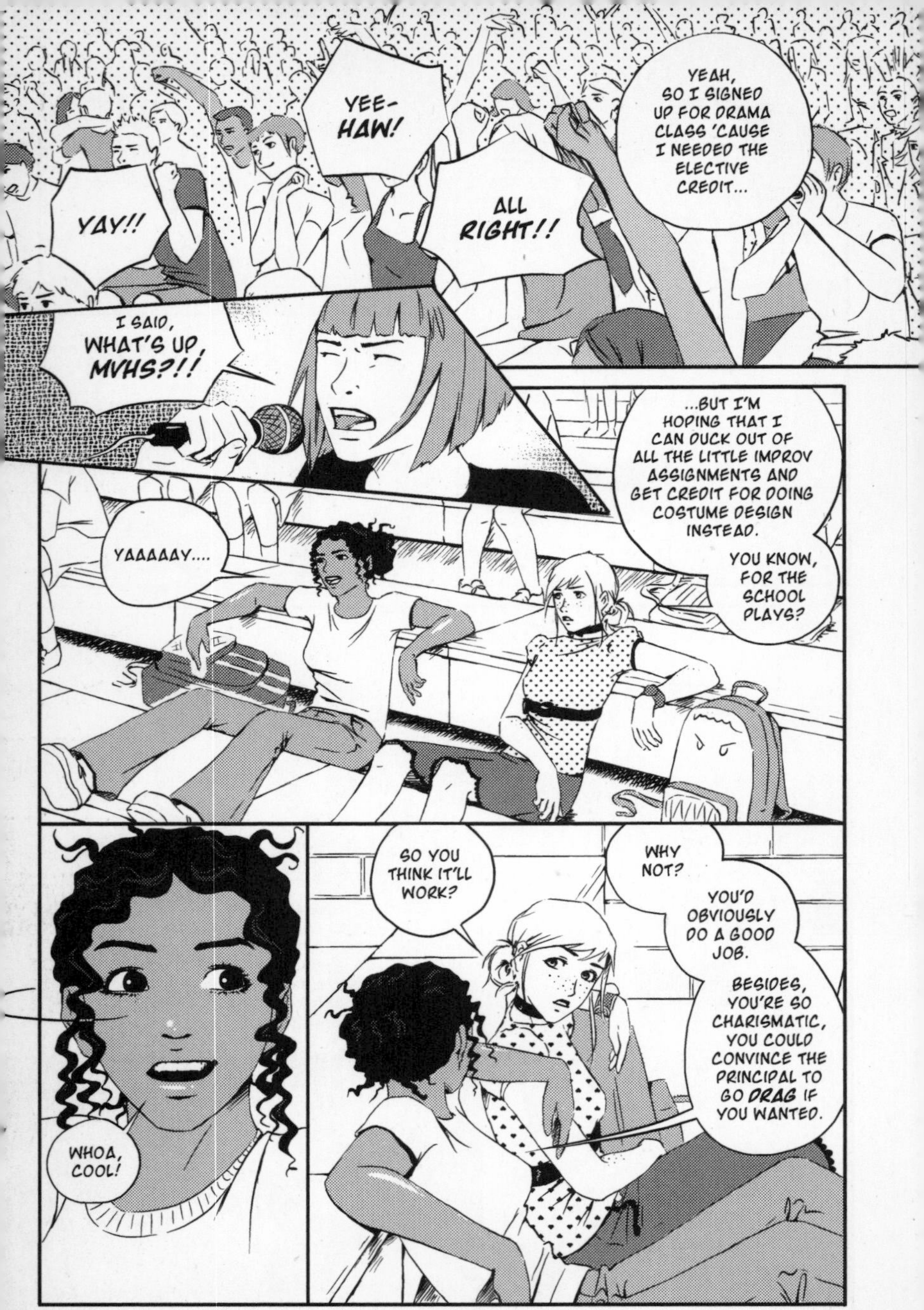
YAY!!
YEE-HAW!
ALL RIGHT!!
YEAH, SO I SIGNED UP FOR DRAMA CLASS 'CAUSE I NEEDED THE ELECTIVE CREDIT...
I SAID, WHAT'S UP, MVHS?!!
...BUT I'M HOPING THAT I CAN DUCK OUT OF ALL THE LITTLE IMPROV ASSIGNMENTS AND GET CREDIT FOR DOING COSTUME DESIGN INSTEAD.
YOU KNOW, FOR THE SCHOOL PLAYS?
YAAAAAY....
WHOA, COOL!
SO YOU THINK IT'LL WORK?
WHY NOT?
YOU'D OBVIOUSLY DO A GOOD JOB.
BESIDES, YOU'RE SO CHARISMATIC, YOU COULD CONVINCE THE PRINCIPAL TO GO DRAG IF YOU WANTED.

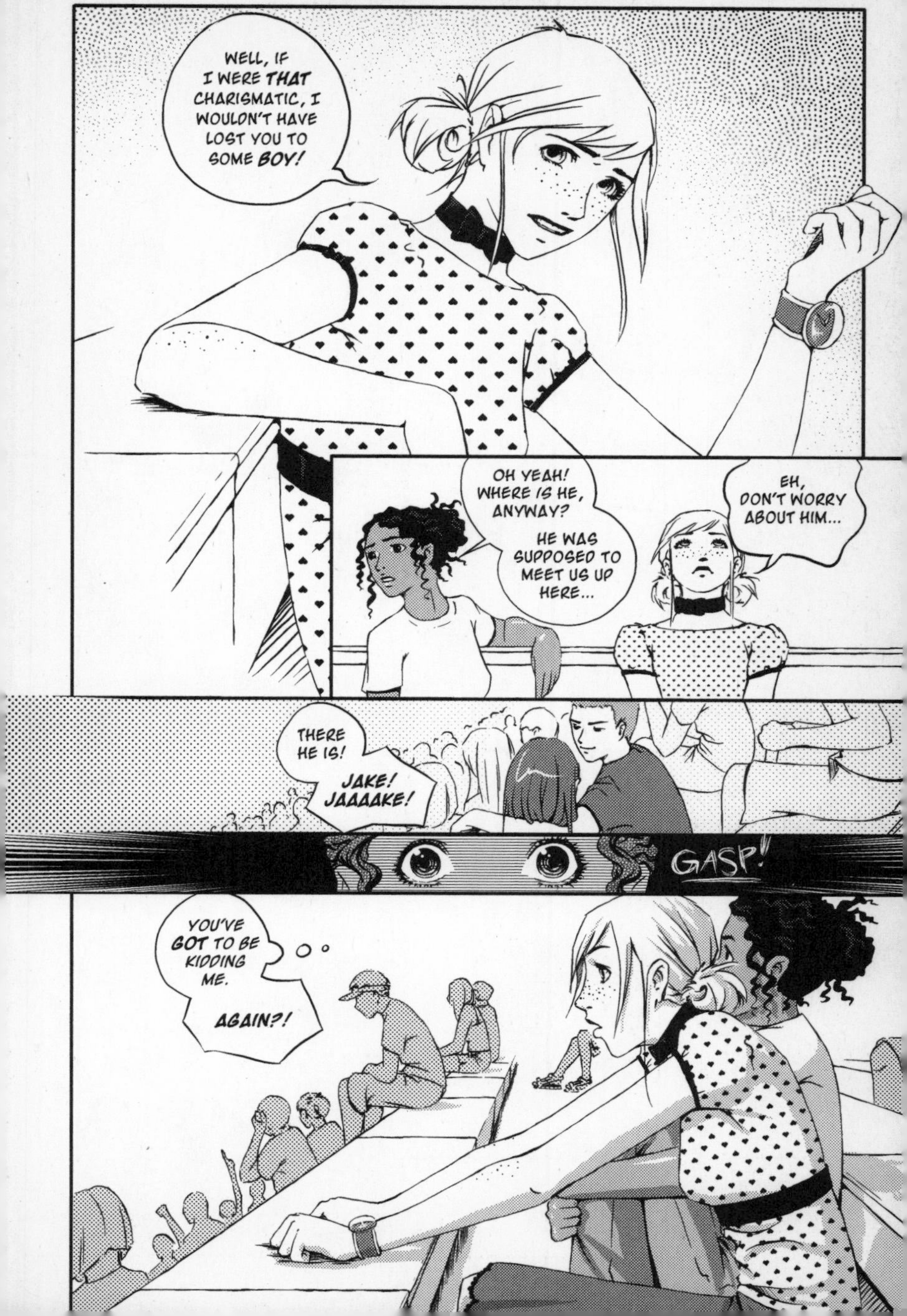
WELL, IF I WERE THAT CHARISMATIC, I WOULDN'T HAVE LOST YOU TO SOME BOY!
OH YEAH! WHERE IS HE, ANYWAY?
HE WAS SUPPOSED TO MEET US UP HERE...
EH, DON'T WORRY ABOUT HIM...
THERE HE IS!
JAKE! JAAAAKE!
GASP!
YOU'VE GOT TO BE KIDDING ME.
AGAIN?!

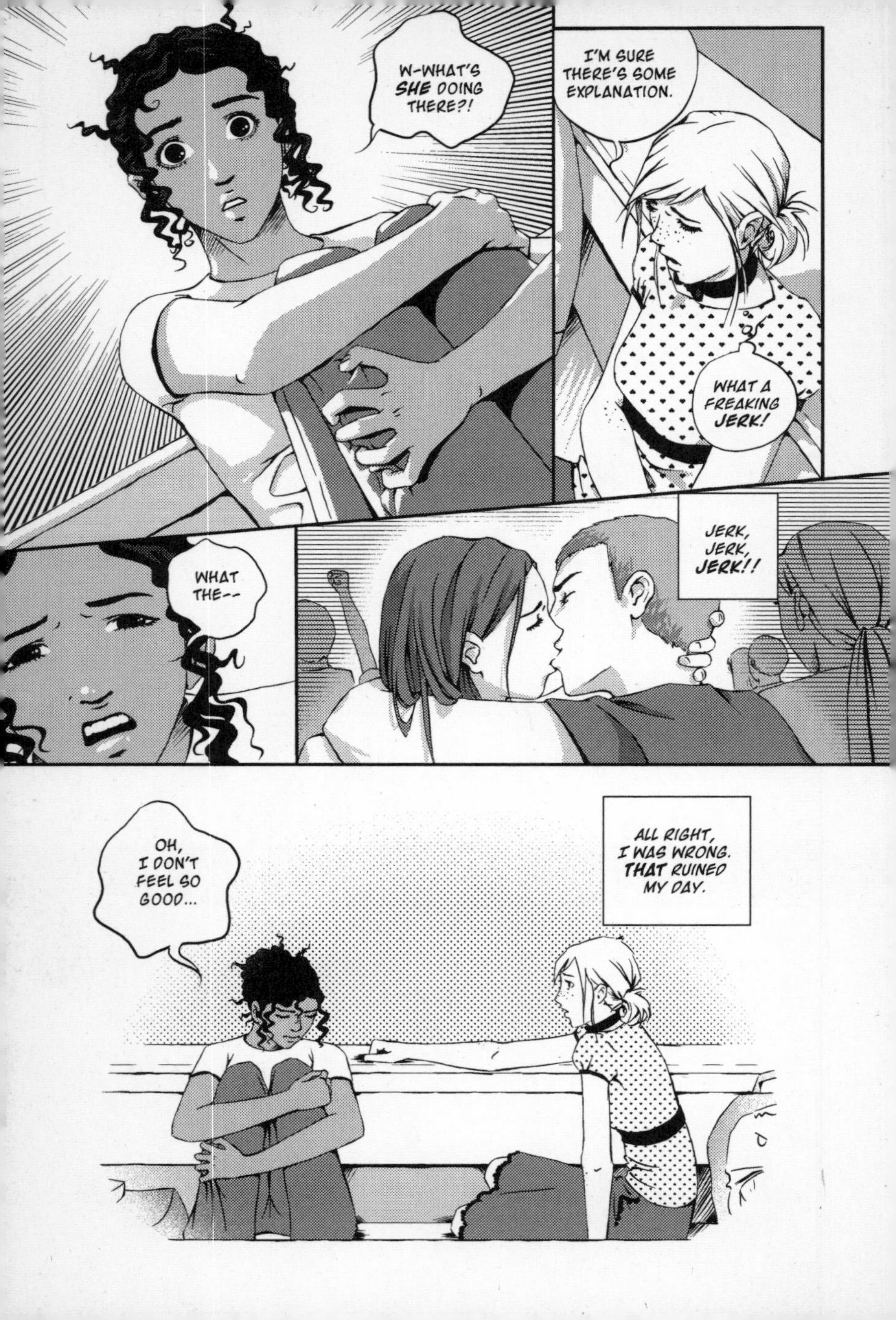
W-WHAT'S SHE DOING THERE?!
I'M SURE THERE'S SOME EXPLANATION.
WHAT A FREAKING JERK!
WHAT THE--
JERK, JERK, JERK!!
OH, I DON'T FEEL SO GOOD...
ALL RIGHT, I WAS WRONG. THAT RUINED MY DAY.

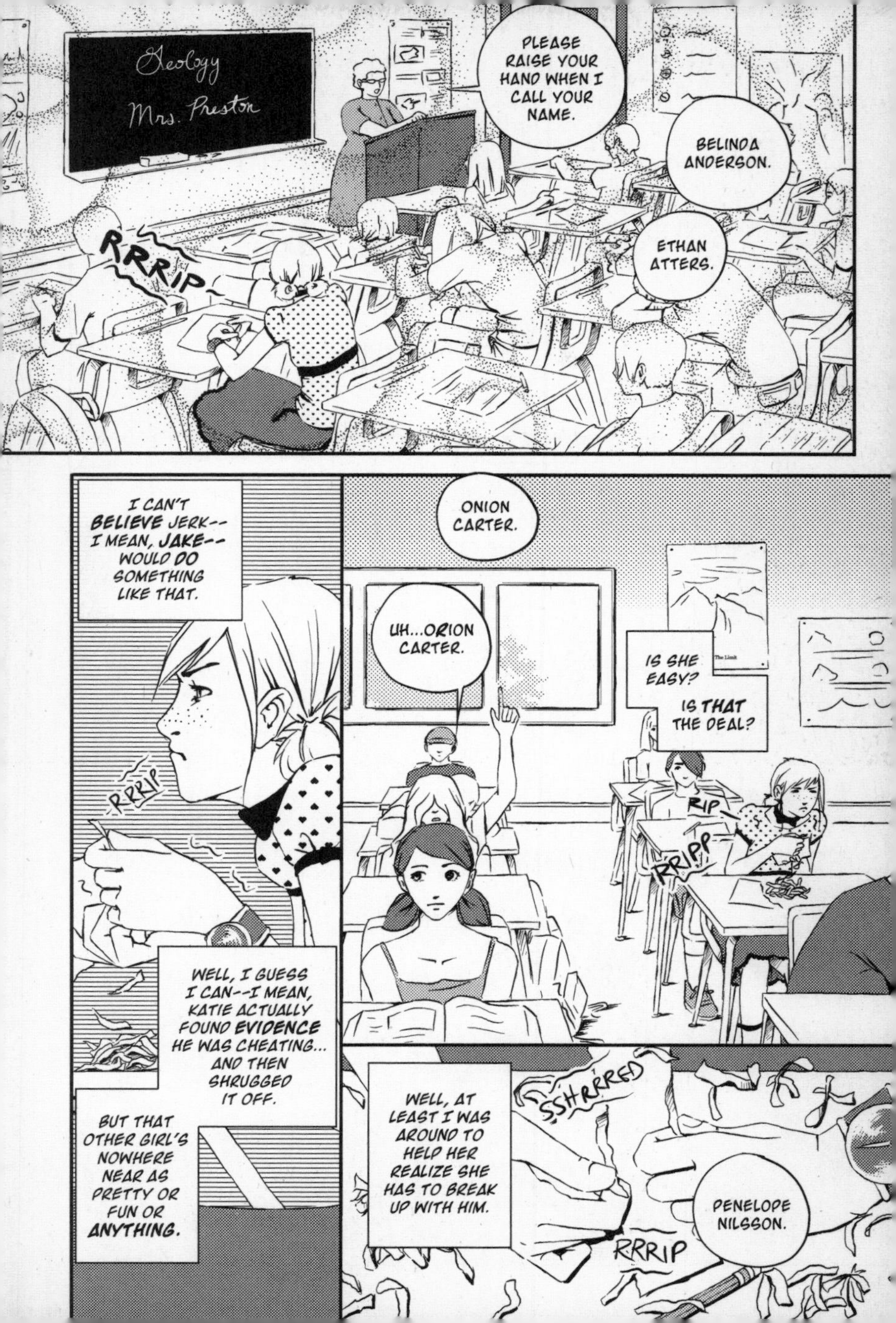
Geology
Mrs. Preston
RRRIP
PLEASE RAISE YOUR HAND WHEN I CALL YOUR NAME.
BELINDA ANDERSON.
ETHAN ATTERS.
I CAN'T BELIEVE JERK-- I MEAN, JAKE-- WOULD DO SOMETHING LIKE THAT.
RRRIP
WELL, I GUESS I CAN--I MEAN, KATIE ACTUALLY FOUND EVIDENCE HE WAS CHEATING... AND THEN SHRUGGED IT OFF.
BUT THAT OTHER GIRL'S NOWHERE NEAR AS PRETTY OR FUN OR ANYTHING.
ONION CARTER.
UH...ORION CARTER.
IS SHE EASY?
IS THAT THE DEAL?
RIP
RRIPP
WELL, AT LEAST I WAS AROUND TO HELP HER REALIZE SHE HAS TO BREAK UP WITH HIM.
SSHRRRED
PENELOPE NILSSON.
RRRIP

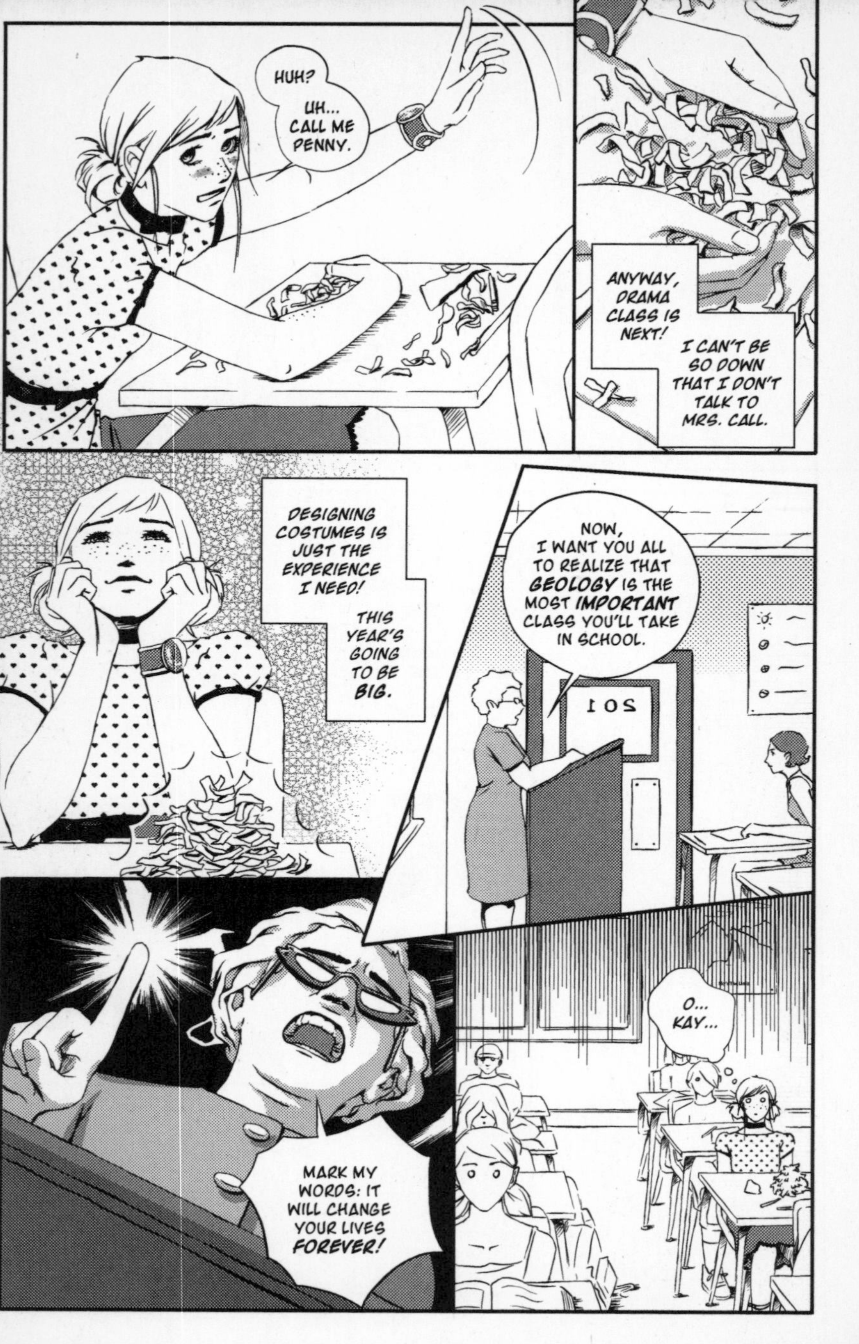
HUH?
UH... CALL ME PENNY.
ANYWAY, DRAMA CLASS IS NEXT!
I CAN'T BE SO DOWN THAT I DON'T TALK TO MRS. CALL.
DESIGNING COSTUMES IS JUST THE EXPERIENCE I NEED!
THIS YEAR'S GOING TO BE **BIG.**
NOW, I WANT YOU ALL TO REALIZE THAT **GEOLOGY** IS THE MOST **IMPORTANT** CLASS YOU'LL TAKE IN SCHOOL.
MARK MY WORDS: IT WILL CHANGE YOUR LIVES **FOREVER!**
O... KAY...

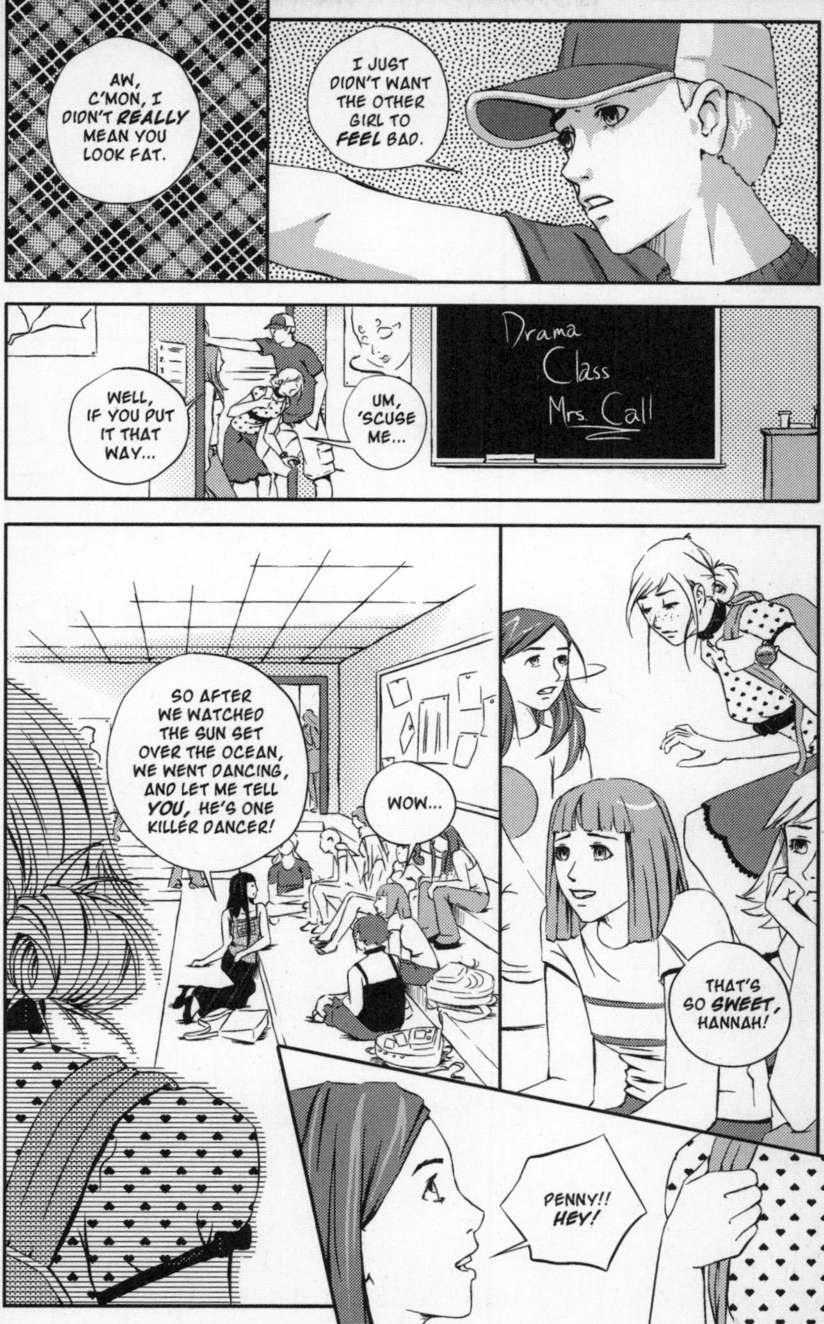
AW, C'MON, I DIDN'T REALLY MEAN YOU LOOK FAT.
I JUST DIDN'T WANT THE OTHER GIRL TO FEEL BAD.
WELL, IF YOU PUT IT THAT WAY...
UM, 'SCUSE ME...
Drama Class Mrs. Call
SO AFTER WE WATCHED THE SUN SET OVER THE OCEAN, WE WENT DANCING, AND LET ME TELL YOU, HE'S ONE KILLER DANCER!
WOW...
THAT'S SO SWEET, HANNAH!
PENNY!! HEY!

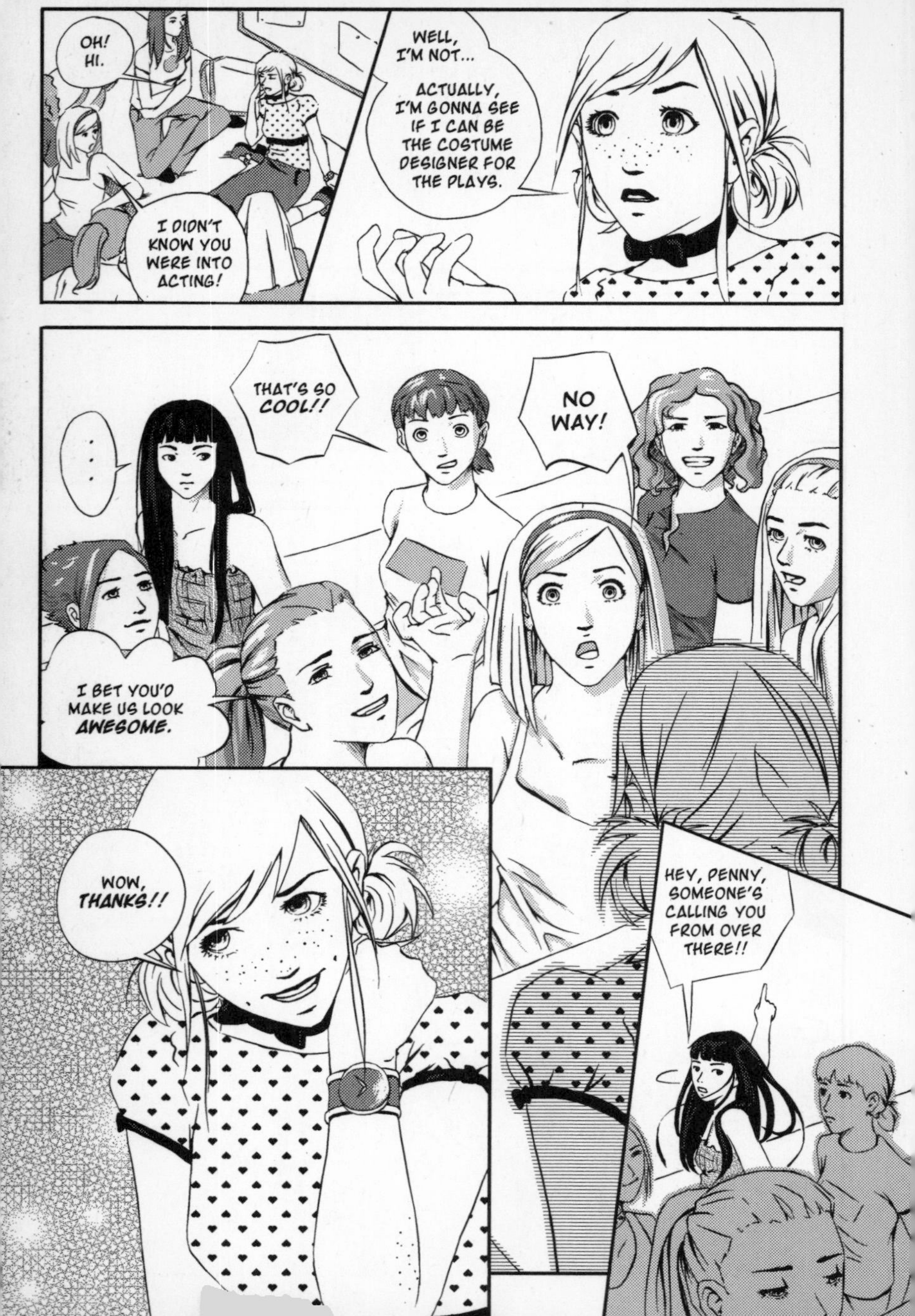
OH! HI.
I DIDN'T KNOW YOU WERE INTO ACTING!
WELL, I'M NOT...
ACTUALLY, I'M GONNA SEE IF I CAN BE THE COSTUME DESIGNER FOR THE PLAYS.
...
THAT'S SO COOL!!
NO WAY!
I BET YOU'D MAKE US LOOK AWESOME.
WOW, THANKS!!
HEY, PENNY, SOMEONE'S CALLING YOU FROM OVER THERE!!

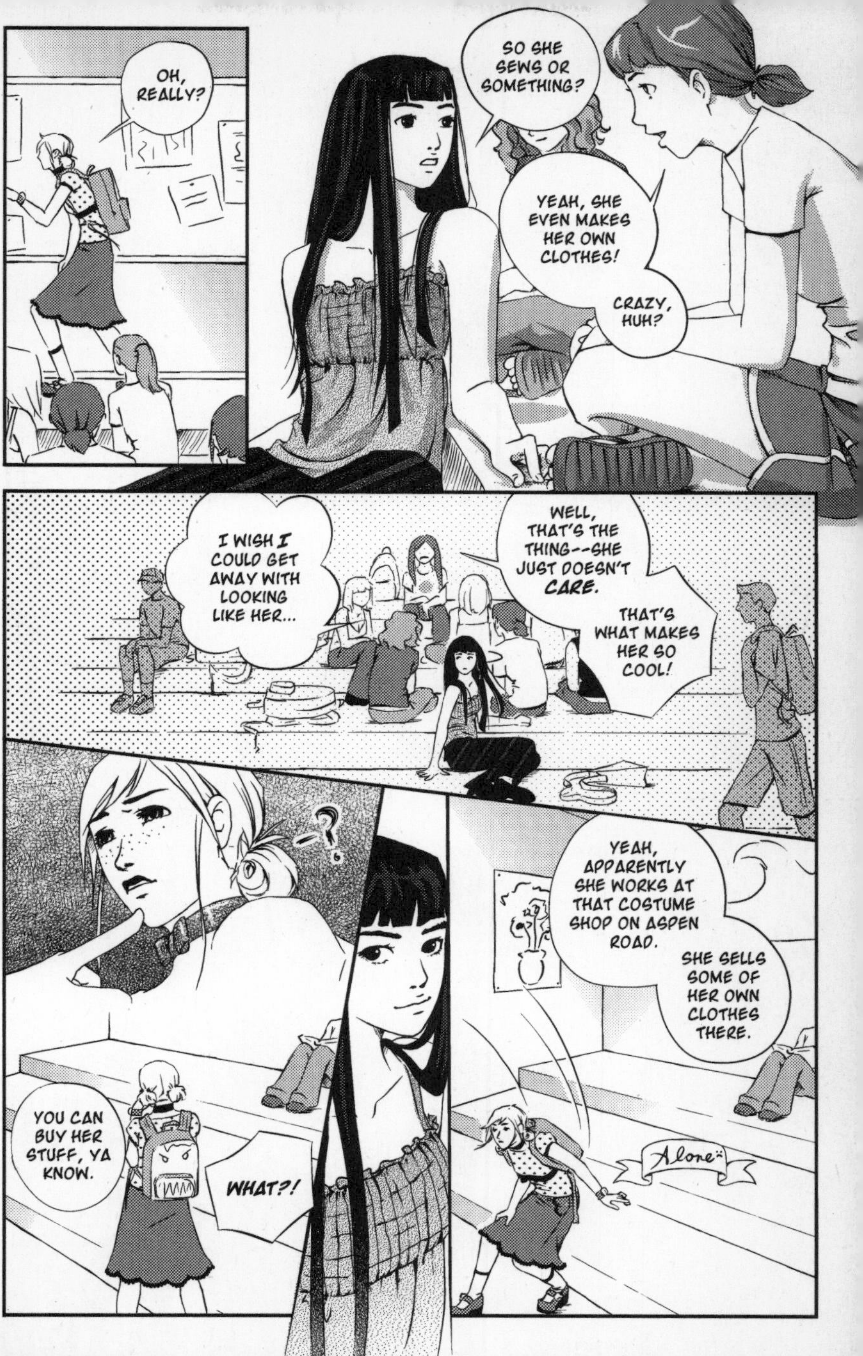
OH, REALLY?
SO SHE SEWS OR SOMETHING?
YEAH, SHE EVEN MAKES HER OWN CLOTHES!
CRAZY, HUH?
I WISH I COULD GET AWAY WITH LOOKING LIKE HER...
WELL, THAT'S THE THING--SHE JUST DOESN'T CARE.
THAT'S WHAT MAKES HER SO COOL!
?
YEAH, APPARENTLY SHE WORKS AT THAT COSTUME SHOP ON ASPEN ROAD.
SHE SELLS SOME OF HER OWN CLOTHES THERE.
YOU CAN BUY HER STUFF, YA KNOW.
WHAT?!
Alone

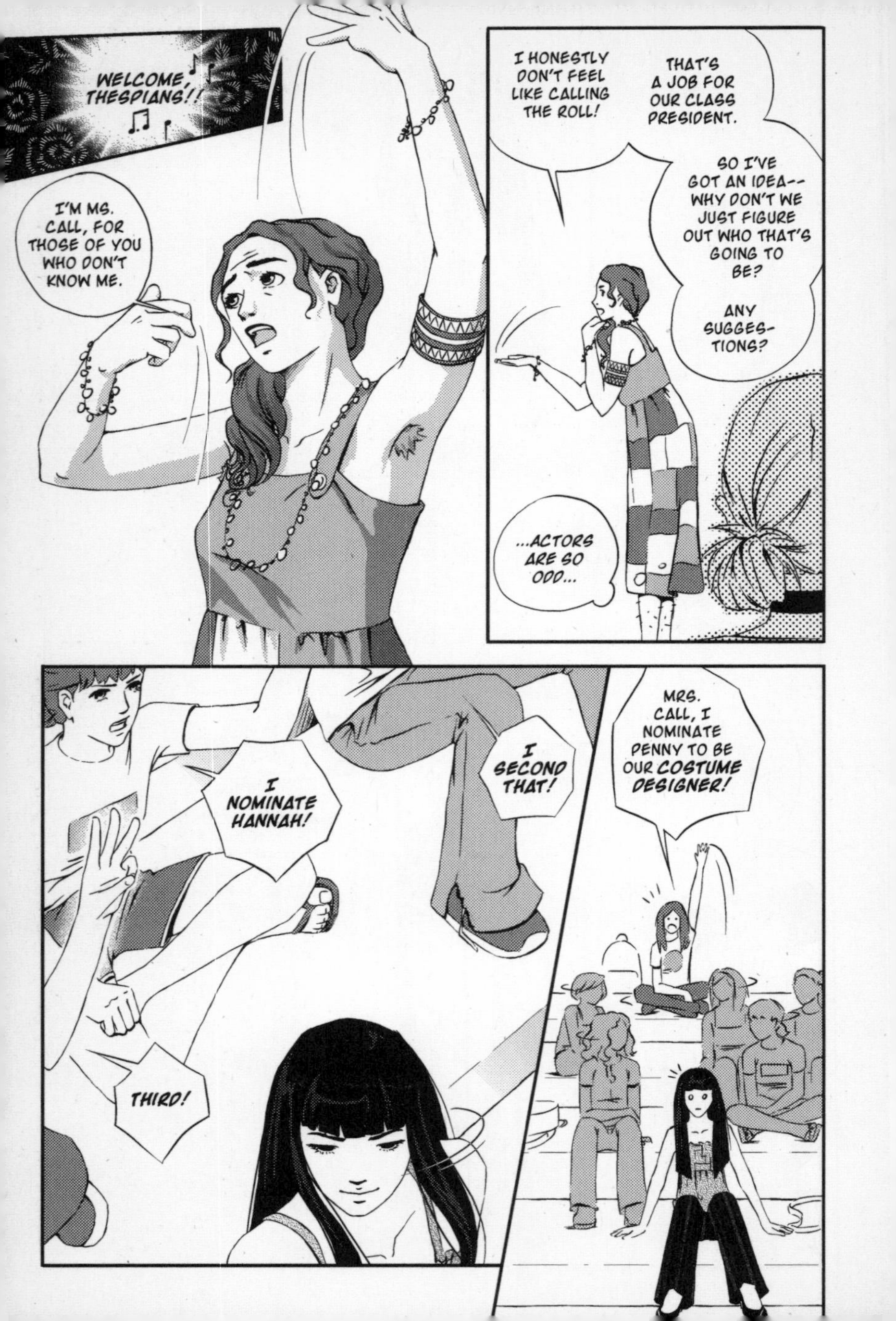
WELCOME, THESPIANS!!
I'M MS. CALL, FOR THOSE OF YOU WHO DON'T KNOW ME.
I HONESTLY DON'T FEEL LIKE CALLING THE ROLL!
THAT'S A JOB FOR OUR CLASS PRESIDENT.
SO I'VE GOT AN IDEA--WHY DON'T WE JUST FIGURE OUT WHO THAT'S GOING TO BE?
ANY SUGGES-TIONS?
...ACTORS ARE SO ODD...
I NOMINATE HANNAH!
I SECOND THAT!
THIRD!
MRS. CALL, I NOMINATE PENNY TO BE OUR COSTUME DESIGNER!

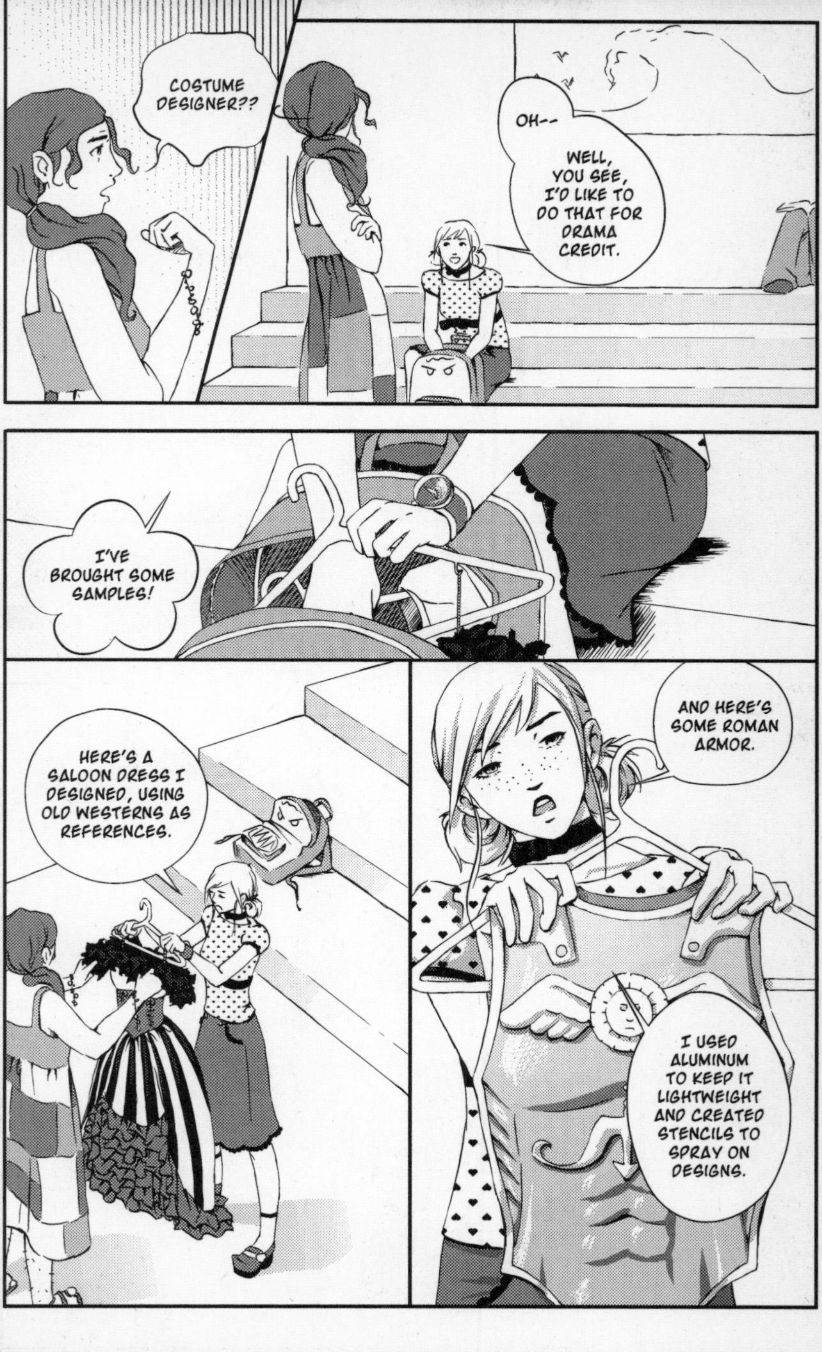
COSTUME DESIGNER??
OH--
WELL, YOU SEE, I'D LIKE TO DO THAT FOR DRAMA CREDIT.
I'VE BROUGHT SOME SAMPLES!
HERE'S A SALOON DRESS I DESIGNED, USING OLD WESTERNS AS REFERENCES.
AND HERE'S SOME ROMAN ARMOR.
I USED ALUMINUM TO KEEP IT LIGHTWEIGHT AND CREATED STENCILS TO SPRAY ON DESIGNS.

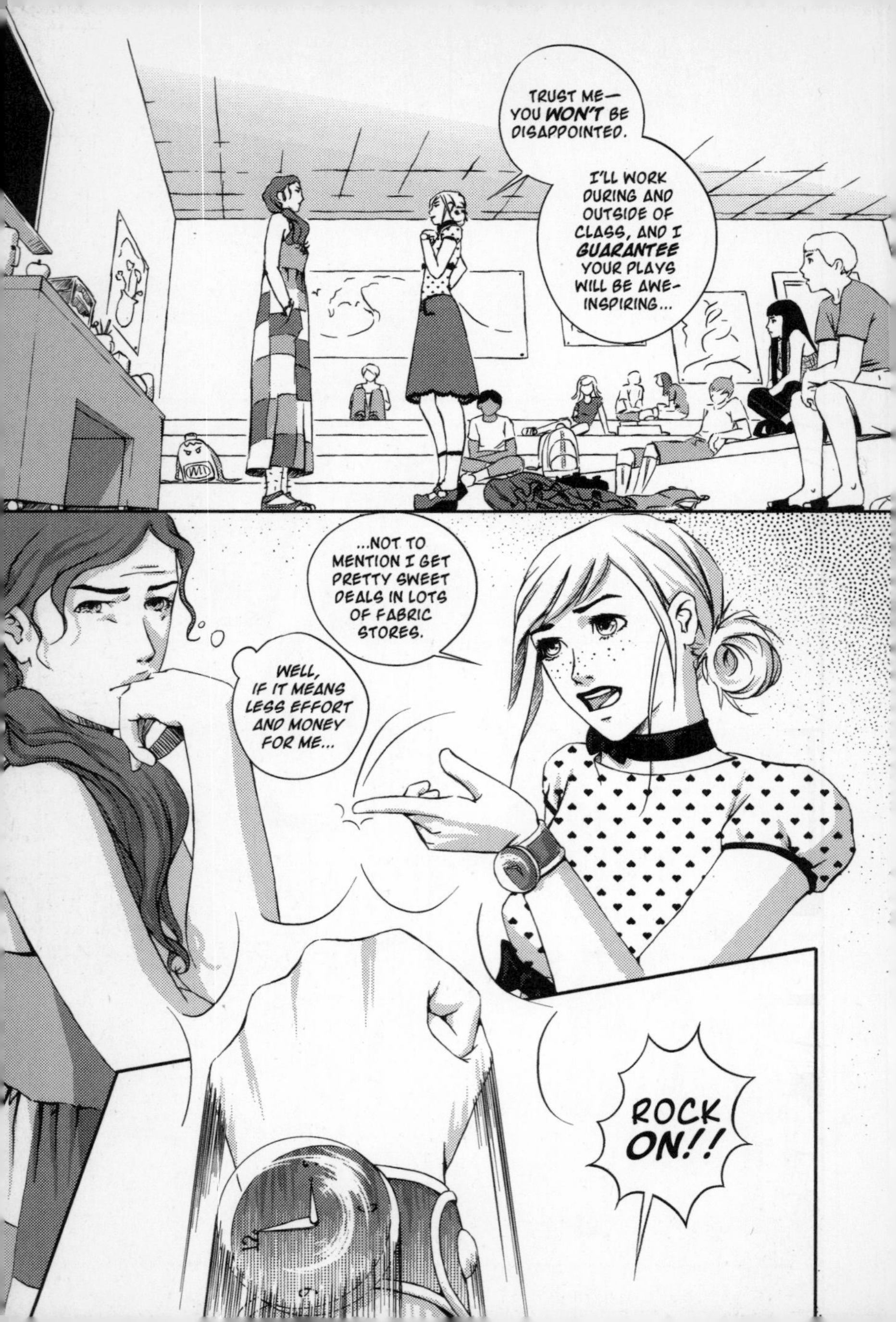
TRUST ME— YOU WON'T BE DISAPPOINTED.
I'LL WORK DURING AND OUTSIDE OF CLASS, AND I GUARANTEE YOUR PLAYS WILL BE AWE-INSPIRING...
...NOT TO MENTION I GET PRETTY SWEET DEALS IN LOTS OF FABRIC STORES.
WELL, IF IT MEANS LESS EFFORT AND MONEY FOR ME...
ROCK ON!!

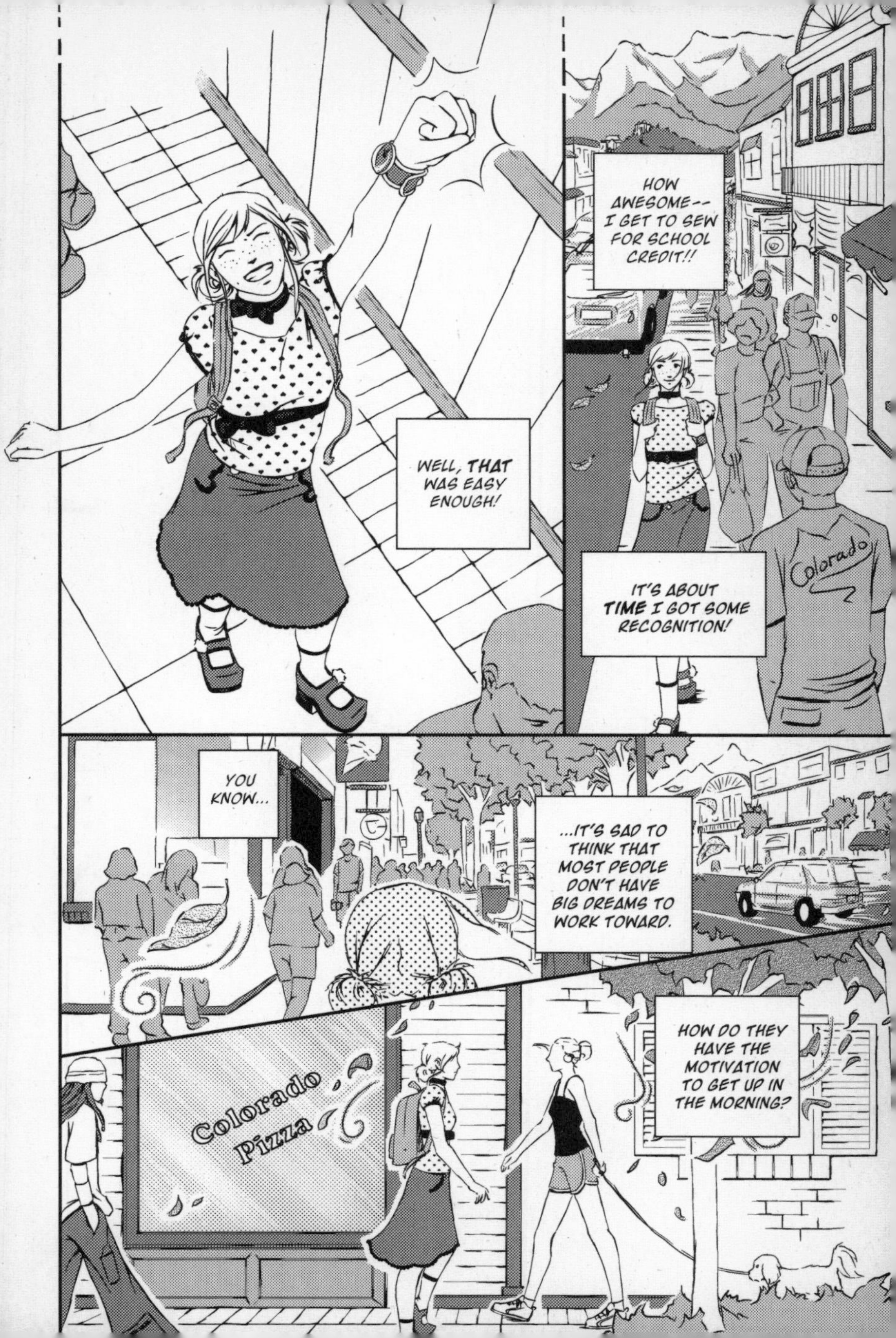
WELL, THAT WAS EASY ENOUGH!
HOW AWESOME-- I GET TO SEW FOR SCHOOL CREDIT!!
IT'S ABOUT TIME I GOT SOME RECOGNITION!
Colorado
YOU KNOW...
...IT'S SAD TO THINK THAT MOST PEOPLE DON'T HAVE BIG DREAMS TO WORK TOWARD.
Colorado Pizza
HOW DO THEY HAVE THE MOTIVATION TO GET UP IN THE MORNING?

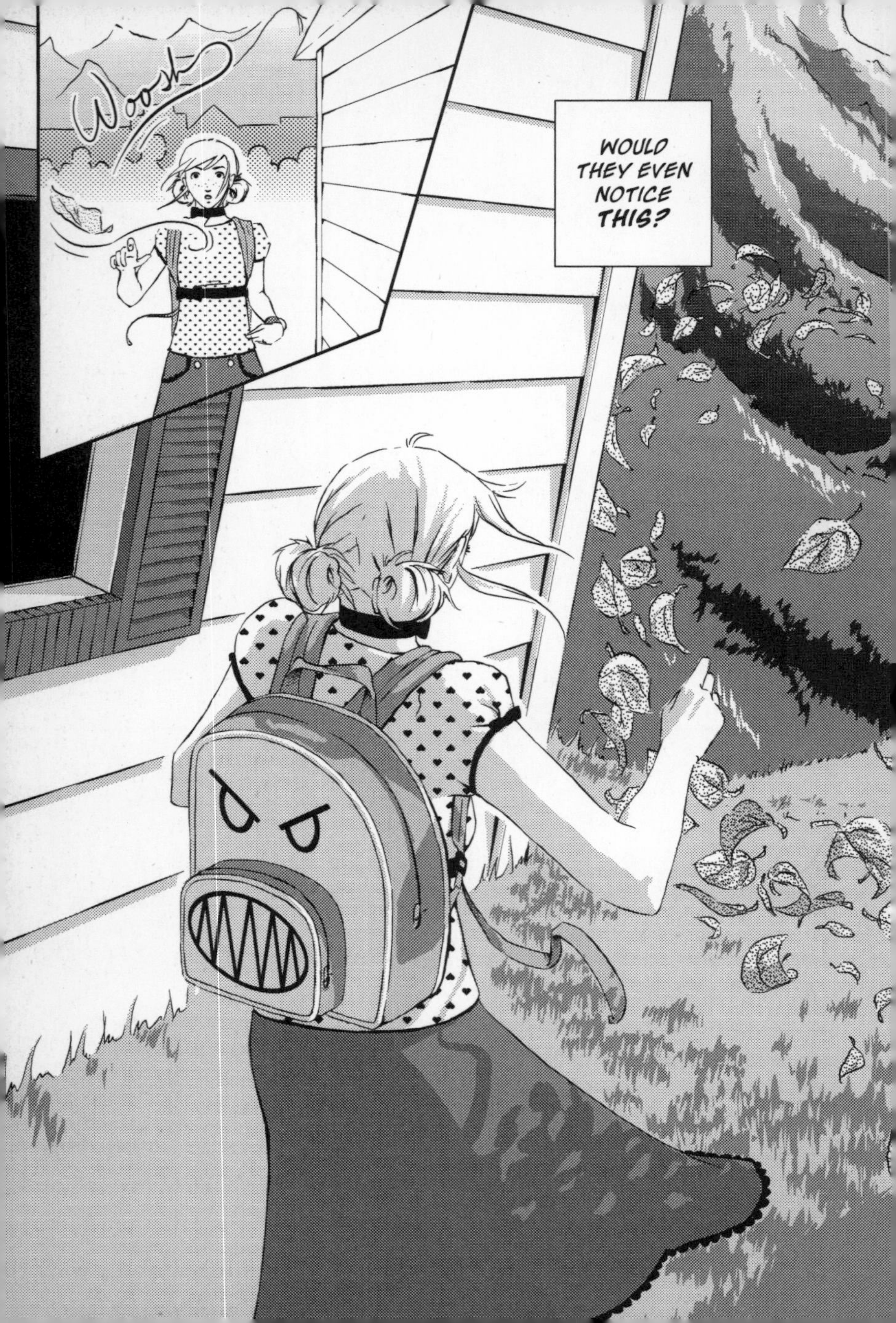
Woosh
WOULD THEY EVEN NOTICE THIS?

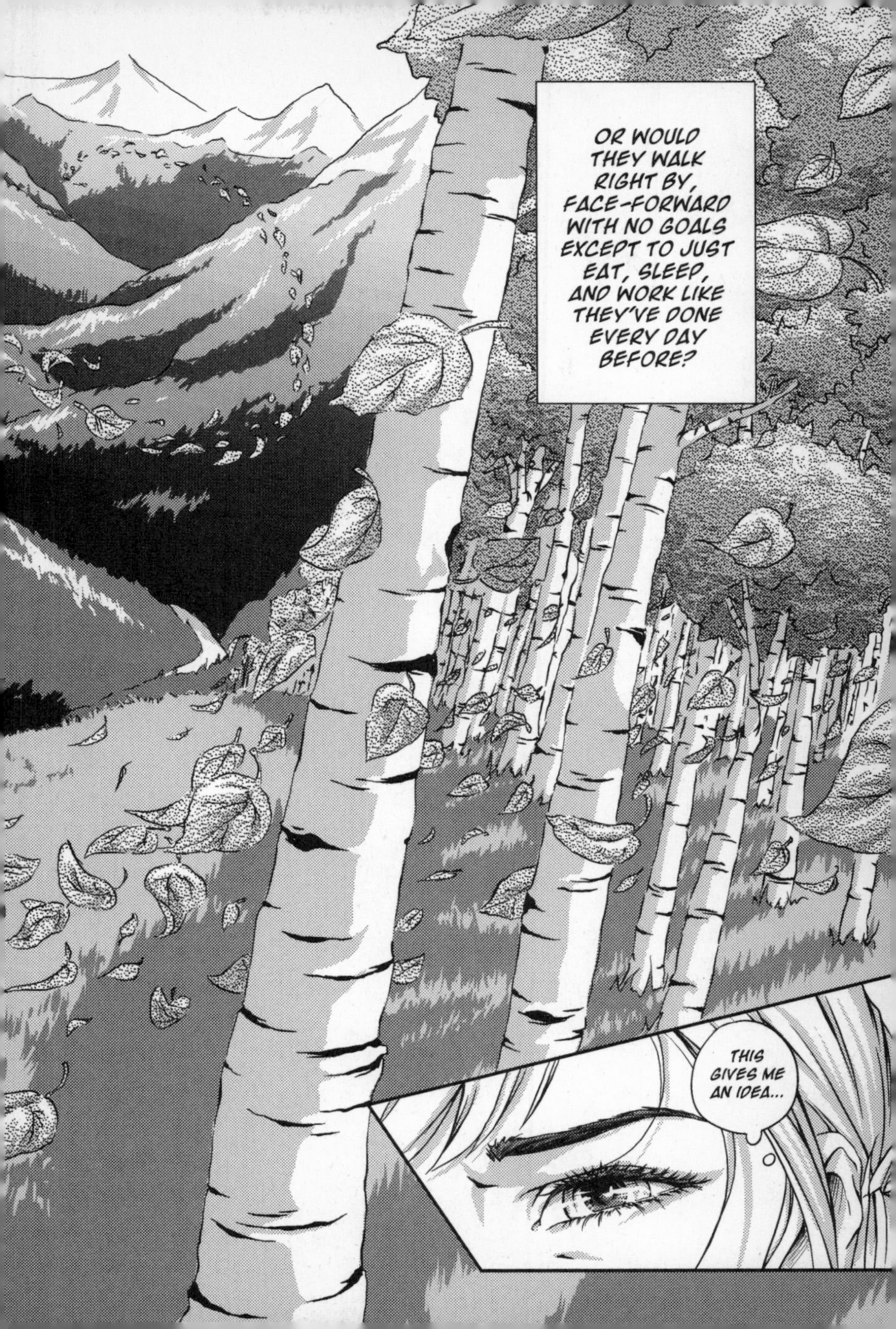
OR WOULD THEY WALK RIGHT BY, FACE-FORWARD WITH NO GOALS EXCEPT TO JUST EAT, SLEEP, AND WORK LIKE THEY'VE DONE EVERY DAY BEFORE?
THIS GIVES ME AN IDEA...

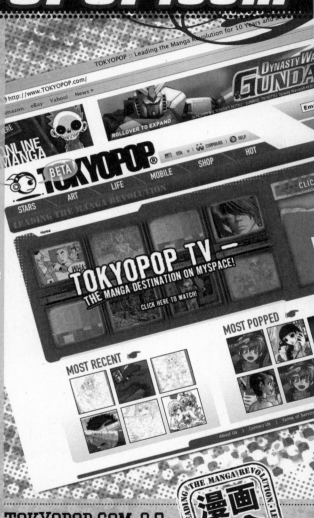

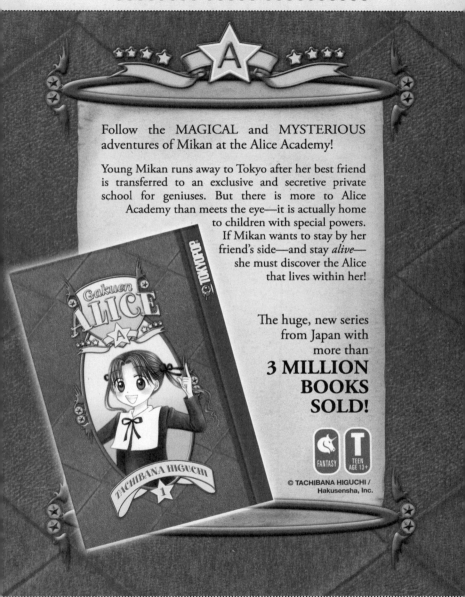